AGE
BECOMES US

SUNY series in Feminist Criticism and Theory
Michelle A. Massé, editor

AGE
BECOMES US
Bodies and Gender in Time

LENI MARSHALL

Published by State University of New York Press, Albany

© 2015 State University of New York

All rights reserved

Printed in the United States of America

No part of this book may be used or reproduced in any manner whatsoever without written permission. No part of this book may be stored in a retrieval system or transmitted in any form or by any means including electronic, electrostatic, magnetic tape, mechanical, photocopying, recording, or otherwise without the prior permission in writing of the publisher.

For information, contact State University of New York Press, Albany, NY
www.sunypress.edu

Production, Ryan Morris
Marketing, Anne M. Valentine

Library of Congress Cataloging-in-Publication Data

Marshall, Leni, 1969-
  Age becomes us : bodies and gender in time / Leni Marshall.
        pages   cm. — (SUNY series in feminist criticism and theory)
  Includes bibliographical references and index.
  ISBN 978-1-4384-5697-3 (hardcover : alk. paper)
  ISBN 978-1-4384-5696-6 (paperback : alk. paper)
  ISBN 978-1-4384-5698-0 (e-book)
1. Aging—Social aspects. 2. Older women. 3. Older people. 4. Human body—Social aspects. 5. Identity (Psychology) I. Title.
  HQ1061.M348 2015
  305.26--dc23
                                                                2014030981

10 9 8 7 6 5 4 3 2 1

Contents

Preface	vii
Acknowledgments	xi

Chapter 1
Constructing the Body of Age Studies — 1

Chapter 2
Deconstructing the Body Through Age Studies:
A Theory Primer — 25

Chapter 3
Ambiguous Loss, Ambiguous Gain:
Age Studies Analyses in Menopause and Beyond — 41

Chapter 4
Changing Bodies and Changing Minds with Doris Lessing's
The Diaries of Jane Somers — 69

Chapter 5
Lucille Clifton's Poetic Perspective and Aging — 93

Chapter 6
Storytelling and Cultural Transmission, with Louise Erdrich's
Last Report on the Miracles at Little No Horse — 119

Chapter 7
Rewriting Death, Rewriting Life — 145

Notes	153
Works Cited	167
Index	193

Preface

This book is a love story. For me, the seduction began with a part-time job I had as an undergraduate. Paying even better than fast food jobs, the Commonwealth of Massachusetts sent me into the homes of retired blue-collar workers to listen to their life stories. I went from apartment to apartment of people who received state assistance, hearing fascinating accounts:

> Mid-Twentieth-Century Uses of a Mill Town's Underground Railroad Hideouts
> Can You Trust a Man Who Forgets to Bring You Flowers?
> The Politics of Holiday Cookie Exchanges
> A Seamstress Cooks for a Hobo and Ends Up Marrying Him
> Lost in a Borrowed Car, with a Happy Ending in a Boston Dance Hall, 1947

I was hooked, happily doing the less-exciting home-health-aide work—assisting with bathing, physical therapy exercises, cooking, and cleaning—just to hear more stories. The passion sparked and smoldered. After graduation, I worked my way up from scrubbing feet, to managing a senior care home, to working for a managed healthcare consulting firm. Instead of listening to stories, I was making PowerPoint presentations. It was time to go back to school.

Even knowing that it would be no bed of roses, I still was interested in pursuing that long-standing relationship. When I mentioned to mentors and colleagues that I wanted to critically explore elders' stories, the responses—"Why? Isn't that depressing?" or "How can you? You're young."—made me nervous. Were they warning me about a ruinous flaw to which I was blinded by a sophomoric infatuation? I had years of secondhand experience coping with the effects of elders' social devaluation, but almost nothing from my undergraduate education suggested a useful way to respond, except for what I had learned of feminism's responses to sexism and other inequalities. Consequently, my research now focused on what one might think of as the equivalent of couples counseling for me and my scholarly interests: feminists' critical explorations of aging and old age.

Pre-Internet, the amount of humanities-based research one could find was severely limited. Among the texts I located, a few offered stellar ideas about re-visioning the social understandings of aging and old age; too many contained classist, able-bodiedist, and ageist ideas, equating old age with disability and social disengagement, and positing old age as a sordid Otherness. On the one hand, I was deeply disappointed. On the other hand, I believed I could add to this field by using feminist ideas about resisting gender inequalities to generate critical responses to the inequalities of old age.

Like a teenager with a crush on a rock star, I learned everything I could about the past history and the future prospects of these ideas. I followed the footsteps and extended the trails of other scholars who combined theories from literature, women's studies, and gerontology with information from the estranged branches of the family tree, including cultural studies, sociology, kinesiology, and anthropology. The relationship was reinvigorated and dazzling, keeping me awake at night thinking through new possibilities of how to make things work and how to explain it all to my friends and colleagues. Four years went by, and then I learned that I had just been playing the field, or it had been playing me.

Finally, I fell in love. Embarrassingly enough, it happened at a conference. During a session on aging and ageism, audience members were paired up for some active learning. In the first exercise, we had three minutes to use as many positive words as we could to describe aging and old age to our partners. I was paired with someone I did not know, and I was to speak first. The woman facing me was nearly twice my age, short and striking, with spiky white hair, laugh lines blending into wrinkles of purpose in her sun-browned skin, and eyes sparkling with humor and challenge. As an English teacher, I know lots of words, but suddenly my mind was empty. All the positive phrases I could recall were mirrors of her face, the vitality of experience embodied. My partner waited patiently. As my cheeks flamed, I hoped she thought I was just too ageist to think of positive words. I was dumb. I was age-struck.

That is why I do this work: for love and passion, for the fullness of the stories, the rich interplays of theory and practical ideas, and the powerful potential for making a difference. Bodies and lives change, twisting, losing, and ripening. Many of the examples in this book are from works of fiction, but none of them are mere abstractions. Every day, each of us is becoming the Other. With any luck, my forty-something body will become fifty-something and eventually eighty-something. I do not yet have the *in se* authority of embodied old age, nor will I wait for that to happen before I speak out. In my work and in my family, I have seen the silencing that can happen to people who are eighty-something. Whether conscious of it or not, we all have ideas about what it means to age and to be old. Age studies scholars and activists must examine their motivation to speak, question the bearing of their location and context, hold others accountable for what they say, and investigate the probable or actual effects of words on the social and material context (Alcoff 111–3). In rejecting essentialism, stasis, and rigid boundaries, in reworking and accepting cross-generational, cross-cultural, cross-disciplinary pollinating discourse, people may indeed—*I* may indeed—offer a text that will be of use.

> The pitcher cries for water to carry
> and a person for work that is real.
> —Marge Piercy

Acknowledgments

It takes a village. . . . My life is rich in people who shared their time and believed in this work, people without whom this book would not exist.

Peg Cruikshank, Helen Klebasadel, Devoney Looser, Teresa Mangum, Michelle Massé, Kate Thomas, and jo trigilio each embodies the spirit of feminism, admirable in so many respects. Donald Ross is a real-life Dumbledore—wise, kind, firm, encouraging, and tremendously talented at keeping the larger picture in mind. Many thanks and much gratitude goes to him, Robin Brown, Shirley Nelson Garner, Rosalie Kane, Mary Lay Schuster, and Madelon Sprengnether, who provided helpful feedback on the first, raw versions of these chapters. Margaret Gullette and Steven Katz contributed vital encouragement, support, and advice—thank you. Susan Squier is a model of excellence in teaching and scholarship. Kathy Woodward, an inspiration in the field of age studies, also is the epitome of graciousness, generous with her time and support; I am always in her debt. I appreciate many things about Roberta Maierhofer, including her keen intellect, skill in social engineering, and delightful wit. For Mike Levy—mensch, mentor, role model, and good friend—I am grateful.

Ylce Irizarry, an outstanding scholar and friend, invited me to play with the big kids and then held my hand when I most needed it. Cynthia Port provided critical 2:00 a.m. moral support and aided and abetted the age studies plotting from the start. I am grateful for her friendship and for her commitment to literature as well as to age studies. Erin Gentry Lamb, a model mentor and the wisest of friends, pushed, pulled, and guided me on, leading by example. Aagje Swinnen is more intelligent, competent, and all-around wonderful than she ever will realize; I am honored to be her friend. In so many ways, I appreciate Valerie Lipscomb's kindness and talents as a thinker and writer. Kelly Hulander's sensitivity, insight, and patience have been a gift. Ellen Weissman, the spirit of sisterhood, shared her home and hot water, let me be not-okay some days, and loves my children. Colette Morrow's intelligence, inner strength, and generosity of spirit are unparalleled. Kate Jarvi and Kate Hearley shared wine, tea, chocolate, good humor, and friendship beyond the ivory tower. Any time I needed advice or moral support, friends salvaged me, renewing my faith in joy and amity. Many, many thanks.

My family deserves credit as well. Ruben Marshall and Barbara Pierce volunteered to help with anything and everything. Julian and Jessica Marshall listened, supported, and consistently reminded me that laughter is the best response. Teaching me how deeply one can love and how much I have yet to learn, Sylvia DuVernois, Mara DuVernois, and Aeden Bard kept themselves occupied when I needed work time, included me in the fun when I had play time, and made sure I went to the playground regularly. Julie McFadden's beautiful spirit and steadfast love sustain my heart and frame the window of my world, now and always. Barbara Veraniam, my first and lasting role model, lived a life of intention and celebration. She was the change she wished to see in the world.

These people inspire me daily to lift up my hands and raise up my actions to be of use. With all my heart, thank you.

CHAPTER 1

Constructing the Body of Age Studies

"The great thing about getting older," said Madeleine L'Engle, "is that you don't lose all the other ages you've been."[1] Perhaps you remember being an age when sleight-of-hand tricks delighted you, when you first held an infant, when you found your first gray hair, when you had your first kiss, when you received your first paycheck or your last one, or when you moved out of a childhood home. Who you are now includes all of those ages. To reach adulthood and then elderhood, the chronological ages through which each person lives are the same—age twelve, age thirty-nine, age eighty-seven . . . The person who experienced those ages and the resulting self who now reads these pages is unique for each individual.

You do not lose the other ages that you have been, but practically, they are inaccessible to people who meet you after those years are behind you. You have become a person who presents an individual sense of self and who looks a particular way. The people who meet you now know you as this person of a certain age. Your sense of self includes all those other ages, but a new acquaintance's sense of you does not. This discrepancy highlights three important concepts. First, self-perceptions about who a person is—that is, self-identity—includes age as well as gender, race, bodily ability, and many other categories of identity.[2] Second, each person has a relationship with her or his younger selves as well as with the now-self. Third, a person's interior sense of self, particularly the individual's experience of embodied age, is not necessarily the same as the visible age of the external self to which others react.

The ways in which individuals and groups of people think about and respond to their own ages and the ages of others, critically examined, form the basis of this field of study. The debate about whether to call the field *aging studies* or *age studies*[3] is much like the debate about *women's studies* versus *gender studies*. *Aging studies* and *women's studies* draw attention to a group that traditionally has been underprivileged, focusing on previously ignored or understudied topics; *age studies* and *gender studies* avoid creating a dichotomy—in particular, *age studies* explicitly acknowledges aging as a continual process throughout life—but both of those terms risk reinscribing the invisibility of a traditionally devalued group of people.[4] Age studies is the analysis of the meanings of age across the lifespan, within specific cultural and historical contexts. Like gender studies, it recognizes that a difference in value requires more than one category; if there were no *male* gender category, the category of *female* would not make sense, and a critical exploration of *old* and *older* can happen only when contrasted with the normative categories of *younger* and *young*. As with gender and culture, age and culture are mutually constitutative. That is, in the biological experience and the social constructions of aging, each element influences the other's structure and development (cf. Brennan).[5] Thus, the binaries are not natural categories, but are cultural constructs that create a hierarchy. Like gender studies, age studies tends to have an activist orientation. Age studies scholars try to move beyond merely identifying social constructions, to instead reduce or eliminate unjust power differentials.

Recognizing the importance of focusing on old age while simultaneously acknowledging that ideas about aging accumulate throughout life, this book concentrates on *age relations* of aging and old age. Age relations, a category of age studies, explores what people of one age range think about people in other age ranges.[6] This book focuses on how and what people of all ages think about aging and old age.

In particular, this text explores the cultural contexts of aging and old age: the performances, visual markers, emotions, regulatory mechanisms, and conceptual understandings that create normative and nonnormative age, and the effects of aging in a particular societal environment. As variable a category as it is, nonetheless, *age*—like gender, bodily ability, gender identity, and ethnicity—is an identity category in literature and in culture, a factor in each individual's self-concept and in the ways in which individuals interact with each other. Researchers can study the cultural vehicles that convey this information, such as the media, fashion, and stage performances, and can "read" them to develop critical, scholarly systems of analysis. In turn, those systems can structure additional scholarly inquiries, and activists can use those structures to develop means of resistance. Because literature can mirror culture, reinforce it, resist it, or do a combination of those things, it provides a laboratory for close examinations of some concepts and testing hypotheses about the effects of resistance. As the complexities of the input and the resulting responses suggest, a comprehensive approach needs to be inclusively broad and multidisciplinary. *Age Becomes Us: Bodies and Gender in Time* investigates the information that North American and British majority and minority individuals and groups acquire about what it means to age and be old. Because this information affects popular and scholarly perceptions of, experiences of, and responses to advancing age and later life. It explores what can happen when the input or understandings change. Critical explorations of ideas about age, aging, old age, ageism, and performances of age lead to greater awareness and appreciations of the myriad factors that influence beliefs and actions.

Professionals inside and outside of academia can use these ideas to expand their knowledge base and their practices, because aging affects everyone. In the 1960s, gerontologist Robert Butler coined the term *ageism*, which he described as a form of bigotry and prejudice. According to cultural critic and age studies maven Margaret Gullette, "ageism is to the twenty-first century what sexism, racism, homophobia, and abelism were earlier in the twentieth—entrenched and implicit systems of discrimination, without adequate movements of resistance to oppose them" (*Agewise* 15). In the United States, ten thousand people turn fifty each day, and it is likely that the majority of people born after 2000 will live to be one hundred years old (Akers; Loe). Census data show that in 2010, 13 percent of U.S. residents were over the age of sixty-five. By 2030, the raw numbers are projected to double, bringing the percentage to 20 percent. People of color, who made up 17.2 percent of the number of residents over age sixty-five in 2002, are projected to be 26.4 percent of that group by 2030 (U.S. Census).[7] Analyses of beliefs and experiences of aging and old age—fictional and factual—must take into account the pressures of the majority culture and the intersections of age with other identity categories. Literary works, self-help books, theory, and practice offer applications for these ideas and data. Most of the ideas in this book fall into one or more of these three categories: analysis, advocacy, and inquiry. These approaches are offered in an effort to expand the reach and depth of age studies, add to the ongoing discussions about these topics, and involve people from a broad range of fields in thinking about, talking about, and working on age, aging, and old age.

Analytical Use

Age, like any other bodily based identity, should be a category of intersectional analysis in literary and cultural studies, and the limitations of using chronological age as a category need to be better understood. Considerations of age, aging, and old age can be critically useful in many fields, including literature, public policy, architecture, sociology, design, and cultural studies. Each field needs to find ways to establish age as a category of analysis despite the instability of the category. *Age*, an often-invisible type of difference in which each of us lives, needs to become more than just an addition to a list of identity categories (Woodward Telephone). A significant factor in personal and national identity, age needs to be more visible because of its centrality to theoretical positions, pedagogy, and research about what it means to be human.

In keeping with Ulla Kriebernegg's methodologies for what she calls *biogerontological texts*, this book uses the concepts of gerontology as the basis for literary critique and the ideas from literary criticism to critique gerontological texts.[8] A deconstruction of fictional and nonfiction texts can further understandings of how aging and old age are created, and provide examples of what a reconstruction of aging and old age might mean, both in literature and in society.[9] Although advancing through the years does not necessarily lead to insight or resolution (cf. Woodward, *Statistical Panic* 62), "aging can be a psychic cure for youth's prospective terrors of the life course" (Gullette, *Agewise* 218). Analyses and literary texts may vicariously inoculate readers against such terror, helping them appreciate the ways in which the critical concepts of age studies are applicable to their own experiences and scholarship.

Age studies distinguishes itself from literary gerontology specifically because age studies does not isolate its focus on old characters or old authors. Applying age studies to film, for example, scholars might notice that the triumph of Katniss and Peeta in *Catching Fire* (2013) reinforces ageist conventions, as the actors playing those roles were the youngest of the named competitors in the arena; that *Kung Fu Panda* (2010) bolsters stereotypes connecting wisdom and old age;[10] and that in *Argo* (2012) and *Captain Phillips* (2013), the treatment of age difference supports an ideology of Caucasian American cultural superiority.

In literature, consider how readers might be inclined to change their analyses of Chinua Achebe's character Ogonkwo if he were sixteen, rather than an experienced, and therefore more aged, chief. People who enjoyed Dickens during their college years might read his depiction of Miss Havisham differently when they, like her, are in their mid-fifties.[11] Until 2012, the only known image of Emily Dickinson was made when she was sixteen;[12] the mystique of her work might be altered if the representative visage was of Dickinson in her fifties, Amherst's reclusive grande dame rather than its maiden belle. Could Huck Finn have been seventy-five and still embodied the spirit of America? Nobel laureate J. M. Coetzee's novel *Disgrace* (1999) focuses attention on age starting with the book's opening words: "For a man of his age, fifty-two . . ." However, until Kay Heath's conference presentation eight years after the book's publication, critics had not considered how age functions within Coetzee's novel. Literary and cultural textual analyses are enriched when scholars consider differences of age, as well as of race, class, gender, and other elements of identity. Encouragingly, many scholars are "discovering" the use of age-based analyses; an engagement with the framework of age studies can bring additional depth to their work.

An experience that Atwood scholars have had when considering age without the benefit of age studies may be instructive. The 2005 Modern Language Association convention included a panel on age in Margaret Atwood's writing. To an audience of about seventy-five people, four respected scholars from across North America and

Europe gave insightful, close readings of Atwood's poems, essays, novels, and short stories. One presentation explored depictions of wisdom in Atwood's aged characters. In 2002, *Cultural Critique* published Kathleen Woodward's excellent article, "Against Wisdom," which explores the powerful potential of anger,[13] and one can find additional critiques of the connections between aging and wisdom at least as far back as 1983, in Macdonald and Rich's *Look Me in the Eye: Old Women, Aging, and Ageism*. Another presentation considered how Atwood's portrayals of characters had changed as the author aged. Scholarship from Amir Cohen-Shalev, David Gutmann, Robert Kastenbaum, Gisela Labouvie-Vief, Edward Said, Mary Winkler, and Anne Wyatt-Brown could have provided a context through which to consider the differences. Yet another presentation focused on the ways in which senior female characters in Atwood's work resist ageist assumptions. Atwood's characters use the same techniques as age studies scholars have found in the characters of authors such as May Sarton, Doris Lessing, Margaret Lawrence, and Toni Morrison, so it would have been useful to reference the age-based critical scholarship that had been done about those authors' characters. For more than two decades, literary and feminist scholarship has included scholarly and activist considerations of the speakers' topics. All of those citations were absent.

If that panel had been about Atwood and gender, or Atwood and bodily ability, and the panelists had not referenced earlier critical work on those topics, then as insightful as the presentations were, they still would have been considered irresponsible at best—but no one on the panel or in the audience seemed to know that age studies existed as a scholarly field. Scholars whose work may seem only tangentially relevant nonetheless can benefit from and contribute to the depth of scholarship in their own academic specialties as well as to the breadth of age studies research. In a society that prizes youth over experience, quick thinking over insight, and speed over resilience, it is crucial to develop analytical models and critical theories that inform how the lens of age difference influences the experiences and evaluations of human life. Considerations of literary and nonfiction texts demonstrate many ways in which, even when the author does not posit the association directly, age studies critical work can enrich a text's impact.

Think of the potential of a critical methodology—age studies—with which a researcher can produce an innovative understanding of a Shakespearian text (cf. Hill and Lipscomb), which in turn creates a new range of analytical possibilities in the fields of literature, history, cultural studies, gender studies, economics, and politics. Scholars whose work only tangentially connects with age studies nonetheless can supplement the depth of scholarship in their own fields as well as the breadth of age studies scholarship. Understanding age as, in part, a product of culture creates fresh insights within a range of humanities fields (e.g., Biggs; Hazan; Featherstone and Hepworth). For example, literary history scholars Drs. Christopher Martin, Devoney Looser, and Kay Heath made valuable contributions to early-modern, eighteenth-century, and nineteenth-century studies, respectively, by considering the cultural implications of age in markedly different ways. Martin reads texts from pastoral poetry to *King Lear* in the context of generational tensions during the later years of Elizabeth's reign; Looser reveals misconceptions about literary periodization that resulted from previous scholars' erasure of the later lives and works of women writers (*Women*); and Heath considers the role of middle age in Victorian fiction and advertisements. Studies such as these allow for new interpretations of the texts and historical periods and reveal the continuing resonance of those constructions of age into the twenty-first century.

Analyses of biological concepts through the lens of age studies can be equally productive. For example, consider texts about menopause. Most North Americans think of menopause as a biological phenomenon. As Gullette suggests, cultural discourse frames this event as a tragedy, an end of the so-called natural female state of monthly hormone fluctuation,[14] mainly ignoring the reality that for more than half of their lives, most women are not in that state, thanks to phenomena such as youth, pregnancy, menopause, birth control hormones, other medications, surgery, and the like. Moreover, most medical personnel are taught to connect the changes of menopause to a particular chronological range, around age fifty. Heather Dillaway's research suggests that women in their early forties who visit a medical practitioner because they are experiencing symptoms indicative of menopause may not receive appropriate medical treatment because doctors assume that the woman is too young for menopause, whereas women in their early fifties who have physical symptoms that may indicate disease rather than menopause tend to be undertreated for their conditions because their symptoms are read as menopausal (see also Gullette, *Agewise* 51–3). That scholarship demonstrates material dangers that stem from age-based assumptions. Again, age studies offers a useful lens through which to critique and reconceive such cultural assumptions.

Fifty years ago, the ideas of gender studies, disability studies, queer studies, and ethnic studies were alien to most literary and cultural scholars. People now know what can happen when scholars apply those kinds of analyses to literary and cultural texts, as well as the benefits of collaborations across the sciences, social sciences, and the humanities. The positive, wide-reaching, and on multiple levels, critically significant impact of those critiques explains why many universities now house entire departments on those topics. One might wonder why there are not more research projects, courses, and departments similarly focused on age.

Researchers in the biological and social sciences generate most of the scholarship about aging and old age. Geriatricians consider the medical aspects of old age, whereas gerontologists research the sociological and social policy aspects of aging and old age. If one mapped that divide onto gender, one would conclude that studying gynecology and social work offered researchers a complete understanding of how gender works within society—clearly a fallacious inference. Women's and gender studies have been working to fill the gaps in awareness of how cultural constructions of gendered bodies affect individuals' and groups' experiences. Age studies and aging studies are positioned to fill similar gaps of knowledge about aging and old age.

Comparative studies demonstrate the effectiveness of some responses to ageism, as well as their limitations. The medical model of aging, which frames aging as disease that leads to a process of decline (e.g., Angus and Reeve; Robinson, Briggs, and O'Neill), posits aging as a problem rather than an experience, and thus is a key purveyor of negative attitudes toward aging. Gerontologists' research tends to focus on data-driven experiments that measure emotional and biological health, with a goal of encouraging "successful aging"; in that framework, the arts and humanities supply useful interventions, but not methodologies (cf. Gerdner and Schoenfelder; Haight and Webster; and Rybarczyk).[15] Age studies scholars can contribute to the field of gerontology by employing feminist methodologies in parallel with more positivist approaches, and gerontology can advance women's and gender studies via data-driven explorations of the storied power structures in gerontological and geriatric care (Waxman, "Literary" 87). Age studies, "in partnership with feminism, can contribute, in important ways, to understanding the 'tension between personal and structural identity and the strategies people use to continue to live and develop in circumstances not of their own choosing'" (Holstein 325, quoting Simon Biggs). Age studies can help alleviate the panic, pessimism, and self-abnegation instigated by ignorance and ageism (Barrett and Cantwell; Blunk and Williams; see also Gullette, Rowles), impelling reconsiderations of the meanings of aging and old age.

Those new methods can help improve self-perception, social status, quality of life, and length of lifespan (Adler "Ageism"; M. Beck; Levy; and Levy et al.; see also Meisner). When younger people Other elders, then live for a few more decades, the distance and disregard for elderhood turns into self-disregard. A cohesive analysis can generate change in readers' understandings of aging and old age, and the concepts of age studies can expand understandings of and resistance to additional forms of Othering. When "some of the deadlocks of antiracist efforts are linked to . . . preoccupations with mortality and self" (Woodward, *Statistical Panic* 56, quoting Srivastrava), age studies analyses can advance social justice in multiple ways. With a greater awareness of the harmful and depressing constructions of aging and old age come more, and more effective, paths of resistance.

Barriers and Words

The levels of sophistication developed in theories of other identity categories, however, may hamper critical considerations of age. In the fields of women's and gender studies, handicapped and bodily ability studies, and race and ethnic studies, for example, several generations of theory evolved before those disciplines grappled extensively with the critical impact and the essentialism of the monikers. Terms that once were acceptable—*half-blood, retarded person, AIDS victim*—are now discredited, as are essentializing definitions of *woman* or a *person of color*, for example. With an awareness of those critical developments, age studies scholars may agree about the problematic value of suggesting life as a linear progression from one age class to another (e.g., youth, young adulthood, middle age, old age).[16] Dividing people using indicators of social significance, such as the age of retirement, or of biological origin, such as the onset of menopause, is critically unsound. Uncomplicated alternatives in this field, as in others, remain elusive.

Terms such as *old, aging, advanced age, later life,* and *aged* are considered acceptable, but their definitions still are problematic.[17] Most Western cultures calculate aging as beginning at birth. One might wonder how long the aging process needs to proceed before a person could be called *aged*. Such questions have been critiqued as being positivist (Gullette, "Age" 223), yet there is a strong compulsion to quantify how much time it takes to get old, as if the developmental milestones of the early years of life, such as learning to walk and cutting a first tooth, should have similarly well-defined and predictable parallels at the other end of life. An identity of agedness does not necessarily reflect some inherent self within that person, but scholars of aging tend to denote multiple social performative axes of aging.[18] Arber and Ginn talk about three types of age: chronological, physiological, and social (5–12). Calasanti and Slevin use four divisions:

1. Chronological: a quantitative measure of how long an individual has been alive
2. Subjective: how old an individual appears to be in relation to the individual's age peers and other people in the immediate environs
3. Occupational: how old an individual is in comparison to other people who have similar vocations or avocations
4. Functional: how much an individual can do or does compared to others, or stereotypes of others, of the same chronological age; and the age or stereotype of age of people who participate in the kinds of physical or intellectual activities the individual does (*Age Matters* 17)

The distinction between old and not-old for any one of those age vectors, however, remains imprecise. Recognizing that aging is a process, in *Agewise* and in other venues, Margaret Gullette suggests that the generic term *aging* should be inflected using phrases such as "aging beyond youth," "aging into the middle years," and "aging into old age," but the question of how to define *youth*, *middle years*, and *old age* remains.

Some gerontologists use chronology to further subdivide these categories, discussing the young-old, middle-old, and old-old. Ironically, attempts to quantify the stages of aging highlight the impossibility of taking such a positivist approach. Depending on the experiment, a category such as old-old might start at age seventy-five, eighty, or eighty-five. Outside the field of gerontology, the number of years that put a body into the *old* range varies even more widely. For example, a study of voting habits reports, "Election day turnout averages about 69 percent for older adults, and 39 percent for younger Americans"; the 69 percent includes everyone over the ripe old age of thirty (Pattock). Erin Gentry Lamb, a medical humanist, surveys her undergraduate students, asking when they think old age begins. Students' answers range from thirty to eighty ("Polyester"). Contrast that survey with a 2005 study in which "boomers defined 'old age' as starting [at age eighty,] three years after the average American was dead" (Adler "Turning"). These data suggest that a person's middle age spans years thirty-one through seventy-nine and that most people will die before they exit middle age. Connecting a fixed chronological range to a particular age category is inherently arbitrary.

Scholars in this field resist establishing a particular chronological delineation of the end of *young* and the beginning of *old* because establishing a nonarbitrary connection is quite a challenge, and for a few other reasons.[19] One is this: age, aging, old age, and ageism are simultaneously culturally and biologically constituted. Beliefs about old age and about how old people behave differ from group to group and individual to individual. Also, ideas about old and young tend to be based on bodily ability and performance. Factors that influence physical ability include, but are not limited to, calendar age.[20] Third, a person's age is situationally relative. That is, a fifty-something person might be deemed—and feel—*old* at an elementary school in the morning and *young* at a senior center later that same day. The variability of the categories of age makes their definitions fluid, at best.

The words for people-of-advanced-age are similarly problematic. For instance, *citizen* can be paired with *senior* to yield *senior citizen*, but that reinforces the normativity of youth—*citizen* as the normative term, whereas those outside the norm are too young for citizenship or too old: *senior* citizens. Using *senior* by itself has the advantage of pairing well with *junior*, but few use the word *junior* frequently. Also, any dichotomous pair (senior/junior, old/young), leaves little room for situational and other nonlinear oscillations or for middle ground between the two opposites. Groups such as the Old Women's Project and the Old Lesbians Organized for Change reclaim the term *old*, asserting that "as long as it is humiliating to be *called* old, it will be humiliating to *be* old" (Garza, Keaffaber, and Rich, emphasis added). I tend to use *elder*, a term I consider imbued with respect for those who have at least a generation of life experience more than I have. However, some reject *elder* as "too churchy" (Graham). Quantitative studies in 1975 and 1985 reported *mature Americans* as the favored term (Stock). A recent anecdotal poll suggests that older people prefer the term *older people*; some respondents proposed alternates such as *vintager*, *AARPeggios*, and *seasoned citizens* (Graham).[21] Neither the temporarily young nor the chronologically gifted agree on what would be a consistently respectful and critically sound term. These debates are unlikely to be resolved in the near future, and this book uses the terms differently depending on the context. The logic of incorporating such variability may be explained best using a cosmetological analogy.

From an age studies critical perspective, youth-enizing treatments such as hair dye and cosmetic surgery are not intrinsically condemned or condoned.[22] When people consider those kinds of treatments and procedures, usually they take into account the financial costs and health risks involved. Age studies underscores the importance of deliberating on the social risks and cultural costs of those practices as well.[23] In addition to involving the exchange of money, and thus reinforcing class-based power difference, such procedures also include a trade in social capital.[24] That is, when such a large percentage of people invest time and money in procedures that equate looking younger with looking better, once those procedures fail to hide one's agedness, one rapidly exhausts whatever social power one had that came from looking young.

The procedures do not change the devaluation of *old*; the attempt to act young and look young "maintains the invisibility of old age" (Swinnen "'One'"; see also Woodward *Statistical* 79). Instead of becoming the Other at fifty or sixty, people without visible disabilities and with sufficient disposable incomes can pass as full members of an ageist society until their bodies reveal how fully Other they have become.[25] Only when people understand these hidden costs can they make fully informed decisions. Similarly, the use of words such as *old, aging, senior,* and *elder* needs to involve an understanding of the problematic nature and challenges of those concepts. No adequate set of alternatives yet exists. Just as feminist scholars continue both to challenge and to use *woman* and *man*, age studies scholars employ the terms relevant to the field even as they problematize and deconstruct the language.[26]

In addition to age studies's challenges arising from having had a later start in academia than many other identity-related disciplines, a certain amount of cultural amnesia hinders the advancement of the subject and limits the development of additional critical work. Although researchers in this area have had decades of ongoing exchanges of ideas and appreciation for how the field has developed, that progress seems nearly invisible in the larger academic arena. In 1973, the *New York Times* hailed Simone de Beauvoir's examination of women and aging, *The Coming of Age*, as a text that "confronts a subject of universal public anguish and universal public silence" ("Five"). The back cover of Barbara Macdonald and Cynthia Rich's 1983 *Look Me in the Eye: Old Women, Aging, and Ageism*, shows that May Sarton welcomed it as "extremely rare," and Robin Morgan called it "courageous." Calyx Books's 1986 "groundbreaking" anthology of art, fiction, and nonfiction, *Women and Aging: An Anthology by Women*, collected works from unknown and known artists including Baba Copper, Elizabeth Layton, Meridel Le Sueur, Ursula K. LeGuin, Barbara Macdonald, and Marge Piercy. On the back of Kathleen Woodward's 1993 gerontological psychological literary theory text, *Aging and Its Discontents: Freud and Other Fictions*, the book is saluted as "pioneering." Betty Friedan's 1993 bestseller, *The Fountain of Age*, which she wrote in response to her own menopause, was seen as "groundbreaking." In 1997, Margaret Gullette's analysis of middle-ageism, *Declining to Decline: Cultural Combat and the Politics of Midlife*, was called "original," a book that "establishes a new domain for research" (Woodward, "Reviews"). In a quotation on the back cover of *Figuring Age: Women, Bodies, Generations*, a 1999 anthology of feminist gerontology edited by Woodward, Marianne Hirsch praises the "amazing feat" accomplished in making older women visible. Margaret Cruikshank's impressive *Learning to Be Old: Gender, Culture, and Aging* (2003), was saluted as "important" and "pioneering" (Gillispie). *Publisher's Weekly* wrote that Margaret Gullette's wide-ranging 2004 *Aged by Culture* "begins to lay out the groundwork" for age studies, and her 2011 *Agewise* is deemed an "eye opening . . . call to arms." With Valerie Lipscomb, I edited *Staging Age: Performances of Age and Aging in Theatre, Dance, Film, and Advertising*. In 2010, when I saw the publisher's promotional materials declaring the book to be "groundbreaking," a few moments of weak laughter followed. Forty years of scholarship and still we are just breaking ground—what rough territory this is! The ruggedness of this terrain and its feminist foundation form a decided contrast to the smooth topography and heteronormative aesthetics of youth-oriented ageism. The power generated by accepting young adulthood as the social norm both reflects and creates age-based discrimination. Also hindering this field are the variability of individuals' abilities at different ages; the myths of old age as a time of loneliness, depression, sickness, and death (Barrett and Cantwell; Blunk and Williams; Gutheil, Chernesky, and Sherratt; Joyner and DeHope; Lamb, "20"; Palmore 89); the relative lack of visibility for those who resist (e.g., Gullette, *Agewise* 108–11); and the money to be made by the so-called anti-aging cosmetic industry and the medical-industrial complex (Estes; see also Marshall and Katz; Gullette *Agewise* 103–23).[27] The other side of the anti-aging industry's largesse: the relative dearth of financial rewards for critical explorations of that work. Those economics restrict the research possibilities and entice scholars in many fields, from geriatrics to the humanities, to focus their energies somewhere other than on age studies. Moreover, the sheer volume of anti-aging messages dilutes the impact of whatever critiques appear. As the Atwood presentations suggest, the shortage of scholars' awareness of critical considerations, applied theory, and prototype analyses forms an additional barrier to the field's development within academia. Hence, the importance of more visible models.

Analysis, Advocacy, and Activism

Age Becomes Us: Bodies and Gender in Time considers the cultural messages that individuals and groups receive about age, what they do with those ideas, and how responses to the cultural messages affect experience. An investigation of how old people are positioned and depicted, and the psychological and physical effects of a variety of cultural venues created specifically for those who are in later life, can lead to a greater depth of analysis and to considerations of opportunities for change—that is, to advocacy and activism. Expanding the range of literary and cultural scholarship has the potential to create a counterdiscourse among primary texts, authors, and readers. In her essay, "The Emergence of the Aging Female Protagonist in Literature," Evelyn Pezzulich suggests that *reifungsromane*—novels of ripening—bring readers to ideas of aging and old age with a mind-set of "self-acceptance rather than self-hatred" (7).[28] When Barbara Frey Waxman coined the term *reifungsroman*, she explicitly connected it to an "endorsement of Frank Lentricchia's view of literary critics as social critics, to foster social change regarding old age" (*From* 2). Many age studies scholars have similar goals.[29] As I have argued elsewhere, an improved awareness of these elements creates the possibility of *conscious aging*—that is, of "aging with an awareness of age studies concepts and an activist response to ageism, with an understanding of one's self-identity and social identity as variable, and with an appreciation for the possibility that the self can remain undamaged even as those identities develop" (Marshall "Ageility").[30] As with other aspects of identity, these concepts are relevant in academic considerations and in each person's life.

As a social experience, aging slowly changes how others perceive and respond to an individual. Those differences may be experienced as positive transformations, as tricky adjustments, as unpleasant disparities, or as some combination of constructive, challenging, and unwelcome. When an individual is not aware of the variations he or she may encounter in aging and old age, or declares those differences unacceptable, the change can become even more difficult. Individuals who have lived longer are more experienced, but not necessarily wiser—and not necessarily not wiser. These many factors multiply the understandings and misunderstandings about aging and old age.

Too many individuals find that with aging and old age, they encounter yet another "problem that has no name" (Rubenstein 3). This is not the same nameless problem as Betty Friedan's, or as Mary Pipher's, although they are analogous. As with adolescent girls (Pipher) and young women (Friedan), women and men may experience the changes of age as personal failures. The experience can feel isolating and can result in withdrawal from social participation. As Woodward suggested (*Statistical* 50), Alison Jaggar's description of a response to such nameless problems illuminates one possibility for activism: being fueled by a "feminist anger" that begins when "the perception that the persistent importuning endured by one woman is a single instance of a widespread pattern" (160; see also Gullette *Agewise* 61). Jaggar focused on sexism and racism, but her point applies equally well to ageism.

As individual a process as aging is, nonetheless, people frequently encounter similar aging-related phenomena, yet often individuals feel as if their own circumstances are anomalous, outside the normal processes of aging. For those who know that the features of their situation are part of a widespread pattern, aging can be a shared experience. More conscious response equates to greater potential for change. The materials in this book advocate for critically based change, encouraging readers to be more educated about and more involved in the processes of aging and in a reconceptualization of old age—for themselves, for the people they love, and for the people they educate. The expectation (the hope!) is that such involvement spills over into readers' research and regular interactions with people across the age spectrum.

Inquiry

Aging is an experience in variability. Undergraduates may take classes on aging "to learn about my mother's menopause" (Mangum Telephone), but whatever happens with a forty-something or fifty-something body is literally half a lifetime away from the experiences of a centenarian. Some critical concepts vary across that spectrum of years, whereas other ideas can be usefully applied to the full range of ages. Some equate changes that happen to the young and the old, such as the experiences of menarche and menopause, whereas others question the value of such parallels.

Most of the researchers doing age studies analyses of literary and filmic texts focus on the age or relative ages of the characters rather than on the life stage of their creators. Some scholars, such as those mentioned in the discussion about Atwood, have addressed how authors' creative works change over the course of a lifetime, but this arena remains undertheorized.[31] Of the three key authors whose work this book explores, Clifton embodied the subject position of the age about which she wrote; Erdrich and Lessing did not. Younger authors trying to imagine elders' roles succeed in doing so to varying degrees; the amount of success partly depends on the assumptions that the writers make about their readers. This area also would benefit from additional academic inquiry. As chapter 6 demonstrates, in addition to considering how people of a certain age act and are treated and what people's thoughts are about that stage of aging and old age, the *roles* assumed to be enacted by elders—what they are expected to do and suggestions of other ways that those goals can be accomplished—is another arena ripe for consideration. There are gender-based differences in aging experiences. The majority of this book focuses on women's aging. Statistically, the majority of old people are women. Many theories about gendered bodies map usefully onto critical concepts of aging bodies. Woodward suggests that "in our profoundly ageist society, gender and age structure each other in a complex set of reverberating feedback loops" (*Statistical* 79). However, as detailed in chapter 2, gender boundaries may blur, reverse, or collapse in cultural and physical constructions of age.

Considerations of intersectional identity are enriched with the addition of age, because with more critical apparatuses, researchers can explore texts more "deeply and closely, increasing the power and reach of the texts' impact" (Waxman "Literary" 103). The literary texts in *Age Becomes Us: Bodies and Gender in Time* do not portray the past as better than the present, and their characters of all ages are unquestionably flawed. As with gender studies, age studies does not make a clear distinction between biological aspects of aging and those aspects that are socially constructed. For example, many women in North America consider menopausal hot flashes to be biological phenomena, but most women in Japan do not have hot flashes (Lock). Having "senior moments" is a culturally accepted part of aging in North America, but studies of other societies demonstrate that such moments are a cultural response to aging (Savishinsky). Loneliness and isolation are not natural outcomes of old age, but reflections of the social state, stemming in part from geographic mobility and an emphasis on the nuclear family. Cultural and biological, historical and visionary: the factors that create, replicate, and have the potential to transform ideas about age difference are complex and impossible to fully differentiate. Nonetheless, as many age studies and aging studies scholars have pointed out, individuals are held responsible for their own signs of aging, as if gray hair, wrinkles, changing eyesight, and even the socioeconomically influenced potential of ill health are the result of personal choice rather than a combination of social, genetic, and environmental factors.[32]

Broadly speaking, the individual and the society in which the individual lives are mutually constitutive. Aging and old age are a complex series of gendered experiences, reciprocally created and reflected in and by the individual and the larger society; neither the individual nor society holds sole responsibility for the vagaries of age. The multiplicities of aging and old age lead to many possibilities for critical concepts and responses.

A Roadmap

Age is a useful and necessary category of literary and cultural investigation—a location ripe for activism, service learning, and participant-observer research, and a rich avenue of future inquiry. *Age Becomes Us: Bodies and Gender in Time* explores the constructions of the aged body. Advancing age and later life are treated in literature and in nonfiction texts that take seemingly oppositional stances to cultural norms, and approaches for response, resistance, and social change. The messages that societies present about age can—and should—affect the scholarship and vocational practices in almost every field, from architecture to archeology, business to social work, engineering to psychology, literature to public policy, theater to design, and of course, gerontology.

Demonstrating how broadly useful age studies scholarship can be, *Age Becomes Us: Bodies and Gender in Time* examines writing from members of several ethnic and racial groups, including African Americans, Native Americans, AngloBritish, and European Americans; nonfiction, fiction, and poetry texts; literary, feminist, and cultural criticism; and methodologies from diverse disciplines. In all stages of life, people encounter a great range of experiences of aging and old age, which makes selecting a particularly representative text or author quite challenging—a challenge that this book does not aim to meet. Rather, this book considers works that depict aging and old age as a theme or trope; it uses age studies criticism to explore how the texts' and the authors' standpoints on those topics suggest points of adherence and resistance to normative conceptions of aging and old age; and it demonstrates a range of concepts for which age studies explorations are relevant. Through literature, readers connect with collective histories, and by extension, with shared futures, a potential that can create in the reader a vital and empowering obligation.

The second chapter serves as a basic primer of age studies theory. It explains how and why those who are not yet aged nonetheless are involved in age studies. The ideas in this chapter establish age as an interpretive category that locates each individual in a particular intersectional social position, demonstrating some of the ways in which agedness gets constructed as "not only a bio*medical* but also a bio*political* category" (Kunow 31, emphasis in the original). The chapter examines contemporary intersectional cultural and social contexts of aging, specifically focusing on age in relationship to other embodied categories, the aged body as a socially constructed body, and the intersection of those two topics in the production of a gendered, aged body. The differences of age arrive via two matrices: self-perception and social perception. The construction of age in relationship to the mind/body split, the inscription of time on the performative aging body, the way subjects are constructed in European American cultures, and the regulatory aspects of choice:

these phenomena function in a multitude of ways to limit agency as people age, thereby impeding their ability to participate in normative human activities. Adding to the uncertainties of age are the challenges—some would say the impossibilities—of performing agedness and gender simultaneously. Age studies can transform the performative possibilities.

The third chapter explores how age studies methodologies apply in a broader cultural context, focusing on popular culture self-help and age studies texts, and on the cultural texts of menopause and ambiguous loss. Menopause is billed as a universal female experience, but individual women experience menopause in dramatically different ways (Dillaway; Lock). The popular texts about menopause treat the variety in women's menopausal experiences with little enough depth that many women believe their experience of menopause is outside the norm (Claman). Deviance from the so-called norm may lead to silence. Social messages about menopause are erratic, contradictory, and very much dependent on the specifics of a person's community and the source to which a person turns for information. The physiology and the psychology of menopause are thoroughly intertwined, which makes problematic the ascription of symptoms either to the body or to the mind, rather than to the complex interdependence of both. This chapter explores many of the social messages that offer negative constructions of aging and how they do so, remaining mindful of the artificiality of the division between nurture and nature.

Those who seek guidance about menopause and other aspects of aging-into-old-age may encounter some purportedly feminist texts that inadvertently validate or recreate the ageist social structures they find problematic. In such books, readers may find ways to change the age at which they are labeled *old*, but little to help them challenge or change negative stereotypes of elderhood. Other texts, based in feminist age studies, re-vision and revalue aging and old age, exploring the social marginalization of age, the intersectionality of identity categories, and the impact of de jure and de facto regulation of aging processes. These texts also form the foundation for humanities-based age studies. The concept of *ambiguous loss* explains some of the trepidation that accompanies the uncertainty of aging-into-old-age, a process that forecloses some possibilities yet opens new potentials for self-development.

Chapters 4 through 6 demonstrate how works of poetry and fiction, as well as analyses of those works, can effectively counter subtle and not-so-subtle ageism. In these texts, readers find productive literary considerations of aging and old age; engaging those ideas in teaching, research, and other work can expand the reach and depth of those activities as well as of age studies. Given the role of cultural production in the experience of aging, texts from a variety of minority and majority American cultures can more broadly explore what social and analytically based resistances to negativity about aging can look like. These readings are not exhaustive; instead, they use the lens of age studies to demonstrate a form of literary critique, providing context and a sample of the positive outcomes of such study.

For example, Doris Lessing's *The Diaries of a Good Neighbour*, a text targeted at a Caucasian American audience, suggests the benefits of creating a personal, individual connection between readers and their understandings of aging and old age. Chapter 4 discusses Lessing's novelistic dyad, which she crafted with the goal of provoking change in readers' conceptions of aging and old age. In *Diaries*, Lessing effectively confronted and debunked many of the standard Western negative and divisive stereotypes about of old age. Lessing's text, although fictional, employs the conventions of autobiography to create the effects of a *roman à thèse* (didactic novel), invoking the readers as the narrator's doppelgänger in discovering how valuable an increased understanding of old age can be. Building on Lessing's own political beliefs, her text considers race, class, gender, bodily ability, age, and the many strata of social power their intersections create. The results reflect the gendered element of care work within family relationships. The book replaces traditional kinship roles with familiarly dysfunctional, quasifamilial relationships between a younger woman, as an *otherdaughter*, and the female elders in her community. In detailing the material consequences of ageism, racism, classism, and other negative stereotypes at the individual level, this book impels readers toward personal change.

Moving from prose to poetry, chapter 5 explicates the poems of Lucille Clifton and other African American authors, which offer positive conceptions of aging and old age. Their texts tend to locate the speakers as part of a continuum linking generations past and future. That connection encourages readers to appreciate the self-respect and the information handed down to them, and to serve as models from which the next generation also will learn proudly. African American women are less likely to need self-help books about aging, instead learning about the changes of age from biological or social kin. This chapter builds on the concept of fictive kin—othermothers as well as otherdaughters—to posit advancing age as a time of women's ripening into roles of racial pride and verdant sexuality; the poetry of Clifton and other Black female poets of her cohort reflect this potential. Cultural factors such as assimilation may damage the suitability of this model; for people of all races, age studies scholarship can build on the concept of racial pride to develop more constructive ideas about aging and old age in the twenty-first century.

The literature of Louise Erdrich and other First Nation authors offers yet another alternative method of forming relationships, as chapter 6 details. In considering narrative as a form of cultural transmission, their texts take on some of the important social functions traditionally held by elders in their societies, showing both the potential of age-related power, and how such power need not be—and sometimes should not be—anchored to an individual's chronology or personal heritage. These texts invoke storytellers as otherelders and readers as learners responsible for using the information they learn. Erdrich's texts consistently separate wisdom from agedness, instead connecting insight to the degree to which a character employs the collective knowledge of the tribe.[33] Through the blurring of seemingly solid boundaries of difference, Erdrich's stories speak to a disasporic readership, facilitating access to this larger body of information. The texts do not specify the identity of Erdrich's targeted reader, an openness that some First Nations authors and critics decry as a serious flaw. Repeatedly, Erdrich's narratives generate opportunities for reconnection to a larger culture, creating both incentive and obligation in the reader to enact change.

Each of these chapters develops the reader's understanding of how age studies augments the available possibilities of analysis and inquiry. The models reveal the breadth and depth that interdisciplinary age studies analyses add to literary and cultural criticism. The need for critically sound criteria with which readers can evaluate potential age studies role models, fictive or real, continues to grow. As fields such as women's and gender studies, race and ethnic studies, disability and bodily ability studies, and queer studies have demonstrated, incorporating analyses from a wide range of cultural traditions yields results that are useful to more people and applicable to more characters. Clifton's and Erdrich's connections to community can serve as the basis for a critique of the more individual parts of Lessing's text; their standpoint as people of color contrasts with her racial and ethnic location. The results of both the analyses and the inquiries can generate personal change in critical readers' beliefs about aging and old age, and thus expand the options in their personal lives, their teaching, and their scholarship.

Feminist literary gerontology, suggests Woodward, may move people beyond the ability—simple but crucial—of merely *naming* their experiences and into a realm in which they are able to *narrate* their experiences of aging (Woodward, *Statistical Panic* 80, emphasis in the original). In doing so, they further expand the boundaries of what can be said and what can be done. Similarly, demonstrating that one's age is affected by biology, culturally produced, dependent on context, and open to deconstruction and reconstruction, the contents of this book explore how the differences of age influence people in a wide range of ages. This information explicitly, intentionally blurs the boundaries between the youth cult(ure) and the Other of old age, suggesting that most individuals can benefit from additional information about the cultural aspects of age: the temporarily young, who can benefit from seeing the pressures of age-based social erasure; the middle-aged, to expose how active dissociation supports the Otherness of old age and to show the cost of that distancing; and the old, to help decrease internalized ageism. These pairings of age and potential benefits may be synthetic, but people of all ages can work to connect perspective and narrative, improving understanding about what it means to age and to be old. To speak across age boundaries builds connections and dismembers false assumptions. That is why I teach and write about age studies. Wherever this book highlights gaps in the field, reveals flaws, generates questions, and inspires ideas, please use that as an opportunity to respond. Scholarship is a conversation. Let's talk.

CHAPTER 2

Deconstructing the Body Through Age Studies:

A Theory Primer

When people learn that I—a queer, feminist, Jewish mother in her forties—study aging and old age, they usually respond with one of two questions: "How can *you* do that?" or "Why do you do *that*?" Would that more would ask, and then, primed for theory, engage in a discussion that answers the question. Scholars do not need to be old before they can engage with age studies. Anyone old enough to participate in a social exchange knows something about age difference.[1] Age studies is not just about elders.

If one accepts the supposition of a focus on elders, however, the questions still highlight a need for critical reconsideration. After college, I spent nearly a decade working for and with seniors in various capacities, from Massachusetts to Oregon, and to say that older and old people are Othered in American society is putting it mildly—they are devalued, ignored, and ridiculed. Age studies concepts, including those in this book, can continue to boost cross-boundary dialogue, creating a space for action and reaction. Wholesale inequalities require a systemic response—men speaking up about gender equality, Caucasians addressing racial prejudice, heterosexuals working for queer rights . . . the list could go on. I do not write or speak *for* old women and men; my scholarship focuses on ideas about aging and old age from across the age spectrum, and I have been doing this since I was in my twenties. Until more people are involved with age studies, can anyone's silence on this subject be respectful?

Few claims should rest on essentialized authority; a group's "'epistemic privilege' does not inherently include a privileged knowledge of the *causes* of their situation" (Harding 130, quoting

Uma Narayan's phrase, emphasis in the original). Being old does not generate the ability to produce critically sound age studies analysis. "When opinion claims to be unassailable because it is based on experience . . . criticism becomes an extension of personal essence" (Roof and Weigman 93). This delineation also solidifies the boundaries between groups (see Sollors 255; Callaghan 196)—the opposite of the work *Age Becomes Us: Bodies and Gender in Time* seeks to accomplish. Also, the groups about which one might be barred from speaking usually are groups already experiencing cultural oppression and Othering. Thus, those groups' voices already are marginalized; requiring marginality further limits the number of people who may speak, which can lead to more silencing.

In classroom teaching, for instance, this effect plays out across multiple identity categories. My ability to teach Walt Whitman's writing has never been questioned, even though I did not live in the 1800s, have not experienced the American Civil War, am not a man, and when Whitman was writing, my foremothers were in Eastern Europe. However, because my progenitors are not from South America, colleagues have felt justified in questioning my feminism and my ability to teach Isabel Allende's works, even though she and I share a gender, a century, and a country of residence. The culturally produced fog of normativity—in this case, of dead White men—"reinforces the invisibility on which its dominance relies" (Callaghan 201). When marginality and authenticity are equated with ability, they reinforce the current power relations. The invisibility of age privilege leads to similar situations. A twenty-something first-year graduate student may be asked to teach a text written five or ten centuries ago by an author who was decades older and of a different gender than the student. I have been in meetings in which the same people who did not question that student's capability expressed reservations about a full professor's ability to, as they phrased it, bridge the generation gap, to teach contemporary texts by emerging authors, such as a Karen Russell story from *St. Lucy's Home for Girls Raised by Wolves*. Some professors might have trouble with Russell's text, but many would not. Questioning the professor's ability without similarly interrogating the graduate student's ability to bridge the experiential gap with texts such as Plato's *Republic*, Joyce Carol Oates's *A Widow's Story*, or Shakespeare's *The Tempest*, is ageist. Without age-based analysis, the invisible privileges of youth go unquestioned, even as they invert the usual academic hierarchy of presumed competence.

Power relations regulate not only what is said but also what people might think. Judith Butler maintains that identity is an iterative performance—a repetition of acts that simultaneously express and create beliefs. When people integrate new acts and ideas into their performances, they enact transformation. As a perpetually changing identity category, age differs from the other categories, but its many key similarities allow for congruence of theories as well. Judith Butler's *Gender Trouble* serves as footing for building an understanding of the similarities among critical constructions of age and other identity categories. Her work brings into play the ideas of theorists including Douglas, Foucault, Freud, Irigaray, Kristeva, Lacan, Riviere, and Wittig. Working with those concepts creates an environment in which to interrogate many constructions of the aging body: the ways in which agedness inflects the Cartesian division of mind and body, how the performative body becomes inscribed by age, age-inflections in the constructions of social subjects, and the means by which the regulatory aspects of choice limit one's agency as one ages.[2] Each of those differences interferes with aged individuals' abilities to perform normatively and thus to be accepted as human rather than as Other. Western cultures' constructions of advanced age encourage individuals to understand the story of their aging into old age as a decline narrative (Gullette, *Declining*). If instead, age is understood as a continued process of becoming, people can retain agency and humanity throughout the life course.

Constructing Age

To examine how individuals become or are made old, consider Butler's discussion of the creation of sexuality. Biologically speaking, most bodies are born with a physical set of genitalia to which society assigns a gender. Scholars continue to debate whether or not an individual's sexuality and gender form prediscursively. In Freudian thought, a child's physical sex predisposes that person toward a particular sexuality and gender, which language and social and cultural influences then disrupt or interact with to form the child's adolescent and adult sexual identity. Although many feminist theorists do not agree with Freud's assumption of heterosexual attraction as the normative condition, some of the same theorists search for a prediscursive, "real," and "unspoiled" sexuality. Others, including Butler, Lacan, and Wittig, see the debate itself as a socially constructed quest and dispute the existence of a presocial self: "what we believe to be a physical and direct perception is only a sophisticated and mythic construction, an imaginary formation" (J. Butler, *Gender* 114). These debates highlight gender's two main trajectories of origination—the physical and the socially constructed—and the same two vectors can apply to age.

In discussions about the awareness of the construction process for age, compared with the paths to gender, ideas about how a person becomes categorized tend to diverge. Most people spend many years of their lives as aware beings who do not yet consider themselves to be aged, far longer than the time they could potentially be pregendered (if such a condition exists). In many respects, each individual enters into the Otherness of agedness from the outside in, as we first become "old in others people's eyes, then slowly we come to share their judgment" (Cowley 4). Thus, each individual participates in the social, cultural, and physical process of becoming Othered via age. Consciousness about how one comes to age awareness means the process can be tracked, discussed, and deconstructed, a procedure indisputably in the discursive realm.

That each person is an active participant in the aging process leaves open an encouraging possibility for change—at the very least, for entering into the process of construction more deliberately. "When the subject is said to be constituted, that means simply that the subject is a consequence of certain rule-governed discourses that govern the intelligible invocation of identity" (J. Butler, *Gender* 145). Butler's body of work demonstrates the complexity of subjecthood's constitution, yet examinations of the process can be quite productive. Applying these concepts to the aged body leads to some interesting observations.

When students are asked to explain what *aging* means, those who focus on internal elements, such as emotions or spirituality, provide more positive definitions (e.g., "mature over time and build life experiences"). Students who consider aging as a physical process say that aging happens when a body experiences "anatomical degradation" so that a "less efficient" body requires a person to "slow down" (Lamb, "Polyester"). Thus, responding to elders based on visual information—the physical—becomes both a cause and an effect of ageism. This is the "practical inaccessibility" of the earlier self with which chapter 1 began. Other people respond to an individual's performative age (Richeson and Shelton), and individuals learn of their (fluctuating) place in the age hierarchy based in part on others' reactions. Posture, speed of actions, hair color, vocal timbre, attitude, style of dress: all of these, and many other indicators, contribute to the ways in which an individual's age is judged, as do the situation and the characteristics of those who assess one's age. How a person—one's body, one's self—performs every day becomes the person others think one is.

Feminist body theories resist the mind/body split, the separation between nature and culture, and the creation of binaries. Binarity encourages divisiveness by creating distinct categories—you are either male or female, you are either young or old. Such categories also are positioned on a gradient of social value. Differentiations between mind and body generally assign the mind a superior position, offering it the freedom of multiple planes of existence. The body, on the other hand, remains earthbound and maintains a one-to-one relationship to time and place.[3] The conflicting experience of the mind/body split that many, if not most, aged people experience furthers the need for a reformulation of age as a nonbinaristic category.[4]

Most North Americans' conceptualizations of aging and old age, however, continue to follow this dualistic model. In Western philosophical traditions, the ability to transcend the limiting confines of the body helps demarcate an individual as human. As a body becomes physically marked by age, the cultural perception of the distinction between the mind and the body decreases. Many of the common descriptors of the elderly—infirm, feisty, sourpuss, witch, geezer—blur the boundaries between physical and mental characteristics.[5] The perceived decrease in the distinctions between mind and body, as well as the reworking of the expected hierarchy of mind over body, are antithetical to the normative social order. "To look old is to be found morally, socially, and aesthetically wanting" (Hurd Clarke 128), the aged body an unregulated "site of pollution" (Butler, *Gender* 168; see also Marshall, "Through" 61-3), a cultural positioning liable to have a negative effect on social acceptance of the aged body.

Advancing age also is perceived as having a parallel of physical deterioration. Decreased physical ability is often seen as increasing the connection between the mind and the body, confining the mind to the body. This perception decreases or erases the possibility in others' minds that an aged body may be transcendable (Rubenstein). Thus, the aged body seems to subjugate the mind, limiting the mind to the earthly plane.[6] The ladder of spirituality, however, requires people to leave the body "behind" to become fully fulfilled human beings. If others perceive a person as not being able to accomplish this seeming liberation, then that individual can no longer participate in normative human activities. Thus, the cultural assumption that elders have a constrained or nonexistent mind/body split becomes a system for making the inhabitants of aged bodies less human.

Paradoxically, at the same time that exterior dialogues are telling a person that the breach has resolved, that person's interior dialogue may be sending quite the opposite message. The physical limitations of aging bodies can, at times, frustrate the mind. For instance, individuals may not be able to read fine print that they are perfectly capable of understanding. Occasional mental lapses can frustrate a person's physical capabilities. Even beyond such concrete occurrences, many aged writers focus on "the betrayal of the body"—feeling emotionally young and being "betrayed" by the age of the physical face in the mirror, or by the mirror of reaction to their age from others.[7] The variability of age based on one's relative, situational age further destabilizes the category. The normative, "naturalized notion of *the body* is itself a consequence of taboos that render that body discrete by virtue of its stable boundaries" (J. Butler, *Gender* 132-3, emphasis in the original). I add *normative* to *natural*, because according to Butler, the very question of what part(s) are natural always already creates a discursively regulated body. That is, the discursive ability to separate the parts of the body from each other, in and of itself, fragments the perceptions of the body. For example, where does *finger* stop and *hand* begin? Because body parts are "naturally" connected, their separation (as when one separates a finger from a hand) constitutes an unnatural act of (discursive) violence. In distinguishing between *finger* and *hand*, language dismembers, and thus denaturalizes, the body.[8]

Discursive production equals *cultural* production, with nature as the matching and oppositional unit in the binary. The binary relationship supports a "hierarchy in which culture freely 'imposes' meaning on nature, and hence, renders it into an 'Other' to be appropriated.... Nature/culture discourse regularly figures nature as female, in need of subordination by a culture that is invariably figured as male, active, and abstract" (J. Butler, *Gender* 37). Thus, the mind/body and nature/culture binaries reinforce both the distinction between genders and the binary nature of gender itself. The cultural aspects of how the nature/culture binary affects aging bodies begin early in life.

Starting in infancy, each individual receives billions of cultural messages. Some of them are literally spoken; other ideas are transmitted through vision, taste, touch, or smell. In the media, in grocery stores, at school, in cars, at friends' houses, at home, at work, the individual is told how to be a good, socially acceptable, Western consumer. The telling takes place verbally, visually, and socially, millions of times a day in a thousand places. To greater or lesser degrees, an individual has some ability to accept or reject any particular message. One can refuse to purchase products from companies whose ads encourage violence or underage sex or that do not treat aged people, queer people, people of color, or people of a certain gender with respect, for example. Nonetheless, the messages get delivered. Each message physically and psychically changes the individual as the brain forms new neural connections to record the event and the memory expands to place the event into the mental data bank. Each message literally becomes inscribed on the body, leaves a change that marks the individual, informing how the person thinks and acts.

One of the most central of Western cultural values, individualism, intersects with these messages to create what seems to be a choice. That is, free will allows people to make many conscious decisions about how to behave, holding them morally responsible for the choices they make about which cultural messages to accept or reject. The more time an individual has spent receiving cultural messages, the greater the social expectations that the person will accept and live by them as a socially constituted, discursively produced subject. For a subject to *be* a subject, it must always already be socially constituted. Resistance can happen only from a social position, and only at the risk of losing that social position.

The question then becomes how this social constitution works with aged bodies. "From this perspective, physical decline is not merely a threat to personal autonomy; it represents moral failure" (Jablonski 192). Woodward posits that, because aging seems to occur primarily on the body, it has a greater effect on women than on men (*Aging* 169). For each aged body, the quantity of culturally inscribed messages overdetermines the body, as does the requirement to "choose" to incorporate those messages to become a socially acceptable self. On the other hand, part of what constitutes an aged body has to do with the physical (rather than social) changes of the body through time—with the messages that the aged person's body inscribes on itself. For women who have tried to achieve "a closer approximation to idealized beauty [in an effort to increase their] social power and opportunities, anti-aging discourses and the fight to preserve a youthful appearance starkly belie the supposedly benign nature of engaging in beauty regimens. Clearly, older women are compelled to engage in beauty work, irrespective of the futility of their efforts, or face social eradication" (Hurd Clarke 136). Eventually, the passage of time becomes inscribed on the aged self in ways that are not socially acceptable—wrinkles, liver spots, joint pain, farsightedness. These alterations are different from, say, the ones that come from working out in a gym (or not working out) because—Oil of Olay, Retina A, and sociodemographic differences notwithstanding—ultimately the body has no choice about whether to make the physical changes of age. The temporally induced modifications undermine or etch out the social inscriptions on the palimpsest of the body.

The agent performing those inscriptions remains murky. At the risk of reifying these ideas, it seems clear that those who participate in the American regulating ideological apparatuses of *culture* or *society* (à la Althusser) obviously do not condone or accept the age that becomes written on the body. Most of the inscriptions of advanced age—the presence of gray hair, the changing reflexes—are directly contrary to the messages people receive about socially acceptable presentation and action. *Culture* knows better than to write such unacceptable messages. Western society has been telling each person, almost since birth, that wrinkles are not okay. Since culture knows that it should not create such inscriptions, then such an antisocial action must be a process of culture's binary opposite: *nature*. At a time when the self should be choosing to make itself more culturally inscribed than ever before in its life course (because one should always "choose" be at one's peak—cf. U. Beck; Schilling; Turner), the embodied self becomes partially reconstituted by a noncultural agent, by the natural body.

Degendering Age

Thus, not only have aged bodies lost part of the agency required by social expectations, but such bodies are continually reconstituting themselves, refusing the static form of the normative subject. Bodies change continually, but the aged self is not self-constituted, because the self is a social agent. The aged are seen as seemingly more natural in a framework that simultaneously removes or reduces self-agency. According to all social rules, at some point in life, each person should choose to stop aging. Of course, one *can* not, but a social perspective only records that one *does* not. As with the mind/body split, the violation of the cultural norm—in this case, the lack of agency that causes an *increased* divide between the cultural self and the natural body—becomes a system for making the inhabitants of aged bodies less human.

An individual may not be as able to act as a static, unaged subject, but one is supposed to try. Advertising slogans reflect the predominance of that project: "Maybe she's born with it; maybe it's Maybelline." "I don't just color my hair; I *revitalize* it." In North America in the twenty-first century, amid a massive array of variety and abundance and a theoretical celebration of difference, paradoxically some choices are more required than ever before. "The key to ageism is the notion that if one *can* discipline one's body so as to forestall aging, one should do so—or else be deserving of marginalization" (Calasanti, "Bodacious" 341, emphasis in the original). Thus, the seeming choice to "go gray," have wrinkles or grandchildren, and remember the Johnson administration and telephones with party lines, when that person knows that doing so places her or him in a less powerful position—at that point, socially speaking, the person has abdicated a position of power.

Change becomes a social negative because of the performative aspects of age and because of the regulatory aspects of choice. "There is no gender identity behind the expressions of gender; that identity is performatively constituted by the very expressions that are said to be its results" (J. Butler, *Gender* 25). On the one hand, throughout life, gender inflects one's experiences with social institutions as well as interpersonal interactions, so aging is always already a gendered experience. On the other hand, for a text to claim that it focuses on women and aging, or gender and aging, is somewhat ironic, perhaps even disingenuous, because the intersection of advanced age and gender can create a social location that distorts the ideas of gender such that "one cannot be a man or a woman *and* be old" (Calasanti, "Bodacious" 348, emphasis in the original; see also Thompson 1). Indeed, for much of Western culture, one might argue that gendered aged human subjects do not exist.

From the perspective of ideological positioning and power, the body becomes both more culturally female and less gendered as it ages (cf. Calasanti "Gender"; Katz and Marshall; Marshall and Katz "Embodied" and "From"; Meadows and Davidson; Richeson and Shelton 180). Aged bodies are perceived as blurring the mind/body boundaries when the body asserts its primacy as inscriptor so powerfully that the discursive self/mind can do nothing to stop it. The body signifies the female aspect of the binary, so the blurring of boundaries makes the aged self culturally (externally) perceived as more female, or less powerful. In the nature/culture split as well, as the body seems to take over, the self becomes more aligned with, or under the power of, nature and the female.

Internally, the message can be quite the opposite, as the aging self experiences a *heightened* mind/body divide. Those who have the mental ability to perceive this widening gap may see the mind as fairly constant while the body's physical and social power declines more rapidly.[9] For example, a professor may spend an hour or more focused on her scholarship or watching a movie, not noticing her body, much as she did decades ago. Hearing the doorbell chime, however, she may become conscious of the physical difference those decades make. The same body that could unconsciously leap up and bound downstairs to answer the door might respond differently now, as her knees need a moment to unbend, her legs take a few smaller steps before they are ready to stride forward, and at each stair, her hand connects lightly with the banister for balance. The professor's awareness of how her actions (or, her performance) would be perceived in a public setting reinforces the correlation between social power and physical prowess, which is to say, performativity—in particular, the performance of youthfulness. The aged body, relative to the aged mind, becomes less powerful—allied with "female"—while the aged mind becomes relatively more powerful—associated with "male." The mind/body split expands in part because of the gender divides of the internal versus the external experiences of self.

The categories of *male* and *female* in this context, though, especially for women who are not active participants in the reproductive cycle,[10] are problematic. The so-called *natural body* may be closely associated with the female, but the normative-natural female body performs reproductively; the normative-natural male body *performs*, potently. When a female body is defined as a youthful, reproductive body attractive to men of all ages, then as women mature past youthfulness and beyond reproductivity, their bodies become coded as not-female.[11] "Aging poses a huge threat to women's sense of identity, perceived femininity, and sexual desirability" (Hurd Clarke 2, 128). Similarly, as men's bodies pass beyond youthfulness to the point that their virility may come into question, they too can be stripped of gender.[12] With the decrease or loss of ability to perform as a normatively natural female or male, the individual becomes less gendered, or degendered. And since subjects are always already gendered, the inability to perform as gendered equates with a loss of subjecthood, of power and agency.

Of course, not all older men experience a loss of potency and virility, and reproductive technologies make procreation a commoditized possibility for women after menopause.[13] However, even when they retain physical capability, aged bodies lose their *social* potency. When aged bodies lose agency and power because they are perceived as being more "natural," and hence more "female," aged men lose the social potency of being the Phallus.[14] As aged women become both physically and culturally "less female," their ability and willingness to act as mirrors for male power may well decrease. Joan Borysenko, a cellular biologist who studies women's bodies, cites studies as well as correlational and anecdotal evidence that, in menopause, women become more aggressive (148, 152, 153, 156). This power shift reflects the double trajectories of age, in which differences are relational to others and to the self. Thus, the reduction of virility, agency, and power for aged men happens in relation to women of their own cohort and in comparison with men of younger cohorts. The ego might mourn the self and desire the lost self, but not necessarily sexually.[15] However, part of that which is lost has to do with sexuality—the gendered self and one's participation in a sexual economy.

Abjection

Theories of the abject provide another explanatory layer to understanding the diminished social power of senior bodies. "Older women . . . are ejected from the social body as abject" (Woodward, *Statistical* 79–80, referencing Macdonald). According to Julia Kristeva, the abject is anything so abhorrent to the members of a culture that it must be constituted outside the realm of culture. In a context where old women serve as scapegoats, embodiments of physical and intellectual realities that society fears and thus represses, old women's presence "challenges the theory of the unconscious" and brings to consciousness that which must be repressed (Kristeva 7–8). Such a stance encourages the social exclusion and invisibility of elders—a familiar reality for far too many.

In Kristeva's discussion of the abject, the subject has neither sex nor gender.[16] Elizabeth Grosz, a significant figure for her work on the female body and its relationships with size and weight, finds this elision problematic and explores how Kristeva's theory constructs the body. Grosz's history of theories of corporeality and subjectivity provides context for Kristeva's work. In this history, Grosz points out, "through the fantasy of a cohesive, stable identity, facilitated by its specular identification with its own image, [the ego] is able to position itself as a subject within the space of its body" (82). To create a stable self, "the subject must disavow part of itself . . . and this form of refusal marks whatever identity it acquires as provisional, and open to breakdown and instability" (86). That is, identity cannot be anything other than imaginary. Lacan's and J. Butler's (*Bodies* and *Gender*) concepts include reminders that this illusion is necessary and integral to social functioning.

The aged social self works at the boundaries of the social, so it also can change the functional social boundaries. "If I am affected by what does not yet appear to me as a thing, it is because laws, connections, and even structures of meaning govern and condition me" (Kristeva 10). By its very existence outside the boundaries of society, the abject delineates the boundaries of acceptability, and thus, of visibility. The abject is an abyss, writes Grosz, that both attracts and repulses (89). Confronting the abject can result in that "burst of beauty that overwhelms" (Kristeva 210). I have argued that this experience has the potential to disrupt the boundaries of self-built-on-illusion with which each person has lived his or her whole life; the ability to re-view and re-envision the self, a broadening of locations available for the self, opens up possibilities that many psychological and cultural theorists considered fixed and sealed at toddlerhood (Marshall, "Through" 61–3). "One does not get rid of the impure; one can, however, bring it into being a second time, and differently from the original impurity" (Kristeva 28). Instead of succumbing to invisibility, one can literally *re*-vision the lived self, perhaps amid thunder and revelation, reconfiguring the realm of the social to include bodies changed by age.[17]

In Grosz's understanding, Kristeva's work identifies three categories of the abject: oral disgust (the urge to dispel the (m)Other's food),[18] the corpse, and signs of sexual difference. "The subject must have a certain, if incomplete, mastery of the abject; it must keep it in check and at a distance in order to define itself as a subject" (87). Elsewhere, I argue that the aged self simultaneously rejects and, through its body, becomes the (m)Other ("Through"). By this reckoning, the aged body is a site of multiple abjections: in its incorporation of the mother, the aged body may solidify the subject's connection to the forbidden; the aged body, in being the

Other to the self, creates the possibility for a death of the self; and the aged body's decrease in socially recognized markings and mirrored reinforcements of sexual difference results in an increased awareness of one's gendered self.

However much that self identifies as gendered, its liminal status may prevent its participation in gendered exchange, marooning a gendered subject in a socially genderless body. Gendered aged figures such as *the witch, the dirty old man,* and *the sage granny* can continue to have some cultural sway, but these are not subjects. As twenty-first-century popular and art-house films reinforce, old women who do not conform to heteronormative narrative expectations—that is, female elders who attempt to assert their agency as gendered aged human subjects—are punished with social expulsion or death (Marshall and Swinnen). In moving through time away from the social acceptability of visible youth, old bodies in effect are read as excreting culture, reverting to "nature."

On the one hand, individuals are held responsible for this seeming choice. Simultaneously, the movement away from a position of power suggests the limits of one's agency and ability to make choices that would return one to power. Since "the question of locating 'agency' is usually associated with the viability of the subject" (J. Butler, *Gender* 142), then as one becomes less normatively performative, one becomes less viable as a subject. As Butler suggests of lesbian bodies, aged bodies lose "cultural legitimacy and, hence, [are] cast, not outside or prior to culture, but outside cultural *legitimacy,* still within culture, but culturally 'out-lawed'" (J. Butler, *Gender* 87), abjected. The aged body becomes the Other.

Potential

When a body reaches a point where it no longer affirms social norms, it is assumed to be regressing, morally as well as physically. In a culture otherwise fixated on the linearity of time and progress, the body follows a circular pattern: childhood, adulthood, second childhood. Thus, being *over the hill* represents a return, rather than progress,[19] an important regulatory construct. Formulating the aged self as one that retraces worn paths erases the possibilities for the aged self to continue becoming. Since one has already been where one is going, there is nothing new to learn, nothing to look forward to. If the aged self continued becoming, then it might know something that the youth cult(ure) cannot. How terrifying. How interesting!

And how true. When asked to describe what old people are like and what they themselves will be like in old age, most young people use largely negative adjectives to describe what elders in general are like, generally positive adjectives to portray the elders they know, and even more optimistic words to depict the elder selves they envision becoming. That is, in comparison with what they think is the usual experience of old age, each of the youths believes that she or he will have a more positive experience (Lamb "Polyester"). "Well-educated people are usually surprised to learn that retirement is generally a *positive* growth period" (Moody, "Overview" xxx, emphasis in the original; see also Carstensen). Those who believe that their lives will be better than the negative stereotypes are correct—their experience of aging is very likely to be more positive than the old age they imagined, which was based on inaccurate conjecture. For example, the majority of young people believe that most elders have substantial age-related cognitive decline; few of those youths know that there is a parallel age-related cognitive gain, and their stereotypes of cognitive decline "are more severe than most actual deficits" (Richeson and Shelton 177). Moreover, for Americans over the age of fifty, the older they are, the more they see their happiness as something under their control ("Happiness"). Thus, as they age, people find their assumptions about their own seeming exceptionality confirmed, because their experiences of aging-into-retirement are more positive than what they believe to be the average.[20] Retellings of the story about their seemingly remarkable experience perpetuate the mythos of North American individuality and exceptionalism.

Stories that shape our understanding shape our future, and distorted stories disfigure the future. At the same time that toddlers begin to understand that they have a body, they are "aged by culture," which makes a state of "prelapsarian agelessness" (Gullette, *Aged* 109) as much of a fanciful concept as the "ageless utopia" Barbara Frey Waxman (*From* 3) imagines. The very act of learning about age studies creates a cascade of possibility. As a field of study, a theoretical framework, and an activist stance, age studies reintegrates agedness into the realm of the social. Much like other identity studies do, age studies makes evident the connections between the mind and the body. Each time another scholar takes up the topic, it is as if the ideas have been moved from a dank corner of the root cellar to a well-lit workbench. Even as it is evident that much work remains, the very act of bringing this topic to a new location adds to its potential. The more light that is shed on how overdetermination by inscription proscribes aged subjects' choices about their aged bodies, the easier it is to de- and reconstruct understandings of aging and old age. Instead of abjection, degendering, and erasure, a well-examined process of aging-into-old-age can lead to a revision of beliefs about aging. Remarkably, with age studies it becomes possible to envision how much we have to learn as we continue to become.

CHAPTER 3

Ambiguous Loss, Ambiguous Gain:

Age Studies Analyses in Menopause and Beyond

> I live deeply with the knowledge that my choices are narrowing, but that all my life they were much more narrowed when I bought into society's denial of death. My wrinkled face now reminds me of what the terms were every day of my life.[1]

Aging into middle age and then into old age makes one conscious of the changes of time. Birthdays, as a marker of time progress, might once have been joyfully celebrated as one's cumulative chronological age led to increasing levels of grown-up privilege—thirteen, sixteen, eighteen, twenty-one—but might now lead to embarrassment or denial that the continued advance of time eventually challenges one's sense of self.[2] Women who ignore or deny their own aging try to maintain an unchanging idea of who they are, a "fixed, abstract identit[y]" (Schlib 208), even though society and chronology will not and cannot grant them a stable reflection of self. Moreover, aging offers a real potential for release "from the fixity of dominant unified subject positions" (Komesaroff, Rothfield, and Daly 11). The "dominance" in that concept may be more relevant for straight White women than it is for queer or Black women, as discussed in chapters 1 and 5, respectively. Whether the physical aspects of the change are pleasant or unpleasant, and no matter how others react, when a woman notices an age-related difference in performativity, it reminds the internal self that something has changed.[3] Recognizing and acknowledging that change has very different consequences than resisting or ignoring it.

However much or little this change is welcomed, something has altered. External and internal markers of identity do not function when they are stagnant. Part of the person, part of the self, is no more, while other aspects have survived. With the negative cultural valuations of aging and old age, it is not surprising that this transition is not always welcome. Women who are unprepared for this change may find the difference particularly traumatic: "Almost half a woman's life lies beyond the transition [of menopause], yet nothing in her education or her conditioning has prepared her for this new role" (Greer, *The Change* 24), especially if she is White. With the change, something has ended, and something continues. People become attached to their younger selves and the accompanying social power; letting go of that internal self-image can be difficult and sometimes painful.

Negotiating with texts that stress the pathology of aging, women simultaneously grapple with issues of self-identity and social identity. No wonder that "women in mid-life are afraid to know—and fiercely resist acknowledging—that menopause can affect *them*" (Sheehy 34, emphasis in the original). People who are skeptical about the value of such a major change, or who think it improbable or unseemly, will find the process more of a challenge, and the dissolution of the old self more of a loss. With the loss of a relatively stable and reasonably cohesive internal self-image, a new self-image is established. Life-changing events that encourage a reformulation of self can create a time of abnegation and refusal, "a time of new development and new beginnings" (Woodward, *Statistical* 66, citing Stanley Hall), or, for women who have long embraced the possibilities of fluid identity, a time that seems similar to the times before it; and there is a vast field of middle ground in which women embody elements of multiple positions.

The first and largest section of this chapter focuses on menopause, an early and particularly noticeable indicator of age-based change. Menopause has, at least theoretically, clear enough boundaries that one can identify as pre- or postmenopausal, even if the actual experience is much more indeterminate. Judging by the number of books available, the transition of menopause seems to be the part of aging about which women (and perhaps the men in their lives) feel the most need for written guidance. Additional contributing factors are that this change seems to have distinct borders, it can be imagined as simply biological, and it has significant potential to be marked as a pathology. The breadth and diversity of ideas about *the change* provide a wide canvas on which to showcase practical as well as theoretical applications of age studies concepts.

Next, the chapter discusses publications that consider a larger, more nebulous change: *getting older*—or, to borrow Margaret Cruikshank's apt term, *learning to be old*. This was my entry point into age studies. The vital old women and men who shared their stories with me were role models, but other storytellers provided examples of how miserable elderhood might be. As a librarian's daughter, my assumption was that someone had written about how to do it right, and if I could locate that text, I would find useful guidance. Perhaps not surprisingly, the recommendations I found varied widely in quality. This discussion provides a generalized view of texts that veer off track, with just a few more detailed critiques. The analysis then focuses on positive models, the foundational texts written in the 1980s and 1990s that many age studies scholars have in common.

The chapter concludes by exploring how the changes of aging-into-old-age connect with the concept of *ambiguous loss*, a slightly more theoretical framework that has practical value in understanding the responses to and the texts about the changes of menopause and beyond. Collectively and in conjunction with the more abstract concepts of chapter 2, the specifics of this chapter form a solid foundation on which to build the ideas about the literary works in chapters 4, 5, and 6.

Menopause

As I was growing up, my mother told me how babies are made, talked to me about menarche, birth control, her two very different birthing experiences, her two abortions, her breast cancer, and her lovers, yet this was the sum total of our conversation about menopause:

> Me: I've got my period. Do you have any tampons?
> Her: Nope, because I don't need them anymore! (Laughs with delight.)

What I heard about menopause from other women also was limited, mostly the occasional, "Is it hot in here, or is it just me?" I am not alone in this experience, especially among Caucasian Americans.

Twenty-five percent of American women hear *nothing* from their mothers about menopause, and talk among peers about menopause often takes the form of humor or self-deprecation; health professionals serve as an information source for only 16 percent of women (Mansfield 98–100; Johnson). Generally, North American women learn about menopause from the media: magazine and journal articles, the Internet, and popular medical books. Caucasian American women of a certain age frequently cite as a source of information the *All in the Family* episode in which Edith Bunker goes through menopause (Mansfield 99; see also Kaplan "Resisting"). "Two-thirds of all American women say nothing to anybody" about menopause (Sheehy 8). In the early 1990s, less than half of American women received information about menopause from others in their cohort (Mansfield). This chapter examines the texts and contexts of menopause—the myths, silences, perceptions,[4] and voices of menopause.

In the absence of hormone doses or other medical intervention, most women begin menstruating between their twelfth and thirteenth birthdays and cease menstruating between the ages of forty-five and fifty-five. However, in North America, between age twelve and age fifty-five, most women experience some form of intervention that temporarily or permanently affects the menstrual cycle. Some birth control methods have that effect. Women who menstruate but who then have their ovaries surgically removed, as well as women on medications such as tamoxifen, experience menopause. Women who menstruate and whose uteruses but not their ovaries have been removed do not have periods, but do continue to cycle through monthly hormonal changes, and usually experience the hormonal changes of menopause, even though they may not have had a period for many years. At one point in time, one-third of American women had their uteruses, ovaries, or both surgically removed (Sheehy 19). Exploring the ways in which surgery and medication change how women experience menopause is beyond the scope of this text; it is important to acknowledge that the experience of menopause has many variations.

The term *menopause* first came into its current usage in the mid-1800s. Depending on who defines it, menopause is either the time in a woman's life that begins when she ceases to have regular, monthly periods (although some women never have this) and ends at the end of her last period, or the time in a woman's life after the end of her last period. According to the *Oxford English Dictionary*, this time previously was called the *climacteric*, a word that came into English from Spanish around 1600. The climacteric affected both men and women as the "period of life (usually between the ages of 45 and 60) at which the vital forces begin to decline (in women coinciding with the period of 'change of life')." In the early 1800s, a "long-established tradition that saw male and female bodies as similar both in structure and in function began to come 'under devastating attack'" (Martin 31, citing Laqueur). Thus, the modification in terminology to a word specific to women's reproductive systems provides a new linguistic model that reflects a change in scientific practice.

Although some contemporary pop-culture and feminist discussions of menopause (e.g., Greer *The Change*) reclaim the term *climacteric*,[5] this discussion uses the term *menopause* for two reasons. First, in agreement with Patricia Kaufert's report that most women use the term *menopause* this way as a "'self-anchoring' definition in which they saw themselves as menopausal when there was a change in their accustomed patterns of menstruation" (Daly 160–1, citing Kaufert 333). Second, this use of menopause refers to a span of time, rather than to a specific moment (ending), acknowledging menopause as nonlinear and as a process (Gullette, "Menopause" 181),[6] just as other elements of aging are.

Menopausal discourse arrives on a body that always already exists within the culture as a fully inscribed site. The power of the discourses of menopause sculpts a body that is compliant to and reconstitutes that same power. Thus, the available discourses about menopause directly affect women's bodily experiences. For example, as the introduction describes, Dillaway's study shows that medical professionals' misunderstandings or misrepresentations of the experiences of menopause, or their insistence on the connection between chronological age and menopause, can affect women's health. Her research further demonstrates that such encounters cause women to question the worth of medical treatment for a broad range of issues and can have significant consequences for a woman's relationship to Western medicine for the remainder of her life, which can further affect her physical health.

Because most consider menopause a women's health issue, it has become a feminist issue, but how feminists approach menopause is quite culturally dependent. In England, for example, feminists worked to get the health system to recognize the usefulness of hormone replacement therapy (HRT).[7] A medical system that accepts the value of HRT must also acknowledge that menopausal symptoms are not merely the products of a woman's mental pathology, but that women's symptoms do have a physiological basis (Rothfield 40–1, citing Vines 140). In contrast, in the United States, "one of the major strategies of feminist discussions of menopause has been to shift the analysis from a form of technical [medicalized] knowledge to understanding that issue from women's perspectives" (Komesaroff et al. 3–4). Even following the HRT scare, American feminists have tended to argue that doctors and women consider menopause to be a medical "problem" for which they accept HRT treatment too blithely, eliding the potential dangers of long-term HRT use.[8] The contrasts between the British and the American debates and feminist actions about HRT highlight the dichotomous cultural camps that women must navigate when discussing menopause.

Margaret Lock's study of menopause in Japan suggests that culture significantly influences seemingly biological menopausal experiences, creating them as well as channeling interpretations of them. This understanding calls into question menopause's status as a solely natural process, one that the body would undergo regardless of cultural influence. Nonetheless, since residents of North American countries hear the "menopause as separate from culture" perspective most often, this analysis begins with that perspective, delving into four common misconceptions about menopause.

Menopause Mythology

One misconception is that women will feel sad and powerless when their periods end because they know they will never have any more children.[9] The majority of women do not feel this way about menopause. Even as some women feel guilty that they are not having the response that they are "supposed to," most express relief at not having to deal with periods and not having to worry about pregnancy; some also report increased energy and enthusiasm (Borysenko; Campioni

82; Gaston and Porter; Martin 175, 177; Sheehy; see also Gullette, *Agewise* 58). Moreover, "the vast majority of women finish having children long before menopause; not menopause but birth-control ended their reproductive" activities (Gullette, "Menopause" 180).

The phenomenon of *involutional melancholia*, a type of depression, serves as an example of how cultural beliefs about the experiences surrounding menopause lead to its medicalization. Listed in *DSM-I* (1952) and II (1968), involutional melancholia occurred almost exclusively in women who were simultaneously menopausal and recent empty-nesters. Further study revealed that this so-called disease was a symptom of the emotional upheaval in social roles, self-worth, and self-definition. Starting with the *DSM-III* (1980), involutional melancholia was no longer listed as a medical condition.[10]

The AARP reports that multiple studies of women pre-, peri-, and postmenopausally suggest that rates of depression do not increase during menopause. "Other events that might occur during midlife, such as divorce, the death of a spouse[, partner,] or parent, children leaving home, and parents needing care, might be stressful and cause some women to become depressed" (AARP). Other studies suggest that so-called menopausal sadness—which receives the label of depression when seen as a pathology—directly correlates with the number of social roles in a woman's life (Bart; Martin). That is, women whose primary social roles and identity have been *mother* and *wife* may get depressed when the *mother* part of that role disappears (for example, when all of the children leave home) at the same time as a key aspect of the *wife* role—sexual desirability—may be encountering rocky ground. Most women do not report feeling sadness about menopause, and most often, the depression they report at this time relates to a change in established social roles.[11] Many women report feeling an increase in energy and engagement, a feeling that anthropologist Margaret Mead called *postmenopausal zest*. Mead considered the collective energy found in the twenty-five years of women's lives postmenopause a vital resource that could be put to collective use (Glennon 147; see also Lutkehaus). Especially when a woman's lived experience directly contradicts the socially accepted myth of sadness—that is, if a woman feels energized and satisfied at a time in her life when a "real woman" is supposed to be sad—she may be less inclined to tell others about her feelings.

Connecting midlife sadness in women to menopause constructs their emotions as stemming from physiological changes. If a woman does experience significant depression, she has to overcome both the social stigma of mental illness and the fear of medical intervention before reporting these feeling. Women going through menopause who confide in their doctors about depression are more likely to be told that their feelings stem only from hormonal causes, so their symptoms are more likely to be treated solely with medication, whereas if they reported similar emotions at another point in their lives, doctors would be more likely to offer psychological treatment as well (Dillaway). Cultural interpretations affect women's lived experiences and thus need to be considered in cultural and literary analyses.

A second misconception: women are understanding of others going through this process. Actually, people who have not yet gone through menopause tend to view the menopausal experience as simply a process of hormonal changes, whereas women who are going or have gone through menopause tend to have a more complex view of the process and often report a mental as well as a physical evolution (Martin 174–5, 177). Male doctors, who both lack the empathy of experience and who tend to hold more negative stereotypes about menopause (Dege and Gretzinger 63; Greer, *The Change* 17), would be inclined to consider menopause a treatable illness, in ways that female doctors who have experienced menopause would not. Physicians without personal experience of menopause (i.e., the majority of doctors) would be more inclined to prescribe drug treatments for the symptoms of it than if they had experienced menopause, and medical school instructors would be more likely to teach students this perspective.[12] The myth that all female doctors understand the complexity of menopause is inaccurate, and that assumption perpetuates the more widespread misunderstandings of menopause.

None of the culturally sanctioned roles to which a woman previously had access—virgin, Madonna, whore—are available to the postmenopausal woman, who is unlikely to have much experience in the crone role. Ergo, to maintain a known place in society, she has to "pass" for premenopausal, abandon her status as a woman, or redefine the category of *woman*. No wonder that "women in mid-life are afraid to know—and fiercely resist acknowledging—that menopause can affect *them*" (Sheehy 34, emphasis in the original). To acknowledge menopause is to acknowledge that who you are is changing. Admitting that one has changed, or changed one's mind, can be hard to do, and in a youth cult(ure), knowing that one has different beliefs and experiences than the majority of younger women can have a silencing effect. Also, an individual whose experience varies from the stereotype may be more hesitant to mention her experiences to others.

Misconception number three: women going through menopause go a bit crazy.[13] When debating if menopause makes women crazy, some postmenopausal women say yes, some say no. Sometimes, the partners or families of women see those women as having had mental changes that have a negative impact, while the women see themselves as having changed but with a positive outcome (Martin 176). Neurobiologist Joan Borysenko, anthropologist Emily Martin, philosopher Mia Campioni, and cultural critic Gail Sheehy offer anecdotal and statistical evidence that, during and after menopause, women become less tolerant of and are more willing to challenge social absurdity and injustice. Even as women in menopause speak out about social justice issues, however, they may not want to attribute their newfound focus to the physical changes of aging, or they may be unaware of the causational connection.

Definitions of mental instability and insanity rely on the implied opposites—the seemingly normal. For most women, the so-called normal state of their lives includes gender oppression, and often other forms of oppression as well. If normal is oppressed, then resisting oppression can seem abnormal, even insane. Operating in a system of oppression, resistance to that system is reasonable—sane—even if it is not normal. Resistance to the norm, however, pushes the resistor toward the margins of society, and because many of the other experiences of menopause involve similar social devaluation, a refusal to relinquish whatever cultural cache one has had may work to muffle women's communication about their newfound "sharper sense of the ridiculous" (Campioni 82). Furthermore, a desire to maintain the illusion that one has not changed will work to silence speech that demonstrates one's new perceptions.

Menopause creates physiological change, and often mental and emotional modifications as well, which leads to a fourth misconception: the changes of menopause are all about endings and lacks. This misperception combines the myth of depression and the medical paradigms that define menopause in terms of the cessation of ovulation and a deficiency in "normal" (i.e., nonmenopausal) levels of regulatory hormones.[14] This narrative of lack and loss works to silence women for the same reason that the "sad" myth does. The changes in family roles are discussed above. Physical desirability serves as a form of social capital within and beyond the family (cf. Hurd Clarke 125). At menopause, women without children often are thought of as having a new and additional loss of possibility—the potential for having children—without regard for the women's earlier experiences, in which she might or might not have made a conscious choice to be childless, that decision might or might not be in the distant past, and the results might or might not be a positive outcome in her life. Defined as stemming from a lack, hormonal changes and childlessness are coded as negative.

The medical-industrial complex and those who gain power from women's oppression have quite a bit to gain from this paradigm: doctors are needed to diagnose and care for this so-called lack, drug companies make money on medical treatments, and women who cannot reproduce are formulated as being in need of treatment, again connecting their use value in society to their reproductive and sexual value and to their value as consumers.[15]

This pithy encapsulation of these four myths belies the enormity of their effect on women's lives. The impact of these misperceptions begins long before a woman experiences menopause in her own body.

With hormonal changes undergirding the rhetoric of menopause as a time of loss, a more in-depth consideration of the mythology of hormones and the consequences of such stories becomes useful in understanding this myth. Emily Martin's influential 1987 study of (among other things) hormonal metaphors discusses the body as a factory and hormones as a "signal-response" mechanism (40). This frames "the body as a hierarchical information processing system," and menopause damages the body's "system of authority" (42). Since then, the discourse has changed, and the more recent discourse about menopause tends to conceive of hormones as messengers (Berkson; Clark, Snedeker, and Devine; Gale; Grimwade, Fraser, and Farrell 45; Gulli; Hendrick; Merck; Northrup 37; Osteoporosis; Rothfield 36; Search). From sources as diverse as Merck, which would ostensibly be in favor of HRT, to the *Gale Encyclopedia of Alternative Medicine*, a potentially neutral reference, to Berkson's *Hormone Deception*, a book billed as the *Silent Spring* for hormones, the metaphor of the messenger seems nearly ubiquitous (*Hormone Deception* makes it a bicycle messenger). When hormones—particularly estrogen—are posited as messengers, they serve as the mobile elements of a communication system. During menopause, this analogy suggests that, at the microscopic level, the body no longer has a team of organized, active envoys; its ability to communicate with itself has been crippled. Some elements of the body become remote and wild outposts, sending sporadic, garbled messages, whereas other components are silenced.[16]

When a woman experiences a change constructed as stemming from an absence, for reasons of vocational or social prestige and power she may not want to let others know. Also, because the culture's ideas about aging are so negative,[17] and because menopause is a sign of aging, a woman may wish to remain silent about *any* menopausal changes, positive or negative. Moreover, the lack of cultural support and of venues for expression not only works to isolate each woman experiencing menopause, but the lack of social acceptance of menopause also reifies the cultural devaluation of this experience.

This book, with its North American perspective, has focused on the myths surrounding the over-medicalization of menopause, but over-*mental*ization of this experience can affect women's experiences just as much, as the example of the British healthcare system suggests. The over-mentalization perspective highlights the presence of physiological changes that accompany the experiences and emotions surrounding menopause. When constructed solely as a natural biological experience, then naturally, menopause should be manageable, and only women who have impaired biological functions would experience the changes of menopause as needing medical treatment. If merely a biological phenomenon, then the experience of menopause should not require medical attention, which means that problems with menopause stem from the mind.[18] Hot flashes, sleep disturbances, and the like will be—should be—untreated by a medical doctor.

Moreover, if menopause is merely a set of biological changes that the body should be able to handle, then any negative emotions that coexist with the changes of menopause would be mental health issues (Daly 161; Rothfield 41). In this scenario, the women who need intervention are those whose brains are getting in the way of their bodies—that is, those with mental pathologies, who should be referred to a mental health professional. Women with menopausal symptoms would then have to overcome the social stigma accompanying mental health problems to seek help, and could be prescribed mental health medications rather than hormones.

Too often, scholars who attempt to combine ideas about over-medicalization and over-mentalization end up trying to figure out what percentage of or what parts of menopause have medical causes and what parts or percentage are attributable to cultural causes (Greer, *The Change* 16 and 94; Rothfield 33). The variations in menopausal experiences create challenges in coalition formation (Rips 85) and make the experience difficult to study. Few theories usefully explore the mutually constitutive medical and mental aspects of menopause.

If the only available descriptives for an experience invoke medical malfunctions, then women cannot discuss their experiences without pathologizing them. The majority of society's speeches and texts about menopause have either a medical or an antimedical focus, which leaves plenty of room for feminist additions to the conversation—women describing their experiences, discussions of the power relations involved in (mis)conceptions of menopause, and re-visions of what empowering and empowered discussions about menopause might look like. Cultural and literary analysts need theories and a vocabulary to apply to the texts and phenomena they study. Widening the available, acceptable discourses on menopause disrupts its liminality; an examination of feared experiences may make them less daunting. "It is only when women unite and make positive discourses of their own that their combined power can have a real effect in the network of power relations" (Sybylla 212; see also

Daly 174; Rich 14). Interpersonal conversations about menopause can become tools by which women can further challenge the myths and prescriptive cultural meanings of menopause.[19]

In working to disrupt the silencing effects of mainstream North American culture, scholars do need to maintain an awareness of the many challenges. One challenge: the *difference dilemma*—"the irony that by calling attention to . . . differences we may reinforce them, but that by ignoring differences we may leave invisible power hierarchies in place" (Schiebinger 3). A second challenge: ensuring an awareness of the multiplicity of cultures and the diversity of effects those cultures have on menopausal experiences.[20] A third challenge: the *call to voice* about a body process is inherently Western.[21] Given the powerful effects socioeconomic status can have on menopause, a further danger is that the "privileged, in speaking in positive ways about the transition, become used as condemnation of those whose circumstances ensnare them in the powerful prevailing construction of menopause as misery" (Mackie 21). For all of those reasons, and many more, explorations and theories of aging issues, including menopause, need to proceed inclusively.

Menopause: Questionable *Wisdom*

The plethora of self-help books about menopause may exist despite the myriad of factors silencing discourse about menopause, or these factors might be contributing to their effect. The sheer number of texts about menopause can be overwhelming. In 2006, a search on Amazon.com using *menopause* as a keyword generated a list of over 600 books; running the same search in 2014 yielded more than 5,100. In looking for a representative text, I used market forces to choose a convenience sample, assuming that the best-selling text is one of those with the greatest impact. A random sampling of several dozen other books on the subject suggests that the content of this text is indeed representative. Beginning in 2001 and continuing through the present day, Christiane Northrup's books on menopause have been top sellers, not just within the category of health but on the *New York Times* bestseller list for more than a year.

Northrup's best-known book, *The Wisdom of Menopause: Creating Physical and Emotional Health and Healing During the*

Change, has been variably received by its lay audience; responses range from exclamations that this book should be required reading, to declarations that the book must be a joke, to protestations that the information in the book is medically inaccurate.[22] Northrup introduces menopause as a natural experience, "exciting and health-enhancing" (7); the remainder of the book, however, tends to belie this perspective. For example, she lists twenty-two common health symptoms, including headaches and depression, as potential evidence of a need for estrogen-imbalance remediation.[23] There are more than a dozen similar lists in the book, each describing the symptoms of a different imbalance, with the need for intervention assessed via inventories that are so wide-ranging that most women and even many male readers may end up with the impression that they need treatment. "In the guise of telling women not to worry, most medical and popular texts tell women what there is to worry about" (Gullette, "Menopause" 184). Such fear works to create a readership and a market for cures. What responsible woman would not to want to know all of her options for greater health, and would not then subscribe to the options she can afford?

The list of supplements that Northrup suggests are needed to optimize perimenopausal health includes vitamins A, B_1, B_2, B_5, B_6, B_{12}, C, D, and E; glutathione, alpha-lipoic acid, coenzyme Q_{10}, DHA, niacin, biotin, folic acid, inositol, choline, calcium, magnesium, boron, chromium, copper, iron, manganese, zinc, selenium, potassium, molybdenum, vanadium, and trace minerals—"ten or more capsules or tablets per day. Think of them as food, not medicine" (220–1). The message is that taking care of one's body includes daily ingestion of each of those elements, and if a woman has not been taking them all, she has only herself to blame for any bodily or emotional harm arising from such ignorance. In books like Northrup's, women are considered so alienated from themselves that they fail to correctly interpret their own bodies. Because the hormones-as-messengers metaphor leads to women's inherent alienation from parts of themselves as the messengers deliver unpredictably, if at all, during and following menopause, the metaphor suggests that women's self-interpretations are almost certain to fail.

Northrup goes so far as to suggest that menopausal symptoms are messages of inner conflict and discontent, sent from a woman's emotions to her self via the body (39–42). Women with any menopausal symptoms, she posits, therefore need medical personnel to act as more reliable and more technically skilled interpreters. The menopausal woman has become interpellated as so distanced from herself as to be a foreigner—or a foreign substance—that needs help inhabiting her body, lest her ignorance of the local language bring harm to herself or the host system. Menopause, with its effects on hormones, continues to be mythologized as a significant lack—as a medical pathology in need of intervention.

The supplement regimen is posited as *natural*, the opposite of medical. Thus, the book interpellates readers as patients in need of the psychic and medical wisdom of the text to interpret women's seemingly natural bodily and emotional ideals. It encourages women to simultaneously take responsibility for the creation and the elimination of their own pathologies. In doing so, it reaffirms many cultural ideas about the pathologies of menopause. This form of self-help therapy offers the hopeful idea that change is possible and both physically and psychically beneficial, because it is a natural part of the body's innate desire for health.[24] That idea constructs a path across the public/private boundaries. There is shame in inhabiting a body that is construed as having been drawn into physical aberrance due to neglect, which is caused when the mind becomes so emotionally distant from the body (which longs to conform to the stereotype of health) that it creates the need for medical intervention to restore the corpus to its natural state. Thus, "Medicine lies on an invisible boundary between the private and the public, between personal freedom and social control" (Komesaroff 55). Negotiating with medicalized texts of menopause, women simultaneously grapple with issues of identity. Each woman must individually navigate the fusion of medicalization and mentalization, a complex locale of mutual constitution.

Learning to Be Old: Help Wanted

Perhaps because menopause is a more tangible experience than aging is overall, and because it is a marker of aging, more women seek information about menopause than about other aspects of aging. Still, there is no shortage of books about aging in general. More than a thousand were published in the decade following 2004. At the end of that decade, according to amazon.com, popular options included the following:

> *Use Your Brain to Change Your Age*, by Daniel Amen
> *Seven Years Younger*, by the editors of *Good Housekeeping*
> *The Hormone Cure*, by Sara Gottfried and Christiane Northrup
> *Man 2.0: Engineering the Alpha*, by John Romaniello, Adam Bornstein, and Arnold Schwarzenegger
> *Bombshell: Explosive Medical Secrets That Will Redefine Aging*, by Suzanne Somers
> *Living the Good Long Life: A Practical Guide to Caring for Yourself and Others*, by Martha Stewart

That the titles omit the word *old* is itself instructive. Imagine looking for books on how to be fit or how to be more organized and not finding those words, or at least synonyms, in the book titles.

When I first began seeking self-help-on-aging books that had a foundation in critical analysis, I turned to the work of women who since the 1960s had actively countered sexism, racism, homophobia, able-bodiedism, and other identity-based power differentials. Having questioned the status quo for close to forty years, second-wave feminist authors, I thought, would have interesting and useful things to say. For these authors, who realized that they now were having birthdays for the same ages they remember celebrating for their grandmothers, gender has become aged for them, or perhaps age has become gendered. As Germaine Greer explained in a lecture, "In the '70s, women carried banners demanding the right to control their own bodies, but no such right can be said to exist for individuals of any sex. Your body is in fact not under your control, and if you don't know it when you're twenty, you'll certainly know it by the time you're seventy-five" ("Women"). Feminists who were active in the 1970s and who have written about the transition into elderhood include Colette Dowling, Betty Nickerson, Letty Cottin Pogrebin, and Gloria Steinem.

Their texts on aging, though, were not what I expected. The self-help-about-age texts of many second-wave feminists aim to question the cultural pressures associated with old age, reconsidering ideas such as the expected actions of a person of a certain age or what retirement entails. They claim that they can change how their readers think about and enact their aging lives. In their books, the authors use their personal experience as a basis for analysis. These books have the stated intention to counter the "coercive age-positive ideology [that] good feminists would welcome aging because (a) it's important to celebrate women as we really are, and (b) feminism has liberated us from the tyranny of youth and beauty" (Pogrebin 17). They make a distinction between middle and old age, with most authors making clear that they and their target audience members are old*er*, not *old*. These authors tend to advocate a consumerist approach as an antidote to being old, as if age is a disease that people can cure when they learn more, buy more, or do more. As these texts worked to understand and reconfigure how society constructs age, they arrived at a new set of answers, but too many did so from theoretically unexamined, underexamined, or underinformed standpoints. In positing a new way as superior to the old way, the expanded options can become a modified, but still rigid, cultural imperative. As a result, they contain material and ideas that are not successful in deconstructing age-based power differentials, instead validating some of the very social structures they found problematic in the first place. Although the age studies criticism that one might cull from these self-help books is flawed, they are important texts in that they had, through the start of the twenty-first century, constituted the bulk of nonfiction texts on aging and old age available to nonacademics.

As self-help books tend to do, these texts have three key elements. First, these books are targeted mainly at female readers (*Man 2.0* notwithstanding). Second, readers are positioned as both completely in control and quite helpless. Third, success rests on individual responsibility and personal change, rather than on social factors. Often, participation in a consumer economy serves as an important element of individual change (McGee; Simonds; Smith). These books do the feminist work of making each reader aware that many others share their ideas and challenges, and may even suggest that readers form some equivalent of consciousness-raising groups; however, the texts fall short of providing "the needed catalyst not only for understanding the present and the past but [of creating] new possibilities in the future" (Woodward, *Statistical* 50).

Requiring people to take charge of the aging process makes individuals responsible for their own performativity—their performance of social expectations. "Buying in" to the idea that a person can choose how to look and act aged serves as the first step toward becoming a consumer of the aging process. Performativity and agency are interconnected in the assumption that a person should be held responsible for all of his or her actions. However, the social self cannot control all of the performative aspects of aging, as discussed in chapter 2.

Simonds argues that women turn to self-help books for assistance because of feelings of cultural alienation, and reading the books helps the women feel less alone, but ultimately "the ideology of self-help books, like the capitalist and patriarchal ideology that is dominant in our culture, denies connection and community-based action" (226–7).[25] That so many of the self-help book authors established a clear demarcation between middle and old age seems unnecessarily divisive, and even counterproductive, reinforcing the lack of community connection among women across age differences. One by one, the fallibility of each woman shows through, and visible agedness impels the individual into the category of the Other. The brief critiques above show how ubiquitous and isolating ageism is, even in texts that consciously take anti-ageist stances, and how often ageism is, deliberately or inadvertently, linked to economics.[26]

A noteworthy age-focused book by gerontologists is Rowe and Kahn's 1999 *Successful Aging*. A significant buzz in the gerontology community preceded the publication of this nontechnical, research-based best-practices book. The book's cover bills the research as the "most extensive, comprehensive study on aging in America." The authors say their goal is to encourage readers to structure the physical, social, and psychological aspects of their lives to extend the active abilities of the aged body. The information in the book considers the results of a longitudinal study that focused on the so-called *risks of aging* and how to reduce them.[27] Vitamins, exercise, companionship, pets, and volunteering figure prominently. Although Rowe and Kahn have said that their project aimed to incorporate an awareness of sociopolitical elements, the resulting text has been widely critiqued for focusing responsibility on individuals rather than on the ways that individuals exist in a society with de facto and de jure inequalities based on factors such as race, ethnicity, class, gender, age, sexual orientation, bodily ability, and gender identity.

At the core of Rowe and Kahn's approach to aging lies the assumption that the body is a project.[28] With this project, each person always strives for betterment, for some unachievable pinnacle of body ability, and how the body performs has to do with how much effort the person puts into the project. Adding to factors such as genetics and socioeconomics, age problematizes this concept; at some point, an aged body will not be able to achieve additional physical prowess. The project of the aged body, then, becomes reducing the rate of backsliding. This suggestion creates a biologically and theoretically based entry point into a performative, consumerist approach to aging. *Successful Aging* is one of many contemporary texts on aging that hold individuals responsible for their own experiences of aging.

Learning to Be Old: Help Found

In contrast, age studies texts that gave the same critical attention to age as so many tomes imparted to other forms of difference, texts that were rooted in a more feminist concept of social justice, were more difficult to find, but they did, and do, exist. Those theoretically sound texts are useful for both their ideas and their bibliographies, which reference other scholars and activists doing similar work. Although each seasoned age studies scholar has her or his own literary genealogy of discovering age studies texts, their bookshelves tend to end up holding similar books, with works by Copper, Cruikshank, de Beauvoir, Gullette, and Macdonald and Rich. Disciplinary differences provide some variety. For example, in literary studies, the shelf might include books by Deats and Lenker, Waxman, Woodward, and Wyatt-Brown; in history, Banner, Katz, and Thane.[29]

Those initial six authors whose writing is on virtually every age studies scholar's bookshelf demonstrate the strong ties between feminist thought and humanities-based age studies. The authors are women who identify as feminist, and their texts establish similarities between ageism and discrimination against other embodied differences. The books recognize aging as a feminist issue. In addition to identifying some of the challenges that keep women of all ages from being able to work together, these texts suggest feminist responses—viable solutions, or at least steps that can lead toward a resolution of the antagonisms.

In her formidable text, *The Coming of Age*, Simone de Beauvoir attempts to trace the causes as well as the effects of society's treatment of the aged.[30] Her text has been much critiqued for using anecdotal evidence in place of studies, offering flawed or inaccurate analyses of other civilizations, and making essentialist arguments. Nevertheless, the book encompasses a wide range of topics, serving as a marker of cultural suppositions to be challenged and of the weaknesses in seemingly logical assumptions about age. The book was praised in the *New York Times*, but largely ignored by academic and feminist communities, perhaps in part because of its flaws and in part because of its subject matter—as mentioned in chapter 1, it is difficult for the public eye to notice or remember texts about aging and old age.

The lesbian authors of *Look Me in the Eye: Old Women, Aging, and Ageism* (1983; Barbara Macdonald and Cynthia Rich) and *Over the Hill: Reflections on Ageism Between Women* (1988; Baba Copper) say they can more easily critically examine the outsider status of agedness than heterosexual women can, because lesbians have more practice being Othered.[31] These texts are not written from within academia or for academicians, but because these authors more closely examine their own standpoints as they confront aging and ageism, and because their texts focus on contemplating past actions rather than on exhorting readers to particular future actions, these books go beyond self-help and into critical analyses.

Copper's text centers on questions about aging and the issue of power. "First men unload responsibility for their children upon women, then women become liberated and unload their children on their old mothers. There are ethnic, religious, and class taboos against anything but the joyful acceptance of these expectations" (9). Exposing the unfairness of such treatment, Copper explores how patriarchy creates a division between women of different ages. For example, in one of her writing classes students authored fictional autobiographies. The students ended their stories with their deaths, either naturally or via suicide, but their fictional selves were not as old as Copper herself. Copper reports being stunned that "they would rather commit suicide than be like me!" Copper spends much of the book exploring two themes. One is the taboo of older women speaking critically or negatively. When women in their thirties talk about their bodies, the experience liberates them, says feminism; when aged women talk about their bodies, they are complaining. When younger women speak of being treated unfairly, they are advocating for gender equality; when aged women do the same, they may be accused of being Bad Mothers—of either not caring enough about the needs of their "children" or of being overbearing in telling adult "children" how to behave. The book also explores how the women's movement discriminates against aged women in ways that it would not tolerate if the discrimination were against women who have other forms of difference. She writes of times at feminist conferences when she took advantage of an open mike to describe some of the ageist treatment she had encountered, saying that her observations were countered and rejected by women visibly younger than her, who self-identified as old and said that they had received no ageist treatment. Copper recalls similar gatherings where individuals from other groups of embodied difference voiced complaints and were heard. Her book explains how seniors become constructed as desexed and disempowered, thoughtfully questioning who benefits from making *over the hill* equal to *out of sight* and how younger women use the power gained by the feminist movement.[32]

Macdonald and Rich's book of nonacademic age theory, *Look Me in the Eye*, pursues these questions and others, exhorting readers to appreciate the capacities specific to elders. Their writing reflects an awareness of and alternatives to repeating feminism's past mistakes: "[T]here were lots of mistakes we didn't make in dealing with our sexism and our racism. . . . White women didn't approach the problem of our racism by setting up consciousness raising groups for Black women. White women didn't set up women's centers for women of color that were separate but equal. . . . So why do we now go back to such obsolete methods for solving our own ageism?" (68). The book also addresses how an unhelpful response to negative ageist stereotypes is to replace them with positive stereotypes—for example, equating aged woman with the wise mother: "as long as we are two women talking together everything goes well, but at the point where one of us thinks this woman could be my daughter or my mother, the conversation is really over. We've gotten into roles that are part of the patriarchal caste system" (Swallow 198). Macdonald believes that anti-ageism gets mired in this caste system, suggesting that women who cannot hear what she has to say about ageism "are bonded with the fathers against me" (Macdonald and Rich 128). Opening up to experiencing aging gives women a clearer vision of the experience. This text recommends women follow the example of May Sarton's fictional character, Caro, who "is not afraid to die, so in a way never possible before[,] she is not afraid to live" (100). As the quote that opens the chapter details, Macdonald reports that her clarity comes from a newfound understanding of what her aging face brings her. Seeing how her identity is reflected to her through society enhances Macdonald's understanding of both her lived and her social Self, as well as of the society in which she lived (Macdonald and Rich 90, 99, 101). The second edition of *Look Me in the Eye* eight years after the book's initial publication, as well as its translation into Japanese, is testament to its influence and continued relevance.

Most twenty-first-century age studies writing cites one or both of these texts, or cites texts that cite these texts, positioning them as foundations of contemporary understandings about aging and old age. These two texts thoroughly ground anti-ageism in feminist rhetoric, and clearly establish the similarities between ageism and discriminations against other embodied difference. Both books show the current separations between feminism in general and age studies, and call for connection building. Most of the ideas in these two books are based on anecdotal data, personal experience, and reflection, rather than on research or critical theory, which can cause difficulties for academics.

Margaret Gullette's award-winning *Declining to Decline: Cultural Combat and the Politics of the Midlife* (1997) bridges the divide between the activist and academic registers. Gullette discusses the relative acceptance of men's aging and exposes many of the ways that capitalism—from the blatancies of the cosmetic industry to the more subtle tactics of the clothing and publishing industries—compels women and men to buy in, quite literally, to the pressure to pass as younger. Some younger readers have read Gullette's book as antiyouthist; a graduate student in her late twenties reported that she felt like she had been "banished to the children's table and chastized for being a younger person." The book makes a distinction between middle-ageism and old-ageism, also highlighting the direct connection between the two; in this text, Gullette locates herself within the boundaries of middle age. The book also makes clear the association between the capitalist urges taught to youth and the extreme discrimination against the aged. It explores the need for narratives to counter the expectation that as women age, they will become more like their mothers, who they see as relatively powerless. The available cultural narratives of aging are all about decline, and women need narratives of aging as progress to view aging more positively.[33] Examples of progress might include going back to school, starting a new company, or leaving a bad marriage. Using autobiography, theory, cultural criticism, and consciousness raising, Gullette exhorts readers to understand that the basis of ageist ideas begins long before one becomes old, and she encourages readers to use their improved awareness to resist proscriptively ageist cultural narratives.

Margaret Cruikshank's well-researched *Learning to Be Old: Gender, Culture, and Aging*, is now in its third edition. Aging, says Cruikshank, "is (1) medicalized; (2) stereotyped; (3) regarded as frightening for both individuals and society; (4) genderless; and (5) stripped of class and ethnicity" (2). A more complex understanding of how conceptions of age are operationalized, Cruikshank argues, enables readers to confront, challenge, and at least partially dismantle the negative effects of cultural constructions of age. This text suggests that readers need to reappraise *being* rather than *doing*, allowing each person to remain valuable even as she or he may become more dependent or less active; simultaneously, it challenges the devaluation of dependency. Although Cruikshank claims to be "favored with only the faintest dusting of postmodern thought" (173), the book demonstrates an awareness of the situational variability and multiplicity of identities and ideals held by those whom society tends to lump together under the label of *old*. Cruikshank's ideas are not all new—Robert Butler made some of the same suggestions in *Why Survive? Being Old in America* (1975). Cruikshank coins the term *gerastology*, which some equate with Roberta Maierhofer's *anocriticism*, to mark the intersections of feminist and gerontological knowledge, simultaneously exposing some of the ageism inherent in the feminist movement. This book argues that it does not offer a new, more subtle, but equally compelling guide for how to age. It educates readers so that they do not merely accept cultural myths. The goal, according to Cruikshank, is not just to be able to recognize and dismantle the cultural constructs of old age, but as the promotional blurb suggests, to teach people enough that we can "to inhabit our age, whatever it is." The body, a vital element of each person's habitat, changes throughout life, and its variability is key in the changes of age that each person learns to inhabit.

Ambiguous Loss

Psychologist Pauline Boss developed the concept of *ambiguous loss* to talk about that experience of letting go combined with holding on—endings without closure and closure without endings. She discusses situations of divorce, military families with a member listed as MIA, a family member with Alzheimer's, and displacement after emigrating from a homeland. Applying Boss's ideas to the experiences of menopause and beyond gives scholars another tool with which to understand the emotional and psychological elements that can strongly influence many women's physical experiences of aging, including menopause.

Boss suggests that people need to have cultural space to mourn that loss of the old self, an ambiguous loss. "Existing rituals and community supports only address clear-cut loss such as death" (20), but with aging, people have trouble moving both into and through a grieving process because the change is not clearly defined, not static, and not terminated (11). Boss suggests that ambiguous loss is confusing, especially for those without experience solving problems under circumstances in which they do not know if the loss is final or temporary. Women going through menopause, for example, often do not know which of their symptoms are part of menopause and which have other causes, and they do not know how long the experience of menopause will last. Some women in their eighties report that their hot flashes have never gone away, other women report "flashing" for only a month or two, and still others never have that experience (Dillaway; see also Lock).

Often, as happens when women try to pass as younger or deny family members' observations about their changed behavior, in situations of ambiguous loss, there can be an illogical hope that everything will eventually reconfigure itself so that things can go back to the way they were (Boss 7). "[T]he absurdity of ambiguous loss reminds people that life is not always rational and just," information that some individuals are unable to process (8). Eventually, people "become physically and emotionally exhausted from the relentless uncertainty [of] . . . a loss that goes on and on" (8). Even as such a change opens up new possibilities for development of the self, the broad expanse can lead to an emotional equivalent of agoraphobia. "The greater the ambiguity surrounding one's loss, the more difficult it is to master it and the greater one's depression, anxiety, [somatic illnesses,] and family conflict" (Boss 7, 10). Dillaway's work gives examples of how the hopes, uncertainty, ambiguity, and exhaustion apply to experiences of aging as well. Those emotions are similar to the feelings that Woodward theorizes can be the root of shame—distress, bewilderment, and humiliation (*Statistical* 83).[34] For some, shame does not register "as an identifiable and felt emotion. Rather shame is [a] *condition*" in which some people live (Woodward, *Statistical* 95, emphasis in the original). Contending with that condition and those emotions can be difficult, especially without social structures for support.

Boss relates that, when a member of the Anishinaabe (a northern Minnesotan First Nation group) cares for a parent with Alzheimer's, at some point the caregiver may hold a funeral for the parent. The parent's body still functions, but the *parent* is gone (17). Some feminists have suggested holding a similar ceremony at menopause. Other feminists counter that such ceremonies assign too much weight to a usual and ongoing process. An age studies approach suggests that the concept of ambiguous loss may allow for a broader, more open social recognition of the losses and possibilities inherent in menopause, aging, and old age. Even though menopause has been socially formulated as a time of loss, the losses that occur with menopause and aging come with a matching possibility of gain (cf. Marshall "Through"; Woodward, *Statistical* 66–7). Theories about aging into old age could include a developmental component founded on uncertainty.

Woodward sees Freud as suggesting that personal loss requires giving up "each memory of the past and of the future.... It is anguishing work and it takes time. For as Freud so profoundly understood, we never willingly give up what means everything to us and has given our life its very shape and meaning" (Woodward, *Statistical* 3). In the gerontological model of *disengagement theory*, people withdraw (disengage) from society as their advancing age reduces their competencies in productive, then social, then familial roles. This theory has been much critiqued, yet Constance Rooke's work suggests that the concept could be reconfigured so that "disengagement or deconstruction of the ego will seem a vital task. Wholeness . . . may require a multiplicity of selves; and [an unaltered] ego may be an impediment to growth. Less radically, we may say that some departure from accustomed behaviors will assist the completion of the human figure" (247). As their development into old age changes their ideas about who they are, people might disengage from some or all of their established connections, then reengage from a new standpoint, one that includes an awareness of the ambiguous losses and gains in their recent past, as well as the impermanence of the self in the future. That supposition might be as contentious as disengagement theory has been, but the conversations about it are likely to be fruitful in developing understandings about age studies, aging, and menopause.

Without more conversation about these topics, for the next generation, the Kardashians' eventual Tweets about menopause may serve as a leading source of information about that experience. Rather than doing solo information gathering through self-help books, websites, or Tweets, women could engage in candid, public discussions that reveal the multiplicity of menopausal and other age-related experiences. Currently, the impact of coping with age-related ambiguous loss may be nearly invisible, but in the U.S. more than two million women reach menopause each year—about six thousand a day (Manson). Hospitals and health clinics sponsor support groups for those coping with chronic illness, the death of a spouse, and miscarriages, and they hold informational discussions about childbirth, nursing, diabetes, and caregiving . . . why not menopause and other age-related ambiguous losses?

On a smaller scale, readers can start individual conversations about menopause, learning from and informing their mothers, daughters, sisters, and friends. Eventually, I asked my mother about her menopause experience. She had breast cancer, started taking tamoxifen, and her periods just stopped. She did not have hot flashes or hormonal swings that felt uncomfortable, and she did not report feeling more lively or aggressive (she always was pretty spirited). On the one hand, I was glad to learn that menopause was easy for her. On the other hand, irrationally and selfishly, I was saddened by her nonexperience of menopause, knowing that unless I begin taking tamoxifen, I will not have her experience to draw on for knowledge, connection, or assurance. Her menopause created an ambiguous loss for both of us.

Menopause is both a public and private occurrence: the assumption is that women over a certain age have gone through it, yet the subject does not often come up in conversation. Menopause happens for almost all women, yet each experiences it differently. Texts about menopause are overabundant, but many women think that their experience deviates greatly from the norm. Social messages about menopause, aging, and old age can be erratic and contradictory, inadvertently ageist and victim-blaming, consciousness-changing and illuminating, or some combination of these. Appreciating the construction of age as a continued process of becoming, individuals can more effectively rework their connections to aging in themselves and in their relationships and work with others. Advancing into old age is an experience full of paradox and potential, which make it an intriguing topic, ripe for complex, fractured, and multiple understandings—ambiguous loss and ambiguous gain.

Theory and nonfiction texts offer many different ideas and models, yet they are limited by the realities in which we live and the perspectives from which we come. Thus, explorations of how the world might be, and of how to create connections between the world that is and the world that might be, become crucial in developing understanding of the differences that age and age studies can make.

CHAPTER 4

Changing Bodies and Changing Minds with Doris Lessing's *The Diaries of Jane Somers*

The discrepancy between the socially visible self and the interior self is one of the most difficult aspects of aging for the temporarily young to comprehend, which positions literature as a highly useful tool for interrogating the experiences of aging into old age. More than most other forms of art, literature offers ready access to ideas and feelings—to the interior dialogue people have as they consider things happening around them. Through literature, readers can see the differences between the lived Self on the inside and the visible, performative Self that everyone else encounters. That difference, in part, creates ageist stereotypes—the subconscious assumption that the visible individual is the whole person, rather than a person who also embodies all the other ages she or he has been.

Storytelling can bridge the gap between the inner and the outer self to show the richness, complexity, and history embodied in an aged physique, as well as the self-perceived age that often belies the chronology written on the body.[1] This further reinforces the use value of literature as a tool for age studies, as a change agent. In particular, books written as *reifungsromane* have engaging, complex, gendered aged protagonists who claim their continued selfhood, leading readers vicariously to experience age as a continuum and to become involved in "that spiritedness, intensity, introspectiveness, anger, love, and deepening enjoyment of life's pleasures [that] are likely to be characteristics of older women" and men (Waxman, *From* 184). Some writers have taken the challenge of trying to write stories that lead the readers into reconsidering their ideas about aging and old age. In the questions that such texts generate, and in the myriad of possible responses, these readers are led to appreciate ways in which people of all ages can be—need to be—accorded social recognition as fully *human*.

If knowledge were sufficient evidence for change, gyms would be busier than malls, smoke rooms would be empty, and greengrocers would be more successful than liquor stores. Obviously, there are some gaps between what people know is healthy and the daily decisions people make. How much less compelling, then, are ideas whose absolute proof cannot be mathematically calculated—vague concepts in the realms of politics, ideology, and self-identity. Yet getting through the day without a justification or a concept of self is much harder than making it from dawn to dusk without ever looking a cruciferous vegetable in the face. In a sarcastic, postmodern society, getting a person to contemplate nebulous concepts such as *happiness* and *doing the right thing* can be a challenge. Encouraging the adaptation of new ideas can be close to impossible, but some politicians, some activists, and some writers decide to try . . . and some succeed.

Never one to shy away from expressing her opinion about large social problems, in her early sixties, Doris Lessing (1919–2013) turned her attention to age in the novelistic dyad *The Diary of a Good Neighbour* and *If the Old Could*.[2] These stories include examples of how people come to think of *the old* as Other, different ways to be pre-old as well as old, the impact of social and economic differences on aging into old age, and the day-to-day routines and challenges of those who have aged into old age. Through these texts, Lessing pushes the target audience of young and midlife women to reconsider their ideas about the chronologically gifted, impelling readers to rework their thoughts and actions concerning aging and old age. Lessing's novel is a standard recommendation to give to someone new to age studies. In many ways, this book is a model entrée into the field, with expertly crafted, engaging text, a rich complexity of concepts, several excellent age studies critical articles, and a wide array of follow-up options.

Lessing's *Diaries* tell the story of Jane "Janna" Somers, a widow of forty-nine when the story begins. Janna has built a successful career as an editor at a fashionable women's magazine. The reader learns that Janna carefully constructed all aspects of her material reality to her own satisfaction, from the flawlessness of her wardrobe to the color-matched, painted blinds in her bathroom. Her interior dialogue, however, reveals a gap in this self-satisfaction, an opening that becomes filled when Janna befriends Maudie, an independent, poor, old woman who eventually dies of cancer. Janna's involvement with and journey toward awareness of the daily realities of Maudie and other old women and Janna's acknowledgment of the reciprocity of her relationships with these women fill Janna's life with value that was previously lacking. Through both vicarious and personal involvement, the reader's attention turns to focus on his or her thoughts about and involvement with people of advanced age.

Lessing's novels persuade in multiple ways, including the following. First, the argument that "the flesh withers around an unchanged core" (Lessing, *Love* 2) intersects with an examination in these novels of the reasons and stereotypes that Other elders. These texts argue that one's material conditions—rather than one's race, family situation, gender, age, or other embodied differences or essential self—create difference. Second, Lessing's own political background—particularly her involvement with the Communist Party—provided her with additional tools to confront, analyze, and successfully challenge ageism as a social problem. Finally, the *Diaries* conform to the persuasive conventions of the didactic novel, the *roman à thèse*. These foundational elements combine to create texts that offer readers necessary and sufficient evidence for personal change in their understandings and valuations of aging and old age.

Text

Although Lessing lived beyond the first decade of the twenty-first century, her autobiographies (*Under My Skin* and *Walking in the Shade*) end in 1962, before her work on the *Diaries* had begun, so they provide little direct information about the influences on her writing process for these texts. In the broader cultural context, the *Diaries* consciously work to counter many of the constructs of age such as these, from the *Journal of American Gerontology*: "With advance in chronological age beyond the early twenties there is likely to be found: a decrement in physical vigor and sensory capacity, more illness, glandular changes, more preoccupation with practical concerns, less favorable conditions for concentration, weakened intellectual curiosity, more mental disorders, and an accumulation of unfavorable habits," and such "decrements" lead to the irrefutably final state of death (Lehman 416).[3] The *Diaries* begin by challenging the connections between later life and death, and work through most of the other items on the list.

In the opening of the book, even as the reader learns about the main character, Janna, the reader hears about the death of Janna's husband, which happened before the text begins. In the first two pages, readers find Janna at the height of her career, physically attractive, competent, intelligent, financially sound—the antithesis of negative stereotypes of age. And her husband, although not presented as drastically different in age, is dead. Juxtaposing these two concepts reminds readers that *death* and *old age* are correlational, not causational. If death can come at any age, then all ages have something in common with old age, and narratives of old age do not have to include death. Starting out dispelling the darkest myth, the text then derails a litany of other negative stereotypical associations, including illness, infirmity, and helplessness.

Otherdaughter: Taking Care

In contrast to the sanitized orderliness and capability of Janna's physique, Maudie is dying of cancer, an illness that literally leaks out of her in the form of "awful, slimy, smelly stools" (Lessing, *Diaries* 132). This illness makes Maudie's body hypervisible for Janna, but Maudie experiences decreased visibility because of the disease, as her symptoms often keep her confined to her home. For all the characters except for Janna, this confinement serves as what Maricel Oró-Piqueras calls a *dys-appearing* condition (413), a shaming and isolating situation. However, neither the disease nor its effects stop Maudie from going about her life. Rather, they add a layer of additional tasks and humiliation to her daily routine: "Maudie gets herself to the toilet, uses it, remembers there is a commode full of dirt and smell in her room, somehow gets herself along the passage to her room, somehow gets the pot out from under the round top, somehow gets herself and the pot to the toilet" (Lessing, *Diaries* 116). The protracted and involved, but not immobilizing, illness of the older woman contrasts with the younger woman's sudden, more thoroughly disruptive affliction.

In Janna's episode of lumbago, readers find more pain, more interference with daily activities, and more physical dependence than Maudie's malady demands: "for two weeks, I was exactly like Maudie, exactly like all these old people, anxiously obsessively wondering, am I going to hold on, no don't have a cup of tea, the nurse might not come, I might wet the bed. . . . At the end of the two weeks, when at last I could dispense with bedpans (twice a day) and drag myself to the loo, I knew that for two weeks I had experienced, but absolutely, their helplessness" (Lessing, *Diaries* 131). Although Janna's description equates her illness with Maudie's, Janna's physical reality is the more disruptive and disabling of the two. Thirty-five pages later, reinforcing this awareness in the reader, Janna again explains the demarcation of difference between physical well-being and its lack: "I know how very precarious it is. My back has only to say No stop! I have only to break a bone the size of a chicken's rib, I have only to slip once on my bathroom floor . . . and there you are, I shall be grounded" (*Diaries* 166).[4] With the demonstration that disabling illness and physical infirmity, like death, are not limited to the old, readers again receive a twofold message: that the negative associations of old age are stereotypes—both the young and the old experience sicknesses that interfere with life—and that the distinctions between not-yet-old and old are less definitive than readers might like to think. The *Diaries* revisit this theme throughout.[5]

In its suggestion that those who are not-yet-old should actively work to care for those who need it (because they are only one slip away from needing care themselves), the text offers multiple options. Janna provides for Maudie the type of aid that a more affluent family might offer its matriarch. Janna's disposable income, available time, and absence of other immediate family responsibilities combine with the onus of care to position her as an otherdaughter.[6] In this new role as fictive kin, she does care work,[7] purchasing food and clothing for Maudie, paying for Maudie's laundry, and hiring an electrician to fix the wiring in Maudie's flat. The text, however, demonstrates that neither such material circumstances nor such a commitment are required to provide support. The "Home Help"[8] personnel in this book are working-class women,[9] many of whom are immigrants, and readers find portraits of these workers' lives, followed by demonstrations of how they, like middle-class Janna, offer what help they can, above and beyond the obligations of their jobs. Bridget, a Home Help, provides material and emotional support by voluntarily taking care of the child of an invalid, even though the child care does not fit into the rules of her job or her daily routine. Although Bridget offers time whereas Janna offers purchases, the two women are classified as performing similar functions of care; the differences in their performance are mainly bounded by their material circumstances.

The representation of caregivers impresses on the reader the gendered, raced, and classed nature of the ideology of care; performing such care work comes at a significant personal cost, which the diverse members of society do not share equally. Learning that Janna, with her child-free, upper-middle-class life, did little to help her lower-middle-class sister care for their dying mother, readers see how the onus of care affects individuals (Lessing, *Diaries* 8, 9). On a larger scale, the whole novel suggests that the majority of individuals of Janna's race, class, and age do relatively little direct care work for the sick, elderly, disabled, and dying, yet shows how participation in such work could enrich human life.

Giving Care

In getting readers to reconsider their ideas about aging and old age, the novel also encourages each reader to appreciate how elders embody all the ages they have been. . Much of the text's argument hinges on differentiating the exterior body from what the author deems the "core" of the self; it therefore becomes important to establish that differences exist between others' perceptions and an individual's experience in the chronologically gifted, just as such differences may exist in the temporarily young. In the autobiographical *Under My Skin*, Lessing described one of her memories "as the equivalent of the pictures of their youthful selves old women put prominently where visitors can see them. What they are saying is, Don't imagine for one moment that I am this old hag you see here, in this chair, not a bit of it, *that* is what I am really like" (205, emphasis in the original). In words rather than visual images, readers vicariously experience the internal dialogues of several characters via descriptions of "a day in the life of" each one.[10] With these accounts, the text connects the physical and emotional challenges that people of all ages face daily, simultaneously adding to readers' understanding of the interior dialogue that can (but does not always) occur across the lifespan.[11]

The first use of this strategy focuses on Maudie's day. A description of Janna's day follows immediately and describes the same twenty-four-hour period. Janna explains: "I wrote Maudie's day because I want to understand. . . . [B]ut what else is there that I cannot know about[?]" (Lessing, *Diaries* 126). Janna's desire for comprehension (which, as detailed below, readers are compelled to feel as well) and subsequent exploration of Maudie's interiority and physical realities impel Janna toward what Mari-Ann Berg might consider a Bakhtinian "creative understanding."[12] Janna's explanation of the two days highlights difference through her omissions. Janna "cannot know about" whatever of Maudie's life Maudie chooses not to mention or perform in front of Janna, and the description of Janna's day does not include the maintenance details of toileting and washing (Lessing, *Diaries* 127).

Daily portraits of Maudie, Eliza, and Annie, three older women whose lives Janna comes to know, highlight how their interior differences create diverse realities in which they each live. "Mental oppression is rooted in the material conditions of our lives," say materialist feminist critics Newton and Rosenfelt (xvi); material oppression can be rooted in psychological realities. Maudie's history of interactions with others—abusive stepmother, capricious sister, humiliating social services representatives, and abandoning husband (who also kidnaps their son)—has taught her not to trust others. This distrust, along with the degrading reality of her inability to control her bowels, combine to make her a solitary person, ravenous for companionship, but unable to bring it into her world until Janna arrives.

Although equally old, Eliza does not have the history or the physical problems that Maudie does. Thus, Eliza's day revolves around her social interactions—morning coffee with a friend, lunch at a senior club, tea with other friends, church outings, shopping partners. Her world is one of "companionableness" (Lessing, *Diaries* 148). Readers can appreciate the difference that physical ability and the interior dialogue, as well as material circumstances, can make. Like Maudie, Eliza feels "low" when others are absent from her life, but Eliza counters this feeling with activity in a way that Maudie cannot. Perhaps Eliza's larger knowledge base allows her to function as a positive model: "Eliza, who has spent the last fifteen years of her life in the company of the old, knows exactly what might happen at the end, the miserable humiliation that might be in store for her" (*Diaries* 189). With this information, Eliza actively works to counter the "tired slovenliness" that Janna thinks of as the "trap of old age" (*Diaries* 217).

A day in the life of a third old woman, Annie, completes the range offered in the *Diaries*. Rage and long hours of loneliness fill Annie's interior dialogue (*Diaries* 414). Whereas Maudie refuses all help except for Janna's,[13] Annie welcomes the full range of visitors available in her home—Meals on Wheels, Home Health, Good Neighbours, and multiple nurses. However, she refuses any interactions outside the home, such as trips to, or sponsored by, the senior center. Although Annie has limited mobility, she could get out if she wanted to, for shopping or involvement in the companionableness of Eliza's circle. Instead, Annie chooses to limit the boundaries of her world, letting the Home Help do her shopping, and even refusing to use the bathroom, having instead a commode next to her bed and insisting on getting her sponge bath in the living room. Although Annie's and Eliza's material conditions (health, income, past social standing, age, race) are similar, their "core" differences create significant disparities in their lived experiences.

Annie, Eliza, and Maudie are about the same age. Each woman expresses strong desires for companionship. Eliza can fulfill this need on her own; Annie allows her mental limitations to be the deciding factor in her relationship with the world; Maudie has both psychological and physical limitations, and although her mobility is more painful than Annie's, it is less limited. Readers see enough disparity among the women to appreciate that aged individuals are more than just their physical and social conditions.

Comparisons of pairs of younger characters further advance

this thesis and blur the line between the old and the not-yet-old. Both of Janna's intimate relationships are with successful, caring men: her husband and Richard. Her husband was an "unknown" to Janna when he was alive, but the sex was good. Janna and Richard come to know each other more meaningfully than Janna and her husband did, but Janna and Richard are incapable of having a positive sexual encounter. Each time they try, something goes awry: they are interrupted, run out of time, are not in the mood, or are not physically capable of intercourse. Janna and her sister Georgie are another study in contrasts, as are the sisters Jill and Kate, Janna's nieces who come to live with her for a time: "Everything Jill does is characterized by competence; Kate bungles the setting down of a coffee cup" (Lessing, *Diaries* 273). Exterior and background may be similar, but interior variations make all the difference.

Material Progress and New Ideas

Similarly, interior parallels are not enough to create comparable exteriors. The book's depiction of the disparities between the lives of Janna and Maudie shows the reader that the differences are not merely a matter of character, but are also materially performative; finances and physical ability are limiting factors. When Janna first encounters Maudie, she thinks, "I saw a witch" (Lessing, *Diaries* 12). Maudie's "dirty and dingy and grimy and awful" (14) house contrasts with the immaculate "perfection" of her own (Lessing, *Diaries* 23). As Janna studies the contrasts, she questions "Why do I go on about dirt like this? Why do we judge people like this? *She* was no worse off for the grime and the dust, and even the smells. I decided not to notice, if I could help it, not to keep judging her, which I was doing, by the sordidness" (18). As Janna goes through the process of discovering, analyzing, and developing a plan of action, the text implicitly exhorts readers to perform similar examinations and come to similar conclusions about the intersections of resource and presentation.

Soon, readers can understand that physical resources are as important as, and perhaps even more significant than, financial ones in determining performance. Maudie did not always live amid filth. "She was wearing a silk blouse, black dots on white. Real silk. Everything is like this with her. A beautiful flowered Worcester teapot, but it is cracked. Her skirt is of good heavy wool, but it is stained and frayed" (Lessing, *Diaries* 15). The items in Maudie's world were once as nice as those in Janna's, but where Janna can clean or replace things, Maudie cannot. "Once Maudie had been like me [Janna], perpetually washing herself, washing cups, plates, dusting, washing her hair" (*Diaries* 50). Maudie's physical ability limits her capacity for activities of maintenance (even self-maintenance), and income (or lack thereof) eliminates her ability to hire others for these tasks. Thus her material reality impedes her ability to self-define—hence, the initial label of *witch*.

The descent of goods and people into social unacceptability is the direct opposite from the narratives of progress that Enlightenment and Marxist narratives value so highly. The phrase *over the hill* implies that elders are in direct conflict with social ideals. That is, as discussed in chapter 2, after a certain point—a pinnacle—one's life slides down an inevitable slope into old age, chaos, and social unacceptability. That trajectory for the old becomes the dark flip side of the belief in human history as continually moving toward progress. The idea of continuous improvement might not be the academic, theoretical concept of history, but it is a widespread commonality—a perspective undergirding history and social studies instruction for many generations of schoolchildren. The requirements for progress, and the bodily changes of advancing age as antithetical to this progress, work together to construct old people as different from the normative culture, as Other. If the human race progresses uphill, those who are heading "downhill" are not part of progress.

Lessing did not agree with the notion that all of history leads toward a higher and better culmination point (cf. *Under My Skin* 16). As she demonstrates in the plot line of *The Golden Notebook*, the passage of time brings an individual toward progress, then away from it, then toward, then away, so that the plot of betterment versus time in a person's life looks more like the tracings of an echocardiogram than an upward mathematical trajectory. The headings Janna uses to condense Maudie's stories into her diary map this "life is full of ups and downs" philosophy in the text: "A happiness" (*Diaries* 88, 89, 93), "Maudie's very bad time" (*Diaries* 97), and "A nice time" (*Diaries* 100, 101)—way up, way down, middling.

In relating Maudie's story, Janna shows the similarities of their narrative trajectories.

Janna's insertion of herself into Maudie's life changes Maudie's existence for the better—Maudie gains positive human interaction, help with daily chores, and things to look forward to. Clearly, Janna benefits from this relationship too, although in different ways from Maudie. These texts underscore the importance of the mutuality by contrasting Janna with her sister, Georgie. Georgie puts significant time and energy into charitable "good causes," but the benefit is monodirectional. Georgie does good deeds so that she can think of herself as a good person, but the activities do not seem to actually enrich Georgie's life. For Janna, the reciprocal relationship of caring she establishes with Maudie and the active role she takes in confronting Maudie's mortality make Janna feel more "awake" (Lessing, *Diaries* 57, 74), more "like a human being" (*Diaries* 11) than she had when, in response to her husband's and mother's dying processes, she erected protective mental barriers. Janna finds that her relationships with the old women makes even *thoughts* more useful (*Diaries* 25).

Janna's imaginative understanding of Maudie's life also leads to a greater creative output for Janna. She writes multiple historical novels and sociological studies loosely based on the details of Maudie's life. In describing those fictitious texts, Janna highlights some of the less pleasant details of Maudie's story as more palatable in a fictional narrative than in documentary format: "I know only too well why we need our history prettied up. It would be intolerable to have the long heavy weight of the truth there, all grim and painful" (Lessing, *Diaries* 141). Speaking of the elderly characters in her novels, Janna writes, "none of them screams and rages, like Maudie, or repeats the same ten or twelve sentences for an hour or two hours of a visit . . . or gets sulky or sullen" (*Diaries* 151). The texts-within-a-text are offered for some hypothetical reader who cannot accept "the long heavy weight of the truth." In contrast, readers of the *Diaries* are posited as more receptive, more intelligent, and more capable of understanding the unpleasant, but still fictitious, reality of old women like Maudie, Annie, and Eliza. Through oblique praise to the reader (*Diaries* 20, 237), the text exhorts the audience to follow Janna in overcoming fear of and aversion to old age.

As if the incentive of increased creative productions and an improved feeling of self-worth were not enough to encourage readers to change their thinking, or perhaps because readers may be skeptical of such larger claims, the novel offers additional reasons for readers to become involved with elders. Janna finds that her reciprocal relationship with the old women gives her a new understanding of time and a sense of astonishment. On leave from the magazine, Janna is "surrounded by oceans of time. I understood I was experiencing time as the old do" (Lessing, *Diaries* 165). The newfound sense of time, a positive experience, brings with it a feeling of "real slow full enjoyment" (*Diaries* 166) that has been missing from Janna's overly busy life. Additionally, her relationship with Maudie gives Janna an ability to see things to which she was previously blind: "Once I was so afraid of old age and death that I refused to let myself see old women in the streets—they did not exist for me. Now I sit for hours . . . and watch and marvel and wonder and admire" (*Diaries* 237). With Janna's acquisition of knowledge comes an admiration for people such as Eliza, who already know these things (*Diaries* 147, 189).

Janna's relationships with Annie, Eliza, and Maudie give her a new perspective on time, and also on age. Again working on dispelling stereotypes, Lessing's *Diaries* encourage readers to appreciate age as a local construction. That is, age defines difference along two matrices: in relationship to others and in relationship to oneself. Janna's interactions with a continuum of characters—Kate, Jill, Hannah, Vera, Janna, Annie, Eliza, Maudie, who range in age at the beginning of the story from midteens to early nineties—show her age as situationally variable. When Janna has lumbago and the doctor visits her house, her interior dialogue foregrounds this concept: "I was wondering what he was seeing: an old woman, an elderly woman, a middle-aged woman? I know now it depends entirely on the age of a person, what they see" (Lessing, *Diaries* 130). Similarly, Janna's interior dialogue repeatedly places her and others in a self-continuum of age (e.g., Lessing, *Diaries* 277). The suggestion of age as situational, rather than chronological, highlights the constructedness of thoughts about age. It also serves to further dismantle any solid demarcations separating the old from the not-yet-old. Lessing's writings on age joined a minority of books that effectively challenge the social devaluation of age.

The *Diaries* create some challenges even as the texts are effective in other arenas. As Rosemarie Garland-Thomson points out, these books "presume a nondisabled perspective even as it deconstructs that very position" ("Learning" 47). Janna could not have helped Maudie if Janna was less physically capable. Similarly, if Maudie were in a wheelchair, her treasured independence would have ended instantly, because admission to her house required an ability to handle stairs. For these novels to happen, the majority of the main characters have to be (usually) able-bodied. Readers without physical disabilities once again find their perspective affirmed; they do not have to fully engage with the realities of life for nonnormative bodies.

Another absent presence: race. Few of the interactions in the book draw attention to racial difference, offering instead a blurring of race and other identities: "A Day in the Life of a Home Help. She may be Irish, West Indian, English" (Lessing, *Diaries* 181); "the worst, of course, was [Maudie's] being washed by a nurse who is black, too young, too old, white" (*Diaries* 206). In this framing, prejudice results from surface differences and a person's core is more important than the flesh around it.

These novels also perpetuate a gendered rhetoric of care for older as well as younger women. For old women, the arguments about the value of care and care work bestow such activities with regenerative power. In her autobiography and through the *Diaries*, Lessing explicitly states that being needed, having someone to care for, extends the lives of those who, without in-house, reciprocally nurturing relationships, will die. Lessing's commentary about her own mother—"she could have lived another ten years, if anyone had needed her" (Lessing, *Shade* 223)—presaged Janna's fictionalized narration: "I sit there [with Annie], as I did with Maudie, and with Eliza, looking at an old woman who I know, if she could be with a family, or even one other person, would live another ten years, another twenty years" (*Diaries* 424). Both statements advocate for the benefits of positions of care and reciprocity for older women.

Lessing's texts reflect a gendered responsibility of care work for younger women as well—an otherdaughter, rather than an otherchild. The social worker, the Home Helps, the Good Neighbors: all of those actively involved in the lives of the old women are women themselves. This may be partly owing to the "Herland" that

Lessing constructed. Janna's lover, Richard, provides an exception to the gendered rule of care, suggesting that men can benefit from engagement in this market of care. His devotion to a son with Down syndrome provides an example of how such relationships can positively affect men's lives, too. In portraying the strongly valued, nonmonetary enrichment Janna and the others get from reciprocal relationships with the individuals for whom they care, the narrative effectively encourages readers, particularly women, to work a triple day, as Bridget and Janna do. The day in the life of Janna shows the energy expenditure and exhaustion of attending to home, work, and caregiving—she literally falls asleep on the job (Lessing, *Diaries* 120, 126). The implication may be that the benefits of caring make such consequences a worthwhile price to pay, but personally as well as theoretically, I question the material effects of this onus.

Furthermore, encouraging women to take on caregiving roles seems to counter the focus of Lessing's other books, as in *The Summer Before the Dark,* which she wrote a decade before the *Diaries*. The protagonist of *The Summer Before the Dark* must shed her caregiving functions at home and at work to appreciate who she is without those socially assigned roles. Perhaps the difference in message in the *Diaries* is the importance of mutuality—mothers are always already engaged in a relationship with their children. Thus, enacting the role of mother can suggest a monodirectional flow of care, whereas taking on the role of otherdaughter mandates reciprocity.

Context
Materialism and Feminism

Lessing's analytic and textual approaches show traces of her relationship with socialism. Since leaving the Communist Party, Lessing had actively worked to distance herself from socialism, calling it, among other things, a form of "collective adolescence" (Lessing, *Shade* 81).[14] Nonetheless, because her history as a communist combined with her rejection of this philosophy to create a specific philosophical and political standpoint—a reformist activist stance—one may argue that the effect of Lessing's *Diaries* falls under the rubric of materialist feminism. Lessing, who also refused the label of *feminist*, found this view of her political philosophy frustrating and American (*Shade*). Despite (or perhaps because of) the connections readers felt to Lessing's fiction and politics, feminists have generally rejected Lessing's rejection of feminism, and one might logically follow a similar path concerning her political and moral philosophies.[15]

Some analysts, arguing that that viable political philosophies must be able to adapt to the developments in the world around them, claim that people who follow the developed ideas (rather than adhering to the original, fixed set of principles) are more authentic in their commitment to the philosophy: "to be Marxist, in the analytical sense, is to once have been a Marxist" (Roberts 217). Others suggest that, if there was an initial philosophy serving as a key progenitor of one's current philosophies, then one can lay claim to being a follower of that initial philosophy: "If by a Marxist you mean someone who holds all the beliefs that Marx himself thought were his most important ideas . . . then I am certainly not a Marxist. But if by a Marxist, you mean someone who can trace the ancestry to his [sic] most important beliefs back to Marx, then I am indeed a Marxist" (Elster 644). Bringing those arguments to bear on Lessing's novels, one could argue that Lessing's reactions to socialism, her drive for social change, and her ability to create connections between disparate subjects, including her awareness of the economic foundations of some cultural constructs, combined to bring her work into the category of materialism.

Furthermore, what she found positive about the Party was that individuals "wanted to know" (Lessing, *Shade* 24) about things. Lessing disliked those people who do not want to know. The *Diaries* offer a reflection of that stance, as when Janna thinks about those who do not know about age, labeling them as fearful, rather than just ignorant (Lessing, *Diaries* 20). Author and activist Selma James says, "Marx's analysis of capitalist production was not a meditation on how the society 'ticked.' It was a tool to find a way to overthrow it" (36). Similarly, Lessing's novels on age are not merely meditations on age; these didactic texts advocate a transformation in readers' ideas about age.

For example, the *Diaries* suggest that readers need to appreciate the individuality of each old person to appreciate elders as a group. Indeed, sociological research tends to find more differences than similarities in elders, who do not vote, think, age, or spend as a homogeneous unit. Age does not create commonalities. For example, issues such as living wages, affordable housing, the war on drugs, and AIDS affect people across age lines. As groups such as the San Diego–based Old Women's Project have demonstrated, to expose the role that public policy plays in turning such topics into issues, visibly multiage groups are more effective than age-homogeneous groups (Garza, Keaffaber, and Rich). Thus, when literary and cultural critics heed Lessing's plea for individuation of old people, it gives individuals of all ages a similar starting place from which they can form groups based on common interests and ideas.

On the other hand, Marx's ideas required a revolution to enact change, whereas Lessing's reformist stance suggests a need to revise ideas about getting and being old, rather than to eliminate *old* as a performed or embodied category. "This way of thinking . . . it is not so much thinking as holding things in your mind and letting them sort themselves out. If you really do that, slowly, surprising results emerge. For instance, that your ideas are different from what you have believed they are" (Lessing, *Diaries* 10): a dictum for nonradical change.

Socialist ideas expect transformations in the collective consciousness, whereas Lessing believed that "it is always the individual, in the long run, who will set the tone, provide the real development in society" (Lessing, *Prisons* 72). Many scholars focus on Lessing's ideas about the individual. For example, Mari-Ann Berg proposes that the *Diaries* are "affirmations" of individualism (Lessing, *Diaries* 21).[16] In her review of Lessing's autobiographies, Jane Miller explicitly connects Lessing's move away from Marxism to Lessing's ideas about individuals: "Her conversion from communism and, indeed, from politics [was a move] toward ways of valuing individual choice and conscience and the sanctity of inner life" (Lessing, *Diaries* 141). Still others suggest that even within Marxism "there is a profound ambiguity between its communist aspirations and its radical individualism" (Lewis 139). In each of these instances, the tenets of socialism inform the concepts promoted in Lessing's *Diaries*.

The *Diaries* fit into Christine Delphy's broad definition of materialism, in which "its premises lead it to consider intellectual production as the result of social relationships, and the latter as relationships of domination" (Lessing, *Diaries* 60). Lessing interrogated how the material circumstances of experience lead to qualitatively distinct engagements with the realm of the social, showing that the variety of visible, institutionalized ways [that] the young oppress the old are effects, at the levels of "society" and "market relations," of the articulation between the two aspects of the mode of production which determine relations between the young and the old that are independent of human will; i.e., relations determined not by what individuals think, believe, want, or need—consciously or unconsciously—or by whatever social constraints the "market" or "society" imposes on them; instead, they are relations mediated by the historically specific relation of young and old to the material conditions of production and of physical and social reproduction. (Gimenez 75)

As much as Lessing rejected the tenets of socialism, the connections in her novels show history, economics, sociology, and psychology in articulation, affecting characters' lives.

Lessing's relationship with feminist thought was as complex as her connections to materialism. A definitive understanding of whether or not the *Diaries* are feminist would require coming to some agreement on what constitutes a feminist novel—an accord likely to be beyond the scope of any text. Some define feminist work as being rooted in examinations of gender, whereas others define it as work focusing on inequitable power relations. Both of these definitions fit with some components of the *Diaries*. On the larger level, the novels work for social change, certainly a part of many feminists' definition of their work.[17] As discussed in detail below, the didacticism of Lessing's novels challenges the "isolation of language and ideas from other realms of struggle," a mark of materialist-feminist writing (Newton and Rosenfelt xxxi). The novels offer many characters who readers may appreciate as feminist: depictions of intelligent, competent women who embody power similar or superior to that of the male characters. Janna, economically independent, has structured her life as she wishes it to be, right down to the tiles of her bathroom. At work, equally intelligent women join her in running a successful magazine. Janna's relationship with Richard contains a mutual balance of power. Richard's wife functions as the key wage earner in his family. These novels are full of positive portrayals of strong, self-sufficient female characters.

Novels in which women are foregrounded almost to the exclusion of men create a system in which women's relationships with each other and with the material world are less mediated by aspects of gender.[18] Creating a feminocentric milieu, Lessing's novels are able to draw readers' attention away from inquiries into how the relationship between the genders affects women's participation in each other's lives. When the female characters interact with men, the contrast is vivid. Maudie's husband left her when her child was small, then kidnapped the child, leaving Maudie to learn self-sufficiency or die. As a working-class woman, her career options are limited, paying barely subsistence-level wages. Janna and Phyllis run the magazine where they work, but their male colleague, "poor Charlie," a "passenger," becomes the editor (Lessing, *Diaries* 202). Not all male characters are portrayed negatively, but the more favorably rendered men, such as the Indian grocer and Jill's boyfriend, are nearly invisible, making no demands, staying out of the way and out of the story. The movers and shakers of the old-women's worlds—Bridget, the social worker, Vera Rogers—have similar arrangements with their male partners. In contrast, when Janna's friend and mentor, Joyce, chooses to let a man run her life, she soon becomes an alcoholic. In the *Diaries*, readers' attention focuses on the interactions and power differentials among women, who work within castelike systems based on race, ethnicity, class, bodily ability, and age. In this society, the women have some, but not complete, choice of how much of this system to perpetuate with their lives.[19] The elision of gendered power relations may detract from both the feminist and materialist aspects of Lessing's analysis, but neither of those camps was a source of Lessing's modus operandi.

Didacticism

Nor did Lessing, in any of the writings that I have found, directly connect her texts and Susan Suleiman's concept of the *roman à thèse*. Lessing's *Diaries* and Suleiman's text on the *roman à thèse* were published in the same time frame, but for widely different audiences. Nonetheless, the *Diaries* contain enough textual and contextual devices paralleling Suleiman's concept of the *roman à thèse* that the correlations can be fruitfully explored—an example of how blending the theories of age studies with the methodologies of another critical approach can lead to observations useful for cultural and literary critics, as well as authors. The characteristics of the *roman à thèse* become devices through which such novels are made even more persuasive.

Suleiman defines the *roman à thèse* as "a novel written in the realistic mode (that is, based on an aesthetic of verisimilitude and representation), which signals itself to the reader as primarily didactic in intent, seeking to demonstrate the validity of a political, philosophical, or religious doctrine" (7). The phrase *roman à thèse* translates as "novel with a thesis." Suleiman suggests that this history of this term carries with it "a strongly negative connotation" (3), but refutes that undertone through her discussion of the *roman à thèse* as an intricate, developed, and historically viable genre. Suleiman's book details three distinct elements of the *roman à thèse*: its goals, the plot category (or categories) used to impart the story, and the relationships established among the author, the narrator, and the audience.[20] Lessing did not use this vocabulary, but the *Diaries* contain the elements of the *roman à thèse*, and those elements support the success of the novels' didacticism.

Lessing's discussion of the writing she admired and the goals of the writing she would like to have done coincides with the first element of the *roman à thèse*. In the *Golden Notebook*, Anna, one of the characters who Lessing acknowledged as an alter ego,[21] discusses her feelings on literature: "Thomas Mann, the last of the writers in the old sense, used the novel for philosophical statements about life" (58). Mann-ish texts are "the only kind of novel which interests me: a book powered by an intellectual or moral passion strong enough to create order, to create a new way of looking at life" (Lessing, *Notebook* 59). Lessing wrote that a good book "refines your knowledge of your fellow human beings" (Lessing, *Skin* 88). Lessing's belief in the individual,[22] her respect and desire for knowledge begetting change on a broader scope,[23] and her concepts of good literature combined to create precisely the type of novel Suleiman describes.

The majority of Suleiman's text focuses on the second element of the *roman à thèse:* the type of plot used to accomplish these novels' didactic goals. As the opening of Suleiman's book suggests, even before reading her text, readers can come to an intuitive appreciation of her points by thinking about parables, which she proposes as being comprised of up to three parts: narrative (story), interpretive (what the story means), and pragmatic (how that meaning applies to readers' lives) (36). As she points out, the latter two aspects are often superfluous, creating redundancy, but this repetition helps eliminate the ambiguity of the story's meaning (55). In a *roman à thèse*, the point or moral of the story is its raison d'être, which makes the elimination of ambiguity a desired characteristic. Indeed, the elimination of ambiguity sets the *roman à thèse* apart from other genres, a point explored in more detail below.

The parable, like the Mann-ish novel, is a genre for which Lessing expressed nostalgic desire even as she re-created the genus in her own work: "once, all our storytelling . . . was myth and legend and parable and fable, . . . [b]ut that capacity has atrophied under the pressure from the realistic novel" (Lessing, *Shade* 336). The *Diaries* combine a realistic setting with a parable-like mode of making meaning. The difference between parables and the *roman à thèse* becomes the degree to which the audience can relate to the reality of the worlds the texts construct. In the verisimilitude and the edifying function of the *roman à thèse*, Lessing offered readers texts that accept that "counter-myths are more powerful than (or as powerful as) economics" (Newton and Rosenfelt xvi) and that conform to the pressures of realism while maintaining the effects of myth, legend, parable, and fable.

These facets are retained through Lessing's construction of the third of Suleiman's *roman à thèse* elements: the relationship that the *Diaries* establish among the author, Janna (both as writer and as character), and the reader. The *Diaries* have a noteworthy publication history, one that locates them solidly in the realistic category. Lessing first published these novels under a pseudonym, offering publishers the name of Jane Somers as the author. The novels were presented as a riff on historical fiction—based in Janna's reality, with allowances for poetic license and character amalgamation.[24] Before Lessing revealed herself as the author, reviews of the novels did not question their authorship. Interestingly, and directly relevant to the construction of these novels as didactic vehicles, reviewers felt obliged to remind prospective readers that these works were not actual diaries.[25] Thus, in the original editions of the texts that comprise the *Diaries*, readers were introduced to Janna Somers first as the author and secondarily as narrator.

This double fiction reinforces the reception of author as

authority, and of "the novel as a 'natural,' innocent representation of the real" (Suleiman 72), thus encouraging readers to accept Janna's experience as authentic. Furthermore, since "the lived experience (or transformation) of a subject over time [is a] means of persuasion no less powerful than the voice of the omniscient narrator" (Suleiman 73), the additional level of the narrator's experiential "authenticity" further supports readers' acceptance of the truth-value of the didactic messages of the text. In acknowledging the texts' worth, readers consent to the ontological worth of Janna's experiences.

These messages are doubly reinforced through Janna's and readers' involvement in producing the interpretive value of the text. According to Suleiman, the *roman à thèse* "calls for an unambiguous interpretation, which . . . implies a rule of action applicable (at least virtually) to the real life of the reader. The interpretation and the rule of action may be stated explicitly by a narrator who 'speaks with the voice of Truth' and can therefore lay claim to absolute authority, or they may be supplied, on the basis of textual and contextual indices, by the reader" (Suleiman 54).

Ostensibly, the events of the *Diaries* happened to Janna, and her analysis of events creates the lens through which the reader views the story. In accepting the stories' verisimilitude, readers must implicitly consent to Janna's interpretation. Moreover, Lessing's invocation of the reader/narrator as a unitary entity (as detailed below) further compels readers to accept Janna's perceptions. Janna is only quasi-omniscient, but since all information is, by definition, interpreted, readers are led to accept her analytic constructions.

Further involving the audience, Lessing formulated the texts as Janna's diaries. The initial audience for diaries is usually the writer, which would make the "original" audience of the *Diaries of Jane Somers* Jane Somers. Thus, the reader is interpellated as the actual person to whom the events of the novels are real. Furthermore, the texts are offered as a midlife bildungsroman—Janna in middle age finally becoming truly human because of her new connection to and understanding of age. If "to see older women and their current social devaluation as somehow separate from ourselves . . . is to lose our humanity" (Hurd Clarke 139), then reestablishing the connection across age difference helps people reconnect themselves to humanity. Such a move does more than counter the stereotype that middle and old age lack possibilities for personal growth. It also generates a story of personal transformation. Since Janna-the-character undergoes this transformation and Janna-the-character serves as a nearly unmediated stand-in for Janna-the-author, and since the reader is figured as Janna-the-author, readers are constructed as undergoing the same transformation. Suleiman suggests that the *roman à thèse* transforms "the reader into a 'real' (that is, pseudo-intradiegetic) helper. What I mean by that is that the reader might continue in his [sic] own life the struggle recounted in the novel" (144). Because the *Diaries* implicate readers on multiple levels, the readers' status as "helpers" becomes similarly engaged.

Janna's finding-of-self happens both within the text and as "real" precursor to the texts; thus, readers' transformation occurs on the textual, pretextual, and posttextual levels. That is, having participated in a change in Janna-the-character's life, a change based on the pre- and extra-textual change of Janna-the-author, readers are pressed to find a pragmatic application for these texts that leads to a change in the context of their own lives. For example, Janna's anger, Maudie's anger, and Annie's anger (Lessing, *Diaries* 31, 151, 251, 253, 414, 425) are impelled into readers' lives, evolving, in this system, from fictional emotions to a stimulus for self- and social transformation.[26]

Additionally, albeit more speculatively, one can argue that Lessing's novels target readers who are *already* capable of identifying with a character like Janna—that is, female readers who find themselves in a "guilt-ridden and successful middle-age" (Grumbach 6):[27] financially sound, concerned about appearances, possibly divorced and/or empty-nesters, perhaps feeling that their lives lack meaning. "According to Lukács, the 'typical' hero . . . in great realistic fiction, is an individual who sums up, most often without knowing it, the aspirations and contradictions of a social group (or more exactly of a social class) at a given historical moment" (Suleiman 106). The character of Janna personifies a version of her targeted readers. Such readers would find a merged identification with Janna to be a nonthreatening, perhaps even a positive, experience. Readers' affinity with Janna's "type" would deepen their level of enmeshment in the texts. Male readers may have a more difficult time accepting the arguments of the text; perhaps the same could be said of male readers of much of Lessing's writing.

So far, the literary devices through which readers are interpellated into the texts are surface devices, foundation for the actual story, and Lessing certainly offered many layers of entanglement there. Within the stories themselves, further levels of invitation and command embroil the reader in the world of age. The audience members are figured as stand-ins for Janna—readers of writing "intended" for herself/themselves (hence, the term *diary*). Within the texts, Lessing "mark[s] Maudie not merely as Jane's foil in time but as her decaying double" (Tiger 9); Waxman's analysis invokes Janna's niece, Jill, as a third generation of continuity (*From* 65). Lessing scholar Virginia Tiger argues that similarities in Lessing's use of bodies, bathing, and anger figure Janna and Maudie as doppelgängers.[28] Garland-Thompson analyzes similar analogues in the women's clothing ("Learning" 46).[29] Berg finds parallels in character traits.[30] Thus, Janna's discovery of herself includes a discovery of herself as old woman, her self-as-Other. This fusion interpellates the reader not just as the middle-aged protagonist, but also as the older and younger women, coming to "feel within themselves, beyond logic, the sensations of women aging" (Waxman, *From* 186). Through this union, readers are personally invoked in the blurring of the boundaries demarking the differences between the old and the not-yet-old.

"And, And, And"

Lessing's *Diaries* offer readers relational connections and textual devices that promote involvement with the issues she raises. In establishing connections partly founded on readers' identification with the novels' characters, Lessing challenged the Otherness of age by blurring the divisions between the old and the not-yet-old. As the *Diaries* draw in the audience, readers encounter deconstructions of ageist stereotypes, which add to their growing understanding of the multiplicity of realities of the aged. As Janna does, readers are invited to take pride in their new knowledge as they learn "*how* to see what was going on: what is developing inside a structure, what to look for, *how things work*" (Lessing, *Diaries* 75, emphasis in the original), and how to make their nonwork time productive of the highest value in their lives.

Readers who participate in these texts can come to understand how economic and historical effects work with age and gender to create a variegated citizenship.[31] Lessing's texts create and rely on readers' identification with the novels and readers' sense of social justice to effect change, circumnavigating the dialectic tension critics such as Frank Lentricchia suggest exists between joyful bibliophiles and savvy critics. Lessing's books engage readers who read for reading's sake, and evidence of her skill as an author is that her stories themselves train readers to be amateur literary critics, so that even casual readers become agents of social transformation. Of the books available that attempt to transform younger readers' understanding of and connection to elders and later life, for readers who enjoy Lessing's writing style, the elements she combined in the *Diaries* make them particularly effective texts and effective role models for other authors interested in pursuing similar methods.

For more sophisticated readers, the *Diaries* demonstrate the range of topics relevant to understanding age studies. This text's content is relevant to people planning to become activists, architects, caregivers, city planners, counselors, economists, historians, medical workers, philosophers, policy makers, politicians, product and clothing designers, social scientists, social workers, or class, gender, or race studies scholars. It underscores the interdisciplinarity of age studies—the many factors outside of the body that affect experiences of aging and old age. It also highlights the emotional power of narrative and the potent value of literature as a teaching tool in fields across the humanities and beyond.

In a National Public Radio interview with Susan Stamberg, Lessing "retorted testily to Susan Stamberg's question about whether she wrote 'to show us the world as it is, or the world as it should be, or the world as it might be': 'Why do you make it or, or, or? It could be and, and, and'" (Lessing, *Interview* 4). Indeed, the *Diaries*' effectiveness increases because they create a wide range of possibilities for both characters and readers, and show the similarities and continuities between the not-yet-old and the old. Lessing's *Diaries* serve as exemplars of relatively mainstream texts for which age studies analyses create possibilities for responses to current constructions, for action, and for change.

Chapter 5

Lucille Clifton's Poetic Perspective and Aging

The intersectional differences of age suggest the importance of cultural context in creating change agents and potential. Lock's research on menopause in Japan, for example, demonstrates the strong influence of cultural environment on a seemingly biological experience. Savishinsky found similar evidence about other aspects of aging in populations across the globe. Activists and scholars do not need to go globetrotting, however, to find people and groups that offer useful alternatives for aging into old age. Copper and Macdonald and Rich explained how their status as cultural Others informed and helped their cultural critiques of aging.[1] Members of the American Deaf culture demonstrate a higher level of respect for elders in the community than non-Deaf people do for elders in their communities. Mexican Americans label themselves as *old* five to ten years earlier in life than Black and White Americans do ("Hispanic"). Several scholars suggest productive connections between age studies and antiracism.

For example, Brent Green argued that self-inflicted ageism, constructed within individuals through their contact with society, creates an effect similar to the racist self-colonization found in First Nation (Native American) peoples. Such parallels suggest that the pressures for cultural normativity in race and age are connected. The work of de Beauvoir and Holloway and Demetrakopoulos suggests connections between African American and Native American oral traditions—a focus on the collective rather than the individual, and on the preservation of heritage. Woodward's ideas about shame (cf. *Statistical* 94–5, 97) and sociologist Sarita Srivastrava's work, in which she posits that "some of the deadlocks of antiracist efforts are linked to . . . preoccupations with mortality and self" (31, quoted in Woodward, *Statistical* 56), suggest that anti-ageist work and antiracist work are mutually supportive and create a positive feedback loop. This chapter centers around the poetry of Lucille Clifton (1936–2010), using her writing as a foundation through which to explore African American concepts of aging, and chapter 6 considers Native American approaches; considerations of other ethnic and cultural groups may well be equally productive, and analyses done by age studies scholars who are accepted members of those groups would add additional richness and nuance to the understandings.

This chapter first examines the historical moment in which Clifton became a writer, including aspects of past and present Black American cultures that influence Black women's experiences of aging and old age. A close reading of Clifton's "There is a girl inside" demonstrates the meaning that an age studies explication can bring to literary studies and the use value that interpretation can lend to cultural analyses. That reading connects the present cultural position with a range of potential future outcomes. Throughout, these concepts are grounded in the specifics of Clifton's poetry, showing how her poems put these theories into practice and how readers can use the ideas in Clifton's poetry as tools for critical analyses of aging and old age.

Exemplar: Clifton

Clifton grew up hearing firsthand accounts of slavery, and she lived through World War II, the civil rights movement, the women's rights movement, and the first decade of the twenty-first century, so she embodied the historical connection between slavery and the digital era. Clifton's poems are relatively short and easily accessible to readers from elementary school on up, but they are not simplistic. Without romanticizing the past or the present, her writing celebrates the heritage of her race, class, and gender. Clifton's widely anthologized poems include "Homage to My Hips" and "Miss Rosie," which is about an aging bag lady.

The world of her writing celebrates Black women's bodies, featuring elements that might be seen as flaws; in the case of large hips, the speaker extols the freedom of her thighs, their size too big to be enclosed in "little petty places." Like other characters who fall on hard times, Miss Rosie and her "wet brown bag of a" body receive not just sympathy, but acclaim, leading the poem's speaker and readers to appreciation for and pride in Black women's bodies: "when I watch you / . . . / I stand up/through your destruction / I stand up."[2] Historically, African Americans have maintained a more positive concept of aging and old age than Caucasian Americans have.[3] Several of Clifton's poems are encapsulated *reifungsromane*, depicting elderhood as a time of evolution, bodily integrity and sexuality, enhanced self-awareness, and continued becoming.

Clifton's poems also include reminiscences about the speakers' departed periods and uteruses. Her texts remind readers of the inevitability and importance of inhabiting aged bodies, of the need to appreciate what she called "older people's wisdom." An age studies analysis of her work includes an exploration of the cultural context from which her perspective arose and the literary and social vistas that stance can produce. The findings substantiate an analysis of Clifton's racial and cultural background as impetus and support for the positive attitudes about age that readers find in her essays and poetry. Clifton's works, formed in a particular historical and geographic location, reflect survival skills and tools for resisting negative, Caucasian Americans' messages about Black women's bodies, especially the menopausal and aged body. Moreover, as exemplified in the ending of "Homage to My Hair," Clifton's positive ideations of racial and cultural identity correspond to positive age identity as well: "when I feel her jump up and dance / i hear the music! / [. . .] she is as tasty on your tongue as good greens / black man, / she can touch your mind / with her electric fingers and / the grayer she do get, good God, / the blacker she do be!" The conclusion of this poem associates a visible sign of the speaker's age, gray hair, with positive racial self-identity: "the grayer she do get, good God, / the blacker she do be!" This is an unusual, and unusually positive, characterization of old age, and a favorable connection between age and race. Clifton maintains this attitude about aging consistently in her poems and her essays.

Historical Context

These ideas, however, are not unique to Lucille Clifton. In examining the poetry of Gwendolyn Brooks, scholar Sylvia Henneberg has argued that "African-American culture . . . regards age as an advantage that can help keep at bay and counteract the damage such discrimination inflicts on . . . black personae." Karla Holloway and Stephanie Demetrakopoulos make similar claims about Toni Morrison's work, suggesting that many African American communities respect older women because of their "spiritual/political significance as foremothers whose survival ensured ours" (13).[4] Thus, Clifton's poems serve as exemplars and as anchors for a larger theorization of African American women's ideas about aging. Clifton's writing on these ideas attracts relatively little scholarly attention. In general, humanities-based age studies considerations of minority groups' experiences of aging and old age are limited. Holladay's *Wild Blessings*, the only volume devoted solely to Clifton's work, mentions older women on five pages. Holladay's other articles occasionally touch on the subject, as does Ajuan Mance's work.

Despite the paucity of scholarly material, Clifton's and others' positive ideations of aging and old age may serve as models for scholars in age studies, literary studies, and cultural studies.

In appreciating that ideas are formed within a particular social and historical milieu, researchers can envision the trajectory that such concepts are probably taking. In studying their writing, scholars can consider ways to counteract the erosion of positive concepts of age, both within the cultural contexts in which they write, and in other contexts. The mutually constitutive character of racial, cultural, age, and gender identities in Clifton's writing also provides ripe grounds for an intersectional analysis that includes age, and for creating critical approaches to age as an identity category.

The concept of African American traditions at least partially elides the heterogeneity of beliefs from which African and African American cultural practices draw. As diverse as the African peoples were, local cultures in America influenced their imported traditions, creating an even broader diaspora of practices and beliefs. In this book, the historical analysis follows cultural theorist Roe Sybylla's idea that documents record people's theories and beliefs, which may vary slightly or greatly from reality (217 n. 10).[5] That is, it matters less how dissimilar African American experiences in Africa were and more how contemporary African Americans perceive and create critical approaches to an African past and a history in America.

Another complicating factor: Clifton and many other Black authors believe that history is not limited to the past. It still exists in the present. In this understanding of time, its flows are "carrying yesterday / Forever . . . dragging forward tomorrow," and those who believe in separating the present from the past "whisper mistakenly" (*Terrible* 37). These quotations are poetic expressions, but Clifton's essays convey the same beliefs. A critical understanding of these works requires a consistent mindfulness of the ever-present fusion of the past and present.

Alice Walker said, "I think my whole program as a writer is to deal with history just so I know where I am" (quoted in Wisker 80). In this conception of it, self-identity requires coming to terms with history. Clifton's poetry reflects a similar desire, and both of these writers' projects are part of an "intensifying desire among African American writers to reconnect with an African past" (Wall 553), as some readers may remember from the Black Pride and Back-to-Africa movements. Showing how one era's beliefs about historical connections influence ideas in later times, this section begins with African spiritual traditions, moves on to the United States and slavery, through nineteenth-century conceptions of womanhood, and into more recent years; in each of these periods, this examination and analysis focuses on beliefs about age, aging, and aged Black women.

Stories about beliefs, whether theistic or atheistic mythologies, form the foundation of culture. "Age within Black culture . . . is not so much a social issue as it is a mythic and political issue" (Holloway and Demetrakopoulos 15). Hence, this investigation begins with mythology and politics. Caucasian Americans are familiar with the possibility of extended families including both relatives and friends, and potentially including multiple generations. For many African peoples, the idea of extended family also includes the dead, the living, and the yet-to-be-born (Holloway and Demetrakopoulos 16).[6] The knowledge of the dead ancestors did not die with their bodies, because their spirits remained with the living. In "prayers of African religions . . . [a] secondary and critical level of prayers features the spirits of departed ancestors" (Holloway and Demetrakopoulos 16), because those are the individuals who embody (or enspirit) knowledge and history.

The concept of respect for the elderly has come into play in European and Caucasian American cultures' understandings of history, particularly for elders in the middle and upper classes. More of a belief than a documented reality, this concept plays a major role in forming contemporary concepts about the differences between the past and the present. Hypothetically, in addition to general decency and emotional connection, Caucasian European and Caucasian American temporarily young people had two material reasons to treat elders with deference. First, the elders usually managed access to whatever money, goods, or land the family owned; those who wanted to inherit had clear motives to treat their elders with deference. Second, in agricultural or gatherer/hunter societies, the elders were repositories of history and knowledge, with information on topics ranging from when to plant the seeds to where to find water in drought. Elders held knowledge crucial to survival. However, once that knowledge was passed along, maintaining deference required respect and adherence to tradition, neither of which was guaranteed.

In many African societies, "older women are magical because of their will to survive, because of their embodiment of the mythology and wisdom of Africa, and . . . in consequence the survival of the Black community" (Holloway and Demetrakopoulos 14–5). Although Clifton asserted that each person has the potential to commune with ancestral spirits, she acknowledged that most people did not commune with those spirits as she did (Hull), and her speakers present this noncommunication as an acute sense of disempowerment and loss: "if our dead / were here they would save us" (Clifton, *Blessing* 16). The oldest members of the community—so old that they are no longer alive—have abilities and power that the living do not. Clifton believed that reclaiming connections with the ancestors would be a potent, empowering action for many African Americans, just as it was for her (Clifton, "The Things"). The living come closest to these answers and ancestors in the personage of the old Black woman, the "conduit of cultural and historical memory" (Mance 132; see also Hill-Lubin) and "the contemporary embodiment of the ancient goddesses, ancestral spirits and earth mothers" (Holloway and Demetrakopoulos 16). An accumulation of age equates with an accumulation of knowledge and power.

As compelling as this connection may be, there are at least two inherent dangers. One is that *all* old Black women will be interpellated as these bridges, whether they want to be or not; the other is that old Black women may be constructed *only* as these embodiments. Clifton believed that each woman has the potential for a spiritual role. She saw that responsibility as a mixed blessing and understood that not every woman would want to take on that task (Hull 112). Reflecting Clifton's belief that in the "ongoing process of time and change, we all bear responsibility" (Hull 112), her texts illustrate other ways of contributing to communal survival, such as providing a solid foundation for one's children (e.g., the mother as the "mountain" in "the lost baby poem" in *Good News*, 60). Examining African spiritual traditions that contain positive connotations for old Black women's bodies makes explicit some tropes, such as *wisdom* and *cultural survival*, that writers such as Clifton, Walker, and Morrison use in their constructions of age.

Another set of Africa-based traditions informing these writers' work is that of history as strength and teacher. Somewhat different from casting the old woman as an historical personage, in this context, history becomes a more nebulous term, a distinct entity, yet still part of each person. "Time," wrote Clifton, "is another name for God" (*Blessing* 120). That is, time shapes individual destinies; individuals are responsible to time for their actions; and time will teach and judge each person. Also, each person has a responsibility to carry time's message to the world.

When a person fulfills that responsibility, she or he demonstrates an advanced level of personal development. "Clifton implies that real insight comes from a mature recognition of one's role at the vanguard of history" (Holladay, "Songs" 283). "Vanguard" makes it sound like a military operation, but Clifton acknowledged the messy, organic nature of the process. In "i am accused of tending to the past," the speaker becomes the wet nurse of history, suckling this foundling baby (*Quilting* 7). Placing her speaker in this role,

Clifton underscored the mutually constitutive nature of African American women and history. History had been lost and needs to be found. Not (yet) full grown, not (yet) able to survive on its own, this "monstrous unnamed baby" needs nurturing and sustenance. The poem suggests that, with this kind of care, history has enormous impending power:

> she is more human now,
> learning languages everyday,
> remembering faces, names and dates
> when she is strong enough to travel
> on her own, beware, she will. (*Quilting* 7)

Like a human child, once history develops enough, it has the potential—and, perhaps, the obligation—to bring forward the entire community.

Given the potential of history, cultures without ties to such a creature risk moral, if not literal, destruction. Caucasian Americans, for example, are seen as being "careless" with history, a casual attitude that apportions self-destruction to those who assimilate (Holloway and Demetrakopoulos 21-2). One of Clifton's speakers "tries on" Caucasian American ways—

> i'm wearing
> white history
> But there's no future
> in these clothes
> so i take them off (*Blessing* 41)

In this poem, the speaker considers the ways of the group that Clifton called the "ice tribe" destructive to her own community. Clifton's poetry holds each reader responsible for coming to a similar understanding of these concepts.

In the poetry, those who embrace the simultaneity of past and present receive access to supportive personal relationships, which are foundational to the larger community. In Clifton's "to merle," for example, the speaker last saw her friend "on the corner of / pyramid and sphinx" (*Good Woman* 171). Their relationship has been interrupted by "ten thousand years," and the speaker recognizes her friend not by visual identification, but by her language. Immediately after comprehending the language, the speaker asks to bring the relationship to a level of greater connection and intimacy ("let me call you sister, sister"), a testimony to the power of words in constituting relationships. Furthermore, the speaker invokes as she requests—that is, on the same line in which she asks permission to use a term of increased familiarity, the speaker interpellates the addressee into the familial community by addressing her as "sister." The expectation is that the family will receive the addressee; as an embodiment of both "downtown" and "sphinx," the character brings with her a welcome history and contemporaneity.

Suckling history, trying on other forms of history, and connecting with friends across the millennia, the characters in Clifton's poetry repeatedly invoke the past not just as relevant, but as a powerful part of the present. This positive attachment to the past, combined with the idea that old Black people embody both past and present, contributes positively to African Americans' concepts of old age.

Of course, a significant part of African Americans' history, one that carries enormous impact, is the history of slavery. A discussion of the relationship that newer generations have with slavery occurs below; each cohort has a different relationship to history and to slavery. Clifton was born in 1936. She and others in her cohort had personal contact with individuals who had known slavery. Clifton recounted speaking with her father about life before the Civil War: "'Oh slavery, slavery,' my Daddy would say. 'It ain't something in a book, Lue. Even the good parts was awful'" (*Good Woman* 22). Slavery affected, among other things, sexuality, family structures, and knowledge systems. Survival skills evolved around each of these areas, and elders were living embodiments of those proficiencies, which led to respect for the elderly, positively influencing African Americans' ideas about old age.

For several generations, Black women's sexuality was not theirs to control. "In slavery, the black female body served as one of the prime technologies of reproduction and commodification" (Bennett and Dickerson 13). White society constructed (and some parts of it still construct) Black women as hypersexual. Many slave owners used that creed to justify their own sexual acts. White people's ageism may have been a positive development for female slaves who survived beyond menopause—slave owners' greater desire for younger women would mean that older women's bodies were less preferred. Furthermore, the end of reproductive capability meant that a woman could have sexual partners without risking her life in pregnancy and childbirth, and without risking the loss of a child through death or sale. Menopause thus may well have served as a form of liberation in the slave community. For free Blacks during the slavery era, the commodity argument may carry less significance, but the claims about the dangers of reproduction remain valid. The past has repercussions in the present; menopause's liberatory potential in the nineteenth century may serve as part of the impetus for contemporary African Americans' conceptions of menopause.

Slavery's separation of families also may also contribute to making African Americans' ideas about old age more positive. Familial separation during slavery, according to psychologist Pauline Boss, is a form of ambiguous loss. As discussed in greater detail in chapter 3, ambiguous loss happens when a relationship has an ending with no closure (as may occur these days in situations such as divorce) or a closure with no ending (as happens with slavery auctions and MIA soldiers). Ambiguous loss can feel particularly challenging for Caucasian Americans, for whom "existing rituals and community supports only address clear-cut loss such as death" (Boss 20). Ambiguous loss can lead to "depression, anxiety, [somatic illnesses,] and family conflict" (Boss 7, 10). A group with experience managing ambiguous loss could develop useful methods for coping with it, making advancing age a more positive experience by giving group members techniques for managing the changes aging brings.

Historically parallel to slavery, and affecting both Black and Caucasian women's bodies, is the historical and contemporary "Cult of True Womanhood"—a cultural valuation that focuses on "piety, purity, submissiveness, and domesticity" (Bennett and Dickerson 6), as well as "isolation within the single-family home" (Mance 123). Any failure to measure up to these oppressive standards regarding race, money, sexuality, and age could be construed as a woman's mutiny against her own so-called true nature. "African American and poor-white (mostly immigrant) women's labor outside the home—and the tenement, multifamily, or extended-family dwellings in which these women lived—was widely interpreted as evidence of their fundamental inability" to be "true women" (Mance 123). Here again, those with experience resisting mainstream culture's definitions of the Self, including those Othered by race, ethnicity, class, or a combination of these, may have built up an array of coping mechanisms. Such mechanisms could also be useful in resisting negative social constructions of aging.

Furthermore, the ruptures slavery imposed on African Americans' families, combined with African concepts of the importance of genealogy, led a large number of African American families to actively claim their predecessors, a focus that takes the form of the "pictorial genealogies" that are "displayed on the walls of [even] the most humble homes" (Wall 554). Clifton's poetry echoes these ideas, simultaneously filling gaps in family histories and invoking a larger African American familial community. In her poetry, the family (like history) is literally holy (*Blessing* 23). Visiting a plantation cemetery in South Carolina, the speaker of a poem calls unnamed buried slaves "foremother, brother" (*Quilting* 11). Claiming these bodies as relatives, the speaker widens her available, known genealogy, and places herself within the context of a community of Black bodies united across time and geography. In the relations it invokes, the poem further collapses past and present.

In another poem, "whose side are you on?" the speaker rides a bus (*Quilting* 18). The speaker's participation in the journey—giving change, ringing the bell—is active, perhaps youthfully so, in direct contrast with the tired immobility of other passengers' passive "hanging" with a "work hand folded shut." The main object of the speaker's gaze is an old man. By the end of the poem, the speaker claims parenthood of the "tired sons," a group that includes the old man. Once more, Clifton's poem conflates generations and creates community through invoked family relations. Both the historical necessity of an active role in retrieving knowledge of one's ancestors and the resulting pictorial genealogies foster feelings of pride and emotional attachments to predecessors. Again, this serves to positively influence perceptions of the aged.

In the bus poem, a genderless speaker identifies others by gender ("busstop woman," "old man," "daughters," "sons"). In her memoir *Generations*, Clifton offers readers a similar construction, charting "familial descent as neither patrilineage nor matrilineage, but a fusion of both" (Wall 559). Some pundits of Black American culture allude to a rift between Black men and Black women—attributed variously to patriarchy and to feminism—a divisive construct that African American authors navigate. Clifton's writing, as in these two poems, creates a gender-free space, demonstrating that all genders share responsibilities for contributing to the community's future.

Slavery's legacy and past and present racism produce the need for an array of African American survival skills above and beyond those needed by most Caucasian Americans. With their depiction as reproductive vehicles, sexual objects, superwomen, and archetypal mother figures, Black women have needed an advanced skill set—"everyday / something has tried to kill me / and has failed" (Clifton, *Book of Light* 25). As this competence in survival becomes honed over time, the skills are passed down as personal strengths. African American women "develop 'respect for their mothers' ability to overcome seemingly insurmountable situations' and tools to do the same in their own lives [because,] . . . regardless of class position, African American mothers reveal the contradictions in their lives, so that their daughters can negotiate survival in a world of white male privilege. . . . This may be particularly relevant for African American women who came of age during the civil rights struggle, which encouraged African Americans to view their family and community as a source of strength in their efforts to dismantle outside forms of oppression" (Agee 82, quoting Carothers 244; Agee 90).[7] Receiving this knowledge from mothers or othermothers can be an additional positive influence on African Americans' notions of old age.

An *othermother* functions as a mother to someone who is not her biological child. The relationship dynamics with othermothers parallel some of those connections made with the otherdaughters in chapter 4. In each of those situations, an unrelated person, who might or might not have been sought out for such a responsibility, accepts the onus of care that usually falls to a family member. Otherdaughters and othersons provide care, services, companionship, and support; othermothers and otherfathers offer guidance, care, support, and information, transmitting cultural values and collective knowledge to an individual. Nancy Naples's work suggests that othermothering is "activist mothering" in both its implementation and its effect.[8] Work done at the level of a neighborhood or town, through which an "ethics of caring and personal accountability move[s] communities forward," Patricia Hill Collins labels *community othermothering* (192). *Otherelders* perform this role on an even broader, diasporic scale, as discussed in more detail in chapter 6.

In many African American communities, the information of those most adept at surviving—knowledge culled from personal endurance through physical and/or sexual oppression and slavery—becomes a valuable cultural commodity. This commodification of knowledge may be able to offset somewhat the trends of the anti-aging market and its products, as discussed in chapters 1 and 2. Such skills are intangible; those who possess them are the physical incarnations of this information. Thus, respect for the knowledge can translate into esteem for those who embody it. Furthermore, reinforcing this appreciation for the aged body, "among traditional African peoples no clear separation is made between body and spirit; rather, the body is conceived as the material form of the spirit" (Peterson x).[9] Logically, then, when one appreciates a mind's knowledge, one must also respect the accompanying body; this factor also counters the mind/body split. Many historical factors contribute to twentieth- and twenty-first-century Black women's relatively positive views of aging and old age.

Contemporary Black women are not detached from the rest of culture and they do experience the reality of age-related physical decline. Nonetheless, negative concepts of advancing age may have less impact on Black women's self-image as they age because of the experiences Black women have had resisting negative body valuations. Copper and Macdonald and Rich argued that lesbians have an advantage navigating cultural negativity about aging because lesbians have spent a lifetime of experience accepting and/or resisting the role of Other. Similar arguments could be made about African American women and aging. Black women's bodies "from slavery to the present, have represented their physical selves in opposition to the distorted vision of the dominant culture . . . [because the Black woman's body has] traditionally not been presented as respected or loved. . . . The black female body has been constructed as profane rather than sacred, other rather than ideal" (Bennett and Dickerson 5–11). Literary and cultural theorist Deborah McDowell writes that Black women have long been constructed "as simultaneously all bodies and nobodies" (298). Black women's experiences resisting being "all bodies" that are "nobodies" may offer some preparation for their response to Caucasian American concepts of female bodies that are not part of the reproductive cycle. Black women also are likely to have experience resisting valuations of their bodies based on cultural standards of gender and race. For example, in slavery there "was a simultaneous masculinization and feminization of the black female body" (Peterson xi). As demonstrated in chapter 2, in old age, Caucasian American women may become similarly more "masculine." Again, Black women have a history of experience in dealing with a particular cultural valuation of their gender in ways that Caucasian Americans do not.

Clifton's poem "Sisters: For Elaine Philip on Her Birthday" addresses these issues, albeit obliquely. The poem shows that Black women can actively claim oppositional racial identity—the speaker and Philip both "got black." Perhaps because of the invisibility of White racial privilege, and because some of its visible parts are so appalling, few Caucasian Americans actively claim their racial identities and "get white." For both Blacks and Whites, race usually remains a constant, but because Whites' self-definition does not consciously include their racial category, most do not and cannot use race to create stability during other changes of self-identity. Many women experience the processes of aging as changes in identity.[10] Black women who claim a particular racial identity have a stable category in which to ground themselves during those changes. Black women who claim multiple racial (or multiple other) identities have more practice accepting the instability of their concepts of the self. Both of these possibilities offer Black women the probability of a greater comfort level with their concepts of self through the changes of advancing age.[11]

Historical relationships with biomedicine are another realm that affects aging bodies. "African American women's awareness of [Blacks] not being well-served by biomedical science causes them to give it less control in their lives compared with women who have traditionally benefited from its technologies"; Caucasian American women have a somewhat more positive history with the U.S. allopathic medical establishment, and may even have used it as a tool for class mobility (Agee 83; see also Agee 90; Nixon et al. 92). Although mainstream Caucasian American culture conceives of old age as a problematic medical event (Rothfield 33), Black women have historical justification in their distrust of the medical-industrial complex's "ideological structures that regulate individual bodies" (Komesaroff 55). A history of resistance offers more possibilities for negotiating or refuting the trend of making aging-into-old-age a medical issue.

Contemporary Context

Contemporary reasons that Black women may have more positive ideations of menopause and aging include the historically based reasons, their family and community relationships, a tradition and mythology of the Black Superwoman, and a further history of oppositional stances to Caucasian American culture.

African American women from across the socioeconomic spectrum report that information they received as young women from mothers and othermothers provided them with "knowledge and power to negotiate difficulties during [aging, and specifically during] the menopausal process" (Agee 74). In contrast, middle-class Caucasian American women related feelings of anger at the lack of warning and information from their mothers about the challenges of menopause and aging, with 34 percent feeling disappointed that their mothers had not modeled or discussed ways to respond to ageism. Working-class Caucasian Americans and middle-class African Americans were not dissatisfied with the information they received, instead reporting that their mothers had supplied information they found helpful in managing the challenges of menopause and aging (Agee 74–9).

Of the fewer than 20 percent of African American women who did not receive advice on menopause from their mothers, many turned to other family members and friends—aunts, sisters, and neighbors (Nixon et al. 89–90). In contrast, 80 percent of Caucasian American women's sources of information about menopause are books, magazines, and health professionals (Mansfield 98; see also

Agee). The widespread kinship network available in some African American communities also contributes both to women's positive feelings about their biological mothers (Agee 82) and to the amount of information available (Nixon et al. 84). Furthermore, "Othermothers . . . provide African American daughters with a variety of female role models within their community" (Agee 81). The presence of othermothers may also affect how Black women think about aging and menopause: "The limited research on African American women's attitudes toward menopause suggests that they may view menopause as a natural transition and more positively than white women do, perhaps because of widespread kinship networks prevalent in African American families that may provide support" (Nixon et al. 84). Thus, both family and kinship networks provide role models, positively influence African American women's perceptions of their mothers, and positively affect conceptions of menopause.

In Clifton's poem "to my last period" (*Blessing* 70), the experience of menopause also positively influences women's communal roles. In this poem, the speaker posits the premenopausal woman as solitary ("i," "girl," "me," "the hussy"). In menopause, the "i" of the speaker becomes accepted into an assemblage of "grandmothers"—plural and in community. This poetic representation reflects the research data demonstrating the centrality of elders in African American communities.[12] The number of group roles that women have—their identities beyond those of mother and spouse—positively influences their mental health status during menopause (AARP; Bart; Martin), as does physiological health, with poor physiological health linked to higher rates of depression. A larger percentage of Black women have occurrences of potentially painful fibroid tumors and other physical symptoms of menopause (Freeman et al. 33) than do Caucasian American menopausal women, yet Black women are more likely than White women are to pass through menopause with no psychological problems (Greer, *The Change* 66; Sheehy 95), perhaps because Black women demographically tend to have a history of community associations, of working outside the home, of church involvement, and of extended kinship networks.

Books by Caucasian Americans about menopause that specifically address African American women's menopausal experiences, such as those by Greer and Sheehy and some culturally informed studies such as that by Nixon et al., suggest that the myth of the Black Superwoman explains some of the differing statistics between Black and White women. The casting of menopause as a more natural experience in some African American communities (as mentioned above) and the invocation of the infamous Black Superwoman myth as an explanation for racial differences can be problematic. The cultural trope of "the black female body" too often has been both "dehumanized as a machine built for endurance" (Bennett and Dickerson 13) and constructed as "natural," as outside of the realm of the social and thus not fully human. In many academic settings, such constructions are no longer considered acceptable, but somehow they persist in the literature of menopause. The rhetoric of menopause needs critical, oppositional attention.

For many years, Black women have challenged Caucasian Americans' body-focused messages; "Considering the prevalence of ageism in white America, one can even see the African traditions as diametrically opposed to U.S. traditions" (Holloway and Demetrakopoulos 15). The earlier part of this chapter highlighted some tactics that Black women can use to resist Caucasian American body concepts about aging and old age. Here, that idea is reexamined, underscoring current cultural theories about Black aging bodies. "Writers and critics have both been attempting over the last few decades to discover the parameters of the black female body when not seen through the bifocal lenses that have tried to limit the view of such bodies to the categories of propriety or perversion" (Bennett and Dickerson 9). Black bodies outside of propriety and perversion have traditionally been rendered invisible to Caucasian American society, except as a caregiving stereotype. Creating a path to social visibility for old women, including old Black women, requires significant change.

Poetic Context

Here, Clifton's work makes an important contribution. The speakers of her poems, publically and positively, claim previously private bodily processes, as in "poem in praise of menstruation" (*Quilting* 36). They equate signs of age with joy—"her hair / is white with wonderful" (*Book of Light* 24). They parallel the acquisition of racial identity with old age ("the grayer she do get, good God, / the blacker she do be!") and with sexuality (waiting "for the second coming / when she can break through gray hairs / into blossom" [*Good Woman* 170]). In Clifton's poetry, "black female bodies replace the marginalizing system of binary relations. . . . Within this new paradigm of meaning, the African American female subject comes into view . . . through those institutions, identities, and ideas that coexist within the boundaries of [her] position" (Mance 126). Mance posits this as a move particularly useful and liberating to African Americans; one might suggest a broader applicability for this oppositional stance. Consider Clifton's "there is a girl inside" (*Good Woman* 170), a sonnet.[13]

Even in its brevity, this poem demonstrates a wide range of age studies concepts. For example, chapter 1 of this book details Calasanti and Slevin's four dimensions of age: chronological, subjective, occupational, and functional (Calasanti and Slevin, *Gender* 17). This poem contains examples of each: chronological in that it repeats the term *girl*; subjective in discussing a *forest of kindling* and *lovers*, plus the contrast between the *girl* in the opening line and the *old woman* at the end of the first stanza; occupational in its references to a *used poet* and the *old woman*'s bones; and functional in the speaker's ability to be *randy as a wolf*, to *break through gray hairs into blossom*, and to *wild* the woods with *damn wonder*.

As discussed at the beginning of chapter 4, one of the benefits of literature is its ability to show interiority. In this poem, the speaker first establishes the presence of the *girl inside*, which readers otherwise would not know existed, and readers learn how the speaker thinks about this girl, who evidently is a wild sexual animal—*randy as a wolf*. As this speaker has aged, she finds that her sexual desires and youthful inner self will not leave. In the play on words with *green*, the speaker blends trees' vitality, innocence, youth, and classical tropes of bacchanalia: a *green tree* is living; a person is *green* when inexperienced; the trees *in a forest of kindling* would be young; the poet's status as *used* suggests sexual experience; a green man, and presumably also a *green girl*, are symbols of abundant sexuality and reproduction. As multiple chapters discuss, aspects of Caucasian American culture decouple advanced age from gender and sexuality; this poem makes those elements inseparable and demonstrates the potency of their combined power.

The poem's third stanza reflects standard social expectations about nuns as unhurried, restrained, passionate about religious experiences, and blissfully married to God. This stanza also continues the double entendres, with a *second coming* that is both a Christian rapture and a sexual experience with multiple orgasms; that experience has the potential to create beautiful fertility, a *blossom*, that belies the *gray hairs* that are a physical manifestation of the speaker's advanced age. Thus, the poem serves as a miniature *reifungsroman*.

In the concluding stanza, the poem becomes an expression of possibility. The side effects of *the second coming* extend beyond the speaker to her lovers, who get to *harvest honey and thyme*—sweet and savory. The poem leaves open the *thyme/time* homonym's possibility that time enriches the speaker's *honey*, so that the lover *harvests* an improved sexual experience, or that the sexual experience may enable the lover to achieve life extension, harvesting time. The union of the speaker and the lover benefits the broader world in which they operate, returning *the woods* to their natural, *wild* form as everything in the world of the poem arrives at a spiritual state of astonishment and, at the end of the last line, *wonder*. Through the poem, the speaker sends a message to potential lovers: "You might not immediately see the randy sexuality in my body, but it is there, and if you are attentive enough to my needs, you will unleash a bounty of personal pleasure and broader environmental benefits." Thus, this text connects the individual experience of agedness with the social context in which the body ages, and it shows the wide-ranging social benefits of appreciating the often-overlooked potential in aged women's bodies.

This poem plays with the connection between spiritual ecstasy and sexual fulfillment, found in textual classics such as Spencer's *Epithalamion* and the passions of St. Teresa of Avila. In the process, the poem establishes the differences between outer appearance and the inner self, encouraging readers to appreciate the potential of each old woman to have a deliciously rich interiority. It challenges conventions about older women and sexual agency. It suggests that, for those who are willing to move beyond the limitations of ageist stereotypes, there is quite a benefit. The poem acknowledge the mind/body split—*there is a girl inside*—then explores the hidden power in reuniting the two elements, with physical ecstasy paralleling an explosive spiritual rapture that yields not collateral damage, but collateral benefit.

Although the poem does not explicitly list negative stereotypes about aging, sexuality, and women's agency, the existence of those stereotypes underlies the text as the poem disproves them. Like "there is a girl inside," several of Clifton's other poems, such as "my dream about falling," and "wishes for sons," also show the dichotomy between the external view of an aged woman and the woman's interior self-identity, equating aging with the process of ripening,[14] noting that both age and youth have advantages and disadvantages, and reminding readers of their always-already aging bodies and of the illusory nature of any thoughts that the state of the body is static. These may seem like relatively simple concepts, but generally they are foregrounded neither in popular culture nor in literature.

Literary and other texts result from and yield influence. As discussed in detail in chapter 2, "The body, as we well know, is never simply matter, for it is never divorced from perception and interpretation. . . . [The body] is subject to examination and speculation. Perception and interpretation come from different sources. . . . The body is then inextricably linked to ideation and subjectivity" (Peterson ix). Discourse about aging and old age arrives on a body that is always already inscribed. "Nothing is more material, physical, corporal than the exercise of power" (Foucault 57–8). The body, as "the locus of all struggles of power" (Göle 474), is doubly constituted as a material location: the tangible flesh is unquestionably material, and the power that acts both from and on the corporal tissues becomes another layer of physicality constituting the human. This chapter then serves as an analysis of that which "reads for the ways persons inscribe on their corporal bodies the culture that produces them and that they mutually produce" (Dickson 298). The power of the discourses about aging and menopause act to sculpt a body compliant to and reconstitutive of that same power. Thus, the available discourse about aging and menopause directly affects women's bodily experiences.

Foucault suggests that, to find the power structures at work, "one needs to study what kind of body the current society needs" (58). In her analysis of Black women's bodies, Deborah McDowell asks a related set of questions: "What is the body we want? What is the body we need? What is the body we have?" (301). Her questions themselves yield power, assuming change. They make the assumption that change will happen; simultaneously, they take on (assume) the power to make that change happen. African American women cannot help but live their lives with some awareness of the effect of racial power differences, and many also have ideas about their location in gender and class structures. Thus, the questions McDowell asks are analytically pragmatic. They begin beyond analysis, starting with empowerment, and mention resistance last, clearly defining the goal and framing the current subject position as a steppingstone on the way to that goal. Similarly, Clifton's writing impels the reader to active engagement with the cultural conceptions of the aged body, her "ability to connect generations of people and to remind them who they are and from whence they came" (McCluskey 49) and her talent for honing in on key tactics that disrupt Caucasian American cultural assumptions.

Counterpoint and Future Context

Clifton's writing skillfully interprets Black cultural concepts and interrupts White ones, but that impact needs to be complicated in at least three ways. First, by the understanding that Clifton's work may be the exception rather than the rule. Many of the Black women poets of the 1960s tended to shock readers, focused on cultural and historical figures, glorified Black nationalism, and disparaged accommodations to mainstream culture. "While others complained of their elders' failures," capitulations, and ignorance, Clifton celebrated her familial ancestors who lived as outsiders within mainstream American culture (Rushing 50).

Second, although it is a reality for many and a stereotype for even more, it is far from universal that Black women live in familial and kinship contexts that support positive ideations about aging and menopause. Many Black women garner unhelpful or even harmful ideas from those they turn to for information and help:

- During menopause, "I thought I was going to die. I just couldn't stand it. . . . I told my minister that I could feel a change in my body. . . . He told me to pray against it" (Nixon et al. 89).

- "I finally went back to the doctor and just broke down. I didn't care. I told him he's got to help me because something is wrong. I was like ready to hang it up, it was bad. He assured me that a lot of it was just from the absence of estrogen" (Nixon et al. 91).
- "When I asked my mother about menopause . . . all she said was 'you'll find out when you get it'" (Sheehy 38).
- New York City's "Department of Health's Pregnancy Testing Centers reported that women in their middle years often presented themselves for pregnancy testing, unaware that their amenorrhea was the result of menopause" (Rips 88).
- The producers of talk shows such as *The Oprah Winfrey Show* (1986–2011) "admitted on the air that they had had an easier time booking guests to talk about murdering their spouses than about menopause" (Sheehy xiii).

Some older Black women seeking information may fall prey to the "considerable misunderstanding" (Nixon et al. 92) that exists. The myth of the Black Superwoman may silence others: "to ask for help from either friends, families, or care providers would be incongruous given their roles as strong, independent women" (Agee 84). Daily fear of their surroundings, mostly owing to high crime rates, is "greater for women, for blacks, for the poor, and for those living alone" (Ragan 33) than for women in the opposites of those categories; one might extrapolate that intersections of those categories produce even higher levels of anxiety. And kinship and communal ties notwithstanding, more than half of all African American women over the age of eighty live below the poverty level (Kane), a factor that affects access to care and quality of life.

Clifton's work and the cultural analysis in this chapter may be widely applicable to women of her cohort, but how much of her work and this analysis are pertinent to later generational cohorts of African American women remains to be seen. "Having never witnessed the Jim Crow South . . . kids can only know this past as a history, not a lived reality. . . . [T]his divergent historical reality will shape the middle-age experience of new generations differently" (Newman 290). Compared with the context of the previous four centuries of oppression, Black Americans coming of age in the

1970s and later have grown up in a context of relative freedom, even though racism is far from eradicated.

The trend toward cultural assimilation furthers the divide between Clifton's and later cohorts: "too many young Black women have the opportunity to westernize themselves so thoroughly that their Blackness . . . is erased by the aseptic masks of western 'culture'" (Holloway and Demetrakopoulos 21). Nonetheless, even though Black women report that they "had negotiated or were negotiating menopause in a very different social environment than that experienced by their mothers under segregation[,] . . . many say that their collective history as African American women shaped important aspects of their contemporary identity, as well as their interactions with the health care system" (Agee 80). The overwhelming majority (82 percent) of Caucasian American women, on the other hand, "stated that they *began* encountering discrimination once they experienced changes in physical appearance, particularly weight gain and wrinkles," and resented their mothers for not preparing them for this moment (Agee 86, emphasis added).[15] In twenty-first-century North American culture, how will these two perspectives influence each other and affect women's experiences of menopause, aging, and old age? Perhaps the techniques through which one might support Black women (and men!) to reclaim a racial identity could work similarly for people of other colors as well, including Whites, creating a stable category of identity that would improve experiences of the changes of aging.

An informed response needs to include considerations of the historical, mythical, familial, communal, and oppositional coping strategies surrounding menopause and age. As with all cultural groups, African American constructs of age are not universal. The strong likelihood of additional cultural convergence further affects African Americans' conceptions of old age and aging (cf. McDonald and Armstrong). Clifton's poetic speakers construct aging "black women as proud representatives of both race and gender" (Holladay, "Songs" 291). The efficacy of these formulations is founded on African American cultural belief systems that encourage positive ideations of aged Black womanhood. With additional convergence or assimilation, what remains of this foundation may be further endangered, and Clifton's ultimate legacy could become her lament of "the lost women," rather than her resistance:

> i need to know their names
> Those women i would have walked with
> . . .
> where are my gangs,
> my teams, my mislaid sisters?
> all the women who could have known me,
> where in the world are their names? (*Next* 29)

Such a future of overwhelming disorientation and bewildering solitude need not be inevitable. For people of all genders and colors, an enduring legacy of pride in community, gender, heritage, and endurance can buffer the potentially negative impact of aging-into-old-age.

Through the breadth of elements that collectively create North American Black women's beliefs about and experiences of advancing age, this chapter again underscores the importance and benefits of age studies' multidisciplinarity. To reach this level of knowledge, which really is just a small first step toward deeper understanding, requires blending ideas from fields as diverse as biology, comparative racial formations, demography, history, literature, medicine, philosophy, popular culture, and spirituality. Such a blend illuminates age studies' parallels with feminist thought: the array of factors that construct, then naturalize, a power differential; the intersectional nature of individual identity; the activist undertone of academic analyses advocating for justice; and the damaging impact on those who perpetuate the denigrating stereotypes as well as those who are stereotyped. That last factor is all the more relevant for age, an identity category that every living person embodies in time.

Because Clifton's poetry honors mainly Black bodies, particularly Black women's bodies, in their assorted shapes, sizes, and ages, for individuals who have other skin colors, her writing may not seem radically liberatory. However, Clifton believed that all women have the capacity to connect with their histories and ancestral knowledge as she had, and she spoke of that connection as the foundational element of a community-building, empowering stance. With that knowledge and with the many other connections her writing develops across age differences and multigenerational divides, perhaps women of all colors will use Clifton's models. Collaborative, cross-racial development of those models could ameliorate the impact that ageist ideations have on sisters and othersisters, daughters and otherdaughters, mothers and othermothers, kin and otherkin, and on ourselves.

CHAPTER 6

Storytelling and Cultural Transmission, with Louise Erdrich's *Last Report on the Miracles at Little No Horse*

Lucille Clifton's work creates an opening for interracial collaboration. Artfully but firmly, Louise Erdrich's texts demand it. Elderhood is not an essentializable or statically calculable quality. A geriatrician handed a human heart cannot conclusively determine whether the organ belonged to a forty-year-old person or a sixty-year-old person. Along with hours and years, a person accumulates beliefs, actions, biology, and material circumstances. As with other identity categories, each individual presents his or her age to the world, moment by moment, and other members of the world, whose bodies similarly perform the identities of their lives, reflect back to that individual the age that she or he embodies. As with gender, part of age becomes a performance, a role each person plays. As age is deconstructed, reconstructing the role of elders within society is only part of the requisite work; the role of the not-yet-old also must alter.

An exploration of the historical function of the aged in multiple First Nation communities, a brief study of elders' roles in cultural transmission, and critical considerations of the impact that the temporarily young can have when taking on functions traditionally associated with elders together provide the cultural context for the main argument of this chapter: Native American authors' texts may be able to serve as textual elders, filling the gap in others' education, performing some of the acts of social transmission necessary for cultural survival, and impelling readers into a familial relationship that carries ethical responsibilities to enact change. Over the last century, the impact of Contact has established the need for making explicit the paths of cultural dissemination and responsibility.[1]

An exploration of key themes in *The Last Report on the Miracles at Little No Horse* by Louise Erdrich (b. 1954), provides specificity for those broad considerations. In particular, Erdich's writing challenges the idea of impermeable boundaries and suggests that each person's value is determined in large part by what that individual can offer to the greater social unit, such as the tribe. The last part of the chapter analyzes how the text positions its readers as culturally responsible for acting as agents of change.

The Story's Story: Old Woman Spider (Cherokee)

The first fire burned on an island in the middle of the river. The council of animals met and decided who should get this new life. Of course the biggest and strongest were first.

First was raven because he could fly and was very strong. He flew to the stump on the island where the fire burned deep inside. He stuck his head in but the heat and smoke turned his feathers black. He became scared and returned to the council without the fire.

Gulegi, the climber snake, went next. He was famous for his climbing abilities. He swam over to the island and climbed up the tree on the outside but when he put his head inside the stump at the top, the smoke got in his eyes. He became confused and fell inside. He wiggled and writhed in the heat and ashes, and luckily found his way back out—but not before his scales were turned as black as the smoke. Today he is called a black snake.

Many other animals went to retrieve this new life . . . all unsuccessfully. The bear tried, the buzzard tried, Oo-goo-koo tried, and even the raccoon tried. Finally, after all these tried, a tiny little voice was heard near the ground. The other animals looked around and finally saw A-ga-yv-li-ge, old woman spider. They laughed. "How could you get the fire . . . a tiny, old woman?" She said, "Each of you has tried with your strengths and talents. My talent and my greatest strength is my mind. I believe I can bring this new life back to the council." They let her try.

She stepped into the river, jumping from crest to crest until she reached the island. There, burning in the center was the stump, caught fire from the Lightning Brothers. She went to the river's edge and there formed a small bowl out of the wet clay she found. She placed this bowl on her back and carried it to the base of the stump. She found a small opening and went inside.

Once inside the stump she took the bowl from her back and scooped up some white hot coals from the fire. She returned the bowl to her back and stepped back into the water. She jumped from crest to crest until she had once again made it to the animal council waiting at the river's edge. She poured out the coals and brought this new life to the Cherokees. From that first fire and the wet clay, came the first piece of pottery. (Masters)

Generational Functionality in Traditional First Nation Cultures

In many Native American cultures, the group has been more important than the individual (Owens 153; John, Blanchard, and Hennessy 292). As Paula Gunn Allen explains, in the "maturation processes among Native Americans, older is valued and younger is valued and each takes the place proper to her age and life phase" (189). When the community functions as the most valuable human unit, each lesser unit—a household or an individual person—works toward the same goal: the continuity of the larger unit. Thus, each person's role becomes defined by what she or he can contribute to the larger group.

Traditionally, children were important because they were the future of the group. Betty Laverdure, an Ojibwe elder, explains that "children are sacred. They are living treasures, gifts from the Great Spirit. You always treated them as if they didn't belong to you; they belonged to the Creator" (130). Because the young were the means of cultural survival, much time and energy were spent educating them correctly, so that they carry on the ways of the tribe. "With children we always have to think about seven generations to come but yet unborn," notes Janice Sundown Hallett, a Seneca elder (145).

Similarly, the middle generations in Native cultures were respected because their functions ensured the daily survival of the group. They were instrumental in obtaining and preparing food, providing shelter, reproducing, caring for children, and taking part in rituals. These activities also prepared them for the role of elders.

In this model, the eldest generation's work ensured the survival of the culture, and this work was publically valued. For example, in the Ojibwe Nation, "those who are wise must speak first" (Broker 7). In this context, wisdom means "possessing applicable information." In addition to the storytelling sessions that occurred on a smaller scale, larger celebrations could include rituals such as the Talk-Dance, a dancing ceremony formatted with intervals in which the dancing stopped and an elder would tell a story. Such rituals served as a way to give the elders a cultural place for passing down "the customs and the history of the do-daim [group]" (Broker 85). Accumulation of knowledge was important not for its acquisition, but because its transmittal improved the survival of the group. Researchers writing about Native American older women pan-culturally report that grandmothers have been respected for their potential "knowledge, wisdom, and power" (John, Blanchard, and Hennessy 303, 307; see also Erben 134).[2] However much Native American or other cultures' grandmothers may be stereotyped as wise women, in real life and in novels their realities are much more complex.

Historically, Native American elders have been the storytellers, and thus, the transmitters of culture.[3] Also, most people of advanced years were biological grandparents or had a cultural role of grandparental responsibility, even for children who were not biological descendants. "Intergenerational patterns of fosterage" (Shomaker 1) are customary in many Native Nations.[4] Thus, *grandparenting* is more of a role description than a strictly biological term. The function of the Native American elder has some similarities to that of the othermothers discussed in chapter 5. Joan Weibel-Orlando, a gerontologist who focuses on aging among Native Americans, conducts research on the variety of types of grandparenting roles that exist: storytellers, mentors, personal and spiritual advisers, and caretakers. Some nations' stories highlight the power of the elders as having both creative and destructive potentials (Weibel-Orland, "Grandparenting" 143), much like Old Woman Spider does. Unfortunately, fewer and fewer Native American children have adequate access to elders who fulfill these roles.

In many traditional Native societies, power comes from the accumulation of years and knowledge, a contrast to most Caucasian American groups, in which power often arises from accumulation of land or money. For example, according to Greg Sarris, the Pomo Nation people[5] believe that each human knows everything at birth. When a person learns to talk, that knowledge falls apart. After learning to talk, a person starts learning again, and by the time "the person gets old, REAL old, it will be all together again" (Sarris 34). Having knowledge that is "all together" does not mean being infallible, but it does mean that elders have some pieces of the puzzle that the temporarily young are missing.

Readers of contemporary popular Native American fiction—works, for example, by Sherman Alexie, Louise Erdrich, Linda Hogan, and Leslie Marmon Silko—encounter old characters who may be experienced, but who are not necessarily considered wise. Elder characters, such Eli, Nector, and Marie in *Love Medicine*, or Zeta and Lecha in *Almanac of the Dead*, are certainly just as human—wise or unwise—as the rest of the characters; in *Indian Killer*, Marie is one of the youngest main characters, and also one of the most astute. Wise or not, old people who remained connected to their culture are likely to have the greatest accumulation of the history and knowledge of the collective. Elders may be judged by how well they translate the individual pieces of this knowledge into action in their own lives and how well they lead the younger generations to learn; they also are respected just for having the knowledge, and for transmitting it, often in the form of stories.

Historically, says Weibel-Orlando, "an Indian elder is not necessarily an elderly person. Rather, to be regarded as an elder implies recognition by the community of one's embodiment of certain exemplary and ethnically valued traits.... It represents a set of the relationships between the elder and his or her constituency (e.g., stewardship, advisory and counseling duties on the part of the elder, and respect and compliance on the part of the constituents)" ("Elders" 152). That is, *elder* invokes a social role rather than a particular chronological marker.[6] This role has the potential to be usefully and respectfully taken up by writers, even those who are not chronological elders.

Additionally, in many nations, "elders belong to everyone. We are to instruct our families because they are being destroyed. We need to strengthen our families, plus our communities and our nations. We must strengthen our nations through the prophecies of our society. We must encourage everyone to be there for everyone" (Laverdure 130; Ojibwe Elder). Elder women in many Native nations move beyond personal family connections and are "able to be mother for all things" (John, Blanchard, and Hennessy 303; see also Erben 130). Understanding the multiple variables invoked in the social role of the elders allows a greater comprehension of the cultural continuance embodied in one of the tasks they perform: telling stories.

Stories' Historical Functions in First Nation Cultures

In oral Native American societies, history lessons and cultural studies, conventionally transmitted through storytelling, are not as strictly codified as different entities as they are in Caucasian American cultures. For example, Ella Cara Deloria, a Yankton Sioux ethnologist who became intimately familiar with the Teton Sioux culture, recounts that historically, even a person's name is a story that contains a piece of collective history (Deloria, *Waterlily* 49–57); Erdrich, a member of the Turtle Mountain band of Chippewa, echoes this perspective in *The Last Report on the Miracles at Little No Horse* (145). A Pueblo elder reports that her culture's language reflects the value placed on the role of stories: "In our language, we have a word that means two things. It means to listen and it also means to behave. So when we're behaving, we're listening, and that's the awareness" (Downey 7). In Dakota, the word that means *to speak to a relative* and the word for *to pray* are the same (Deloria, *Speaking* 28); the act of communicating culture is a sacred task. This reverence for cultural transmission demonstrates the importance of supporting group cohesion and continuity, as well as the value accorded to those who perform these tasks.

As vehicles of social instruction, stories can contain multiple layers of learning, including history, values, survival tactics, continuity, and unity. A Cherokee account of how Grandmother Spider brought fire to the people opens this chapter. Grandmother Spider is a figure found in many different Native groups, including Cherokee/Ojibwe, Navajo, Hopi, Keresan Pueblo, Tewa and Kiwa, Papago, and Shawnee. This brief tale is rich in lesson.

The story tells how the animal community came together to provide fire for humans, thereby also teaching listeners about cultural history. Listeners learn that the human and the animal communities were once joined, and about the importance, power, and interconnectedness of other living beings. Listeners also learn that humans are not at the top of the animal hierarchy. The narrative details the strengths and weakness of different animals, which teaches listeners to appreciate beings of varying physical capacities, and how best to hunt or trap a particular animal. The tale of how Old Woman Spider brought fire and pottery (or, in other nations' versions, fire and weaving) to humans explicates aspects of local and natural culture, accounting for the physical characteristics of some animals and explaining why people should not kill spiders.

It teaches that physical ability is insufficient for survival—that brains can win out over brawn. This tale also fits into a larger cultural context, in that there are many different stories about Old Woman Spider. In some traditions, she is the female embodiment of the creation myth. She weaves and unweaves, creates and destroys. In one legend, she saves the human race from a flood by spinning and weaving a boat for them. Other legends about her suggest that, when minds are open, her intelligence and wisdom enter. Multiple stories featuring the same characters—such as the Grandmother Spider stories, and, more contemporarily, Erdrich's books about the Little No Horse reservation—teach listeners about continuity; a story never ends, because something always happens next (Hill), happened before, and is happening simultaneously. The self can be fluid over time: Carol Patterson-Rudolph, who studies the stories of Grandmother Spider in the American Southwest, shows that Old Woman Spider is, simultaneously and by turns, creativity, spirit, old age, and wisdom (Patterson-Rudolph). Learning about cultural traditions and values provides the solid foundation necessary for positive membership in a society.

Kathleen Donovan, author of a book on feminist readings of Native American literature, posits that, in Native traditions, "power and centricity reside in knowing exactly who you are" (18)—a strong recommendation for the unconventional eldering that can happen through the texts of some First Nation writers. Furthermore, this knowledge works to preserve a healthy interrelationship among human beings, other beings, and environment: a Seminole elder remarks that her people "were always taught to try to keep the heritage and the traditions and keep it going because that was the strength of the land or the earth" (Cypress 92; see also Erben 13; Schweninger). Transmission of culture leads to cultural health, which is ecological and spiritual health. Because the body and the spirit are connected in most Native cultures, spiritual health leads to physical health. "I got my education from my people; that's why I am able to keep going and to keep my health and myself in physical condition," explains a Chumash elder (Centeno 32). With a strong base founded in the lessons of the stories, each individual is more likely to maintain solid bonds to community and land, and ties to spiritual and physical health.

Storytellers' Function in Contemporary First Nation Cultures

Stories were most often passed along orally by the elders: "It has always been the custom for us [grandmothers] to tell what must be passed on so that our ways will be known to the Ojibway children of the future" (Broker ix–x; see also Hallett 159; Sooktis 67; Weibel-Orlando, "Elders" 153–4). Government policies, assimilation, poverty, and the influences of cultural intersections and assimilation, not to mention the diaspora of Native people, have prevented many elders from fulfilling these traditional roles (Beckett and Dungee-Anderson 289; Centeno 45; Downey 3; John, Blanchard, and Hennessy 296; Weibel-Orlando, "Grandparenting" 140; Weibel-Orlando, "Elders" 152–3). Tewa Tesuque Pueblo elder Vickie Downey explains: "Trying to teach the children, it's hard now because we have to compete with the television. We have to compete with the radio and the fashions, the sports, and everything that's out there for them. The video arcades, the movies. It makes it hard to make them aware" (7). Westernization, urbanization, and pressures to assimilate create a situation in which some Native people choose not to claim their heritage (St. John 65). Other "children were born and raised in the urban areas and they do not make any distinctions as to their tribes. They do not say 'I am Ojibway,' or 'I am Dakota,' or 'I am Arapaho,' but they say 'I am an Indian,'" writes Ojibwe elder and author Ignatia Broker (7). Trying to negotiate a Native-centered self-awareness or cultural awareness based on the teachings of elders is, in many cases, no longer possible even for those who wish to claim their heritage.

But already, more than just a glimmer of hope offsets this grim reality; "things which don't shift and grow are dead things" (Silko, *Ceremony* 126). Native American storytellers create stories that resonate with contemporary readers, reaching larger and larger audiences with narratives that "cast long shadows both forward and backward" (Erben 134). Leslie Marmon Silko, whose work is anchored in her history with the Laguna Pueblo people, says, "Our greatest natural resource is stories and storytelling" (Seyersted). The tales are out there, and they are being told.

The discussion of generational functionality posits cultural transmission through story as a fundamental task of elders. *Eldering* is a social role, rather than chronological role, and elders' social roles stem in large part from their accrual of collective knowledge and their responsibility to benefit the larger community. Taken together, these concepts open the possibility for what one might call *nontraditional elders* or, building on the othermother model, *otherelders*. Many contemporary Native American authors, through their predilection for story and the research they do for their writing, gain knowledge customarily maintained by elders. In Lakota tradition, "if someone made you a gift, no matter how valuable it might be, he did not mean for it to grow old along with you. He expected you to use it when and as you chose, to honor someone else, and, indirectly, yourself" (Deloria, *Speaking* 68–9). Knowledge, in such a reciprocal relationship, obligates the recipient to use it, then pass it along. Authors acquiring and employing cultural information in their writing posit their stories as guided or inspired by the traditions of Native elders. Thus, their works assume (in both senses of the word) the cultural power and weight of elders' stories.

For example, Silko begins *Ceremony* by invoking traditional storytelling:

> Ts'its'tsi'nako, Thought-Woman,
> is sitting in her room
> and whatever she thinks about
> appears.

> She thought of her sisters,
> Nau'ts'ity'i and I'tcts'ity'i,
> and together they created the Universe
> this world
> and the four worlds below.
>
> Thought-Woman, the spider,
> named things and
> as she named them
> they appeared.
>
> She is sitting in her room
> thinking of a story now.
>
> I'm telling you the story
> she is thinking. (1)

Such an opening performs several significant functions. To a skeptic, at the very least, it records that Silko claims inspiration via the beliefs, characters, and stories of her culture. Taken more literally, this opening metamorphoses Silko's novel into a traditional story. Thought-Woman, with the power of creation, is no relic of the past; she continues to create in the here and now. She forms the world, and she generates the story of the novel. In positing herself as a mere scribe and the actual author as a character from the old stories, Silko gives the novel a link to history, and thus a cultural weight, more significant than could be found in the stories of any human elder. Also, in the First Nation communities about which Silko writes, time is nonlinear, which makes the past just as available today as it was a century ago. With that construction of time, Silko's invocation of Old Woman Spider does not draw the past into the present. Rather, it prompts readers to recall that the past *is* the present, and vice versa. Additionally, this collapse of linear time reminds readers that age is immaterial in comparison with knowledge—a helpful device for Silko, who wrote *Ceremony* as a woman in her mid-twenties.

Although they do not always use such complex methods, many contemporary Native American novels perform similar tasks, keeping both stories and storytellers alive in the imagination of the readers (Erben 135). In his discussion of the uses of traditional stories in modern times, UCLA professor and Coast Miwok Nation chief Greg Sarris reasons that having contemporary readers and listeners allows stories to continue to evolve and create meaning now, rather than taking the listener back to the time encompassed in the story. "If talk initiates in the interlocutors a kind of internal dialogue where the interlocutors examine the nature of their own thinking, that dialogue can be carried over to an ever-widening context of talk in stories and conversations, such that the inner dialogue can inform and be informed by new stories and conversations" (Sarris 30). Erdrich's Nanapush tells the story of the last buffalo hunt. Alexie's *Indian Killer* incorporates the Ghost Dance into a modern context. Often, novels by these authors are more accessible, both materially and psychologically, than stories from more traditional elders. In this vein, one could argue that a culture's stories should be, *must* be taken up by contemporary writers for the tales, and therefore the values and traditions, to survive.

Nonetheless, one might do well to consider a potential counterpoint. Although Native American writers' texts fill a cultural void and perform a valuable service to a community of readers, they may also contribute to the problem they seek to remedy. Because writers' stories are taking on part of the role of creating community continuity, a role that had been held by elders, those whose needs are even partially satisfied by the work of Native writers' texts may be less inclined to seek out actual elders. In most Native American nations, the elders have held the responsibility for transmitting knowledge of cultural values and identity and for sharing the group's collective knowledge. "Lack of community role contributes to the older Indian's sense of loss, isolation, and lack of well-being" (Weibel-Orlando, "Elders" 166). North American governments' policies creating reservations consolidated First Nation communities in some cases, but other policies and social forces, such as juridical relocations, economic relocations, the trend toward urbanization, and the disruption of family patterns, combine to create a situation in which members of many of North America's indigenous nations grow up with limited access to elders who can share their nations' history and knowledge.[7]

Writers such as Silko, Erdrich, Cook-Lynn, Alexie, Owens, and Sarris are aware of many of their communities' challenges, and through their writing, they contribute more to community building than would otherwise be possible.[8] That is, their texts are read by thousands more people than the authors could personally contact, and readers may gain a sense of belonging to something bigger than themselves. The gains of the written stories, however, are accompanied by the dangers of substitution and transference. The goal is community building; a vital community includes individuals of all ages, and communities must actively work to diminish or eradicate the "loss, isolation, and lack of well-being" too often found among the elders of numerous cultures.

Moreover, some Native American thinkers disagree with Erdrich's methodology. Erdrich's texts do not argue for the necessity or future existence of Native sovereignty. They take as given that Caucasian Americans are not leaving the Americas any time soon and that nations existing within another nation necessarily have some interaction with the outside nation, which makes full Native sovereignty implausible. That is, Erdrich's novels fundamentally accept the presence of Caucasian American culture. For those who believe that Caucasian American culture is antithetical to the existence and stability of an intact Native American community, such a message is an anathema.

Native critics such as Elizabeth Cook-Lynn ardently advocate a separatist message of tribal sovereignty. Multiple authors, including Leslie Marmon Silko, argue that Native sovereignty necessitates the withdrawal of non-Native cultures from the Americas. Silko also has asserted that some stories should not be shared with cultural outsiders.[9] A number of Alexie's texts, such as *The Absolutely True Diary of a Part-Time Indian* and "The Joy of Reading: Superman and Me," suggest ways in which the cultural interactions may be negotiated, while *The Joy of Fancydancing* portrays the damage that Contact has created. Silko's writing contains more assuredness that Caucasian American retreat can happen; her texts and some of Alexie's suggest that this removal is the only cure for the socioemotional illnesses brought on by the interactions between Native and Caucasian American cultures. On the other hand, whatever other disagreements Greg Sarris may have with Erdrich's texts, he somewhat agrees with her approach (121, 131).

Taking what might be considered the middle path, ethnographer Ella Deloria's novel, *Waterlily*, argues for separate societies, but ones that de-problematize the reentrance of those who have left. Each of these thinkers works to build community in different ways.

Group Individuals: Story as Context

In this context, *home* is in the locus of the community. In contrast, since the early-modern era, Caucasian American traditions have focused on the individual as paramount, declaring that stories should be about discrete, particular human beings, and that such entities are important primarily because of their differences. Small wonder, then, that Native people's stories post-Contact are so full of conflict between the individual and the group—not just the nuclear family, but the tribe or the nation. "If anything is most vital, essential, and absolutely important in Native cultural philosophy, it is [the] concept of interdependence," says Acoma Pueblo writer Simon Ortiz (xii). In this framework, *home* means more than just an individual's family or family dwelling place. *Home*, in Native writing, includes one's place in the world—that is, one's relation with the larger group. A significant part of the friction at the interface of the Native and Caucasian American cultures occurs because of that difference. Caucasian American ideas tend to devalue the interrelationships of self and community so vital to many Native traditions.

The ability to go home, then, is not just about being in a particular location, returning to well-known faces and customs, or reuniting with loving or familiarly dysfunctional acquaintances; one goes home to rejoin a whole that is larger than either the self or the family unit, however extended that may be. A significant portion of the conflicted identity that Native writers bring to their writing is not just about genetic lineage, eco-centrism versus ego-centrism, or urban versus reservation; it communicates the challenges of establishing a mutually sustaining relationship between self and community, in which the self both exists as a separate entity and exists for the community.

First Nations' resistance, then, needs to critique and offset Caucasian American culture's insistent divisiveness. Texts of resistance need to effect change on the personal level because the individual cannot act as part of a group unless he or she accepts membership in a group and the group accepts the individual. In addition, such resistance needs to simultaneously address the community, because community vitality and cohesion is the goal. Cultural critic and scholar of comparative racial formations Helen Hoy quotes Chandra Mohanty about the mistake of reducing structural inequities to personal differences (14), and Hoy applies this concept, albeit incompletely, to her discussion of postcolonial analysis: "While postcolonial analysts have long rejected essentialist notions of Native authenticity, we have hovered avidly around textual manifestations of postcolonial resistance" (164–5). For many Native communities, group identity equates to authenticity; to be accepted by the group in which one claims membership, one must know where and how one belongs.

Changing self- and group identities is the goal—a complex task, especially when mainstream culture tends to work against this objective. One might wonder how best to incite self-transformation. Cultural critic Chela Sandoval's ideas of the differential consciousness of resistance may be useful in thinking of *how* resistance can work. Sandoval argues that, to be effective, resistance must operate simultaneously on multiple fronts, and the decision about which tactics are used should depend on which will be the most effective. To combat oppression, the most effective way will use multiple tactics.

For many Native nations, several aspects of oppression have a common denominator: the separation of the individual from the group. Therefore, to some extent, responsible Native literature needs to involve the reintegration of the individual with the group. Uniting the group, the individual, and their potential commonalities in resistance to Caucasian American culture does not necessarily result in "'terminal creeds': those monologic utterances that seek to violate the dialogic of trickster space, to fix opposites and impose static definitions on the world" (Owens 55, opening with a phrase from Vizenor). The concept of differential consciousness encourages a multiplicity of responses. When the two cultures are so intricately enmeshed, they are mutually constituative: as one evolves, the other also must flex. That flexion changes the shape of the first, which changes the shape of the other, and so on.

Because cultures are kinetic, not static, their relationship dispels stagnancy. A more focused consideration of one author and one text will help solidify this point and substantiate the assertion that contemporary storytellers can respectfully assume the role of otherelders, conveying cultural values and models of continuance.

The Story of *Last Report*

The acumen that Native writers have to offer on how to navigate the structural chasm between Caucasian American and Native cultures builds on the values embodied in traditional tales. This discussion now focuses on one author and one text—Louise Erdrich's *The Last Report on the Miracles at Little No Horse* (hereafter called *Report*).[10] Like the story of Grandmother Spider and like Silko's poetic invocation, Erdrich's texts function on multiple levels similar to those found in the older legend at the start of this chapter. For example, *Report* comments on the terrain of community, the importance and power of other living beings, the strengths and weakness of various beings (teaching listeners to appreciate organisms of diverse physical capacities), the interconnectedness of living beings, the explanatory histories of some aspects of local culture, and the fallacy of the notion that physical strength trumps other qualities in struggles for survival or achievement.

Above all, Erdrich's stories about the Little No Horse reservation, much like the story of Old Woman Spider, fit into a larger cultural context, teaching listeners about continuity of community and fluidity of the self. Creating a text that positions itself as teacher, Erdrich takes on some of the responsibilities traditionally assigned to elders. For her to have functioned as an elder when she was writing *Report*, the borders between age and roles needed to be reduced or eliminated; for her texts to develop readers' access to community, readers have to feel that they can cross over the divisions between out-of-community and in-community. The permeability of boundaries also is key in the concept of *othereldering*.

Moreover, in some ways, when the reader accepts the elemental significance of the community, as discussed above, and the permeability of boundaries, as discussed below, that acceptance dislocates the hierarchies of the Caucasian American world. The porous nature of borders, such as the inconclusive distinctions between sacred and profane or between old and young, informs Erdrich's entire text and generates a significant message of resistance. Erdrich's texts suggest ways in which Native Americans, European Americans, and those who claim multiple identities can negotiate the relationships among intertwined cultures. This approach calls for readers to accept lack of a clear distinction between traditional dichotomies, including male/female, Native American/other American, reservation/outside, profane/sacred, right/wrong, old/young, Ojibwemowin/English, saint/Satan, sex/rape, dream/reality, alive/dead, Christian/pagan, and linear/nonchronological time. In this line of reasoning, embracing permeability, part of Erdrich's construction of Native culture, allows a person to access the vital community connections of Native Americans and the individuality of the Caucasian American world, without forcing a person to have to permanently choose either one or the other.

The book begins on the Ojibwe reservation of Little No Horse toward the end of the long life of its resident Catholic priest, Father Damien. Another priest, Father Jude, has been sent to the reservation to report on the life of Sister Leopolda, a nun being considered for sainthood. An example of Erdrich's interruption of boundaries occurs in the disparity between Father Jude's and Father Damien's interpretation of Sister Leopolda's behavior. Father Damien and several parishioners consider Sister Leopolda an agent of Satan. Readers have heard about her as a murderer. That the Church has sent Father Jude to research the passion of Sister Leopolda, a first step in the process of her ascension to sainthood, muddies the distinction between saint and sinner. Moreover, Father Jude's research on the nun leads him to consider Father Damien a possible candidate for sainthood, yet Father Jude believes that Father Damien has committed a mortal sin, further blurring the partition between sacred and profane.

From the start, *Report* eases the reader into the concept of permeability through its chronology. After the book introduces readers to the main character, Agnes/Father Damien, it explains how Agnes came to be Father Damien and relates other incidents of his life, but not in chronological order. The details of the plot are rife with additional porousness. The nonlinearity of the text serves as a

Storytelling and Cultural Transmission

gateway device that helps readers gradually engage with the other nontraditional concepts they encounter. Agnes's transformation into Father Damien, for example, takes several days, and even when complete, is reversible. A short way into the book, readers have seen Agnes's difficulties in building her life. Then, a flood carries Agnes away from that life. Readers have learned enough about the challenges Agnes faces from being female in the first decades of the 1900s to sympathize with the enormity of the task she would face in beginning anew.

When Agnes finds the drowned body of the original Father Damien, whose clothing contains identification and paperwork indicating his appointment as priest on the Little No Horse reservation, readers join Agnes in considering the possibility that she may take on his identity. Agnes "prayed for a sign—what to do? But she already knew" (44). In the full day that it takes Agnes to bury the body, "the certainty grew" (44). Nonetheless, as she journeys to Little No Horse, several times she changes her mind about accepting that identity. As Agnes decides to be Father Damien, her transition develops gradually, from clothing to performance to full self. In the first stage of her travels, on a train, she merely dresses as a man. In the wagon that takes her from the train to the Little No Horse reservation, Agnes begins acting as a man. Once at Little No Horse, she feels with certainty that the correct person has arrived (65). Nevertheless, Erdrich does not make the transformation complete until the next day, when Father Damien begins his work as a priest. Erdrich validates the full change through the use of a masculine pronoun, "*his* hands" (67, emphasis added). Catholic priests are, by definition, male, so when doing priestly acts, Agnes is a man, yet she does not relinquish her birth gender and embodies it when doing things that priests may not do, such as having sex.

Other Caucasian American characters in the story do not believe in this permeability of boundaries, and readers who accept the premise of the story can join with Agnes in appreciating how narrow-minded and restrictive those beliefs are. For instance, another Catholic priest, Father Wekkle, maintains that Agnes must be either a woman or a priest, whereas she believes that she can be both, although not both at the same time (206–7). Nanapush and Kashpaw, two men who embody the authority of Ojibwe values, accept Agnes/Father Damien as a priest, as a companion, and as a woman. Their acceptance represents the acceptance of the Native community, even though the larger community is not aware of Agnes's biological sex. Agnes can become Father Damien, and Father Damien can become Agnes: in allowing a situationally variable, impermanent identity, the text asserts the fluid navigability of gender boundaries.

The divisions between youth and its connotations, and old age and its implications, are similarly conflated. The book opens with the earth marked with a sign of age and chill—"white with frost"—yet offers positive, warm associations, as "the morning air was almost warm, [and] sweetened" (1). Aged bodies flourish aesthetically and physically, "beautifully old and supple" (4), and "powerfully withered" (143), with wrinkles that are "beautifully aligned" (235). The elders in the story retain a level of physical prowess that, as Erdrich notes, defies stereotype: the aged "possess a startling vigor" (206), walking with "surprisingly limber strides" (47), "mov[ing] with strength and economy" (164). The presumed connections between youth and physical fitness, and old age and disability, sometimes evaporate, particularly in cases of ill health. During a flu epidemic, Father Damien can "not tell the old man from the young girl" in one house (80), and finds "old women and brand-new babies . . . all the same" (121) in another. Even in good health, characters confound the usual distinctions. Father Jude, who thinks of himself as young, has "never really had a young man's habits or inclinations" (140). Father Damien becomes "old" and then "past old" (4), until he has the body of a "wrinkled but innocent child" (47). His friends are similarly "old but not old" (133). The physicality and valuation of aging and old age defy conventional Caucasian American narratives of decline.

In this book, even individuals' inner selves confront and resist normative age labels. For example the chronologically young Awun seems devoid of emotions in most scenes, whereas the old and dying Agnes, who "at her age, was supposed to be at peace with the world" instead fills with a "darkling rage" (347). When Father Jude sees Agnes as an old woman, he sees her as a "female of stark intelligence" (139). As Agnes approaches death, "instead of getting duller, shutting down her senses, turning away from life, she found . . . that she was growing keener. Her understanding was more intense, her vision wary and her hearing razor sharp" (348). Especially when juxtaposed with expected norms, these representations of inner and outer senses, combined with the presentation of aged bodies as vital and beautiful, expands the list of boundaries that have become indistinct or nonexistent in this novel, challenging readers' notions of what it means to embody age.

Similarly, the borders separating the reservation from the outside world, sharply defined in the 1984 *Love Medicine*, blur in *Report*. When Albertine drives home from nursing school in *Love Medicine*, she remarks on the distinct boundary surrounding Little No Horse: "At the end of the big farms and the blowing fields was the reservation. I always knew it was coming from a long way off" (11). In contrast, in *Report*, the "land of the Ojibwe" is "north" (45), with no clear demarcation of entrance. The cart that brings Father Damien to Little No Horse crosses a landscape devoid of definitional markings. Father Damien travels *toward* Little No Horse, but at no point does the reader learn that Father Damien arrives *at* Little No Horse until he is inside his cabin. Even then, he arrives at an unspecified place ("here"), rather than a named location (65). As the novel continues, the boundaries blurring on and off reservation continue to be permeable, as Nector Kashpaw, Pauline Puyat, and Lulu Nanapush Lamartine, in her stint at the boarding school, prove. Individuals may leave and return and leave again, or come and stay.

The openness of this community may seem odd in light of the fraught relationships between parents and children in this story. Neglect, abuse, and parental deaths lead almost all of this story's main child characters to be fostered to some degree: Agnes, Awun, Fleur, Lulu, Marie, Mary, Nector, and Pauline; Eli is not fostered, he is merely "gone" (102). Reasons for the parents' actions vary widely. For example, when John James Mauser, through trickery and theft, acquires much of the reservation's land and then gains a fortune logging it, Lulu's mother, Fleur Pillager, appears to hate Mauser more than she loves her daughter. She sends Lulu to boarding school to seduce Mauser into marriage and become pregnant with his child, Awun, whom she mostly ignores. When Fleur decides she wants to care for her daughter, Lulu no longer loves her. Not until the next generation are some of the characters capable of parenting their offspring adequately; Lulu Lamartine's love for her nine children is more tender and lasting than anything she feels for their (mostly unnamed) fathers. The stories of disrupted, yet ultimately salvageable, childhoods across multiple generations, remind the reader of the significant, long-lasting, destabilizing effect of Contact on the Anishinaabe (and scores of other Native Nations) during the twentieth century.

In *Report* (2001) and *Four Souls* (2004), Fleur—the character most connected to tradition and the land in *Tracks* (1988)—is shown to have lived immersed in the Caucasian American world.[11] In the stories of Little No Horse that are set closer to the end of the twentieth century, Erdrich's writing suggests that the demarcations may *seem* to have become more rigid, but permeability happens for those who know how to access it. The choice about which civilization to inhabit does not have to be permanent, and the knowledge of how to blur the boundaries lies in the collective intelligence of the group.

Father Damien, who came to Little No Horse to bring Christianity to this Native group, may have converted some of them, but he also has been converted, both spiritually and culturally. Midcareer, he enters Nanapush's sweat lodge and understands it as a church (215). In old age, he lapses into Ojibwemowin with ease and has to actively remember to use English (51). At the end of his life, Father Damien is considered for Catholic sainthood. During that same period of time, in a conversation with the devil, Father Damien calls Nanapush his confessor, and says that he (Father Damien) will convert, to "become at long last the pagan that I always was at heart" (310). When resisting the devil, Father Damien's actions reflect Native spiritual beliefs as he calls for aid from ancestors and spirits, rather than from the Holy Trinity; Father Damien also comes to see the connection between "vermin, insects, the lowest form of life are manidooens, little spirits, [in a] philosophy that so unites the smallest to the largest, for the great, kind intelligence, the Gizhe Manito, shares its name with the humblest creature" (315). The more Father Jude believes in the power of interpersonal love, the more he questions the love of God (239). Father Jude, Father Damien, and readers are not bound to a set form of spirituality.

The boundaries between life and death and dream and reality are similarly indistinct. Nanapush's deaths and funeral scenes in particular (292–5), and the Ojibwe people's relationship with the dead in general, disrupt Caucasian American concepts about the division between life and death. In Ojibwe tradition and in this novel, dreams and beliefs become reality, and vice versa. Christ himself feeds and takes care of Agnes (42–4, 123). During a famine, the wine and the Host transubstantiate to provide adequate sustenance (69). When Father Damien gets lost in a dream, another character, Mary Kashpaw, enters it to guide him back (213). Agnes turns Father Hugo's dream of a church into a reality (217). A "peaceful scene of twirling popple leaves and new-growth maple" is a "delirium" (228). In *Report*, Erdrich does not distinguish between the stories and realities of the Ojibwe and the Caucasian Americans. In positing as ephemeral the distinctions between the spirit and the material world, between dream and actuality, Erdrich transmits and renews First Nation beliefs. These same concepts support the possibility that the ideas expressed in her fiction can become reality.

Of particular interest to age studies scholars, the age relations in this novel reflect a complex set of patterns. Among the main characters in the novel, often the younger members serve as otherelders to ensure the group's future. The chronological elders may provide guidance that makes the work more effective, but the main responsibility rests on members of the next generation. For example, to remove Mary Kashpaw from a sexually abusive household, Agnes/Father Damien invites Mary to live at the convent, but when Mary arrives, Agnes/Father Damien realizes "with positive prescience, that Mary Kashpaw had come to shield her and heal her" (118). Later, Mary saves Father Damien's life. After his death, she follows his wishes, preserving his legacy and keeping others from discovering the secret of his gender, which would undo much of the good he had done as a priest. Nector Kashpaw, sent by his parents to learn about the Catholic church, comes to realize the importance of keeping track of real estate transactions, "the papers, the titles, the tracks of the words" (99, 169, 171). He is given the task of typing up the handwritten transaction records, which makes him "in charge of history . . . and he was only a boy" (171). Thus, in addition to bringing an important historical reality to the reader's attention, Erdrich names the responsibility that falls on authors, regardless of age: those who write the words are in charge of history. This lesson gets reinforced when Nector and his cousins "borrow" a car that ends up in a lake. Nector's father, Nanapush, reminds his son about the power of words by suggesting they craft an alternate narrative, which they successfully use to literally get away with murder (178). In all of these cases, those who craft the tale control the history of the future, just as Erdrich does.

Othereldering

Discussing the influences of cross-cultural writing, Greg Sarris argues that such representations of interactions between or among cultures create or become occasions for actual interactions (Sarris 5, citing Bleich 418; Sarris 121). In the context of discussing the cultural significance of readers' responses to information, Sarris also points out that, "in nondestructive culture contact, self-preservation presupposes self-transformation, or, more generally, the recognition of otherness/Other induces a self-transforming interaction" (60; see also 131). In texts that assail the intransigence of divisions, Erdrich creates a permeability that allows the cultures to coexist. Significantly, *Report* affirms the connections between the community and the individual, demonstrating that those who uphold Native American traditions do not seal off the possibility of useful interactions with the Caucasian American world. This permeability can dissolve the separation between the individual and the community. The premise of Erdrich's resistance impels readers to reconsider divisions in their lives that they had thought were permanent.

A book that insists on the permeability of boundaries can foster a readership in which re-creating or rejoining a previously nonextant or inaccessible larger community remains a viable option. *Report* goes beyond making it an option. Erdrich, via the act of storytelling, functions as mentor, personal and spiritual adviser, and caretaker of the community, at least partially fulfilling the role of elder or otherelder. Moreover, as the recipients of the story, readers are positioned as fictive, younger kin. Parents take care of their children until the need is inverted; then the children care for the parents. Through the kinship functions the book invokes, in which familial roles are not connected to chronological or genetic delineations, readers become morally obligated to join and care for that larger community. Moreover, this obligation reduces the possibility of racist Othering. Indeed, as Woodward suggests and as discussed in the previous chapter in this book, age-based critical analyses can expand the vista of antiracist work (*Statistical* 56). In *Report*, Erdrich offers readers—Native and others—advice on how to interact with the world. In the usually solitary act of reading, the reader instead becomes engaged in a relationship that mandates reciprocity. In a system of beliefs in which the group, rather than the individual, functions as the principal unit, interactions among individuals create community. Generating that engagement becomes the central task of Native American writers who, like traditional elders, take on the responsibility for cultural transmission.

Erdrich dedicates the book to *nindinawemaganidok* ("my relatives"), explaining that "In saying the word nindinawemaganidok ... we speak of everything that has existed in time, the known and the unknown, the unseen, the obvious, all that lived before or is living now in the worlds above and below" (n.p.). Erdrich's readers do not need to be genetically related to her or her characters, nor do they need to be a particular age. The books' dedication invokes each reader as a relative, positioning that relative as a learner-about-the-community. That is, readers have operational roles as youths. In an Althusserian sense, readers are hailed as kin, then called on to fulfill the younger generation's obligations of support. Thus, Erdrich's text not only gives Native American readers information and access to community; it creates connections with and among readers, producing a larger group of people whose members are morally obligated to share information and caring.

Much as Silko does in her texts, in some ways Erdrich formulates herself as a Divine Being. In Erdrich's novels, some characters, such as the identity-seeking Lipsha Morrisey and the aged Father Damien, believe that the gods are no longer paying attention, and that humans need to actively seek divine consideration (Erdrich, *Love Medicine* 236; *Report* 238). Native writers' books can become mediators of that vital attention. "Whatever she thought, came into being" (Patterson-Rudolph 8; see also Silko, *Ceremony* 1); like Old Woman Spider, Erdrich takes on the creator role. That which she envisions has the power to become real and the potential to create or destroy (Weibel-Orland, "Grandparenting" 143). For readers who did not focus on the story in quite this analytical depth, Erdrich provides a final chapter, "End Notes." The chapter opens with the author breaking the fourth wall to explain that the people and events in the book are fictional. She then tells a few more short stories, one about a fax to Father Damien from the Vatican and one that was "told by Nanapush to Father Damien" (359). On the final page of the novel, she writes, "We Anishinaabeg are the keepers of the names of the earth. [. . .] That is why we all must speak our language, nindinawemagonidok, and call everything we see by the name of its spirit. Even the chimookomanag, who are trying to destroy us, are depending on us to remember" (361). Erdrich's words explicitly interpellate each reader as a member of this Native nation, as someone who controls the history of the future.

The readers who accept the porosity of boundaries that allows Agnes to be Father Damien, who appreciate Nanapush's sweat lodge as theologically similar to a church (215), and who agree that Sister Leopolda's fire makes her a "spiritual arsonist" (238) are challenged to accept the logical consequences of their beliefs: that they have membership in this group of people responsible for the future of the world. Anyone who does not heed this call falls into the category of destroyer. Moreover, the request is couched as being absolutely vital, yet completely feasible: all Erdrich asks is that readers remember. Here, Erdrich's tactics invoke an "ethics of caring and personal accountability" (Collins 192) on an even larger scale than Collins does. *Report* becomes an othereldering ur-text; each reader comes to be an otherdaughter or otherson. In this context, the onus of care falls on every individual, and the recipient of this care is the spirit, *manidoo*, in all living things.

A Possibility: "Regardless of Time"

Another Grandmother Spider story tells how Old Mother Tarantula saves the human race, rescuing the first man and the first woman from a flood by spinning a raft for them (Ramel).[12] Similarly, Erdrich spins her stories, working to rescue readers from the overwhelming floods of cultural disruption. Erdrich's writing suggests that unfamiliar cultures are like water: some amount is a necessity of living, but for full immersion, one must be equipped and maintain an active role to keep from drowning.

In Ella Deloria's historical fictional *Waterlily*, memory, consciousness, and life intertwine intimately; to be alive, a person has to be conscious and have memory; forgetting, becoming unconscious, serves as the first step along the pathway to death.[13] In storytelling, ideas that have disappeared or been forgotten are returned. In stories, says Silko, "there wasn't anything lost, nothing was dead, nobody was gone . . . in the stories everything was held together, regardless of time" (Seyersted). The novels of contemporary Native American writers can take on a significant portion of the instructional responsibilities of cultural, and thus global, continuity traditionally effected by elders. In weaving their stories, Native American writers can provide a life raft for the individuals and the human race, across generations. As grandiose as these ideas sound for the earth, they also highlight the immense potential of age studies as a foundation for activism and as a useful element of sound critical responses to cultural texts.

CHAPTER 7

Rewriting Death, Rewriting Life

Re-membering the Field

A colleague celebrating her fortieth birthday says that she enjoys the newfound freedom that comes with the relative invisibility of her older age. She shares this anecdote with me as an example of a positive way of thinking about aging—and yet her hair, which had been starting to silver, has been dyed uniformly black.

Much as feminist readings, discussions, and actions affected the gendered balance of power, so too the ideas of age studies have the potential to influence the hierarchies of age. Beliefs about aging and old age affect laws and institutions as well as daily interpersonal interactions. This book demonstrates that age is a powerful aspect of personal identity and an important basis for cultural analysis. Cross-disciplinary scholarship demonstrates the use-value of adding *age* to the list of identifiers that serve as foundations for examinations of literature and society. To make age more visible and more socially understood as retaining humanity and agency, part of what is needed is an understanding of *age* as complex, splintered, spliced, and multiple, a postmodern concept. Understanding *age* as a constructed identity leaves open possibilities for de- and re-construction. The bodily changes of age are real and biological, but they are the signifiers, not the signified. As with *death* and *life*, considerations of what *age* means happen in the realm of the social. Rüdiger Kunow says, "it takes two to age," a pithy encapsulation of Toni Calasanti's focus on age relations— on the ways in which individuals of all ages, through their beliefs and actions, structure the social context and power differentials of agedness. *One is not born, but rather one becomes, an elder.*

That concept has been alive and kicking around in the humanities for almost half a century. More than a century ago, the birth of gerontology included a deep engagement with the humanities: in the first book ever written about gerontology as a field, Elie Metchnikoff devoted an entire chapter to Goethe (Katz, "Personal"). For even longer—thousands of years—humanities and the arts have included contemplations of aging and old age. Nonetheless, the biggest challenge for age studies continues to be a general lack of awareness that it exists. Scholars in this field have been working in relative isolation (in contrast with gender, race, or class studies scholars, for example). Anecdotally, it has been interesting to see that across disciplinary fields, historical time, and geographical specialty, many scholars who "discover" age studies generate criticism that does much the same work. Their work emphasizes a set of concepts: that old age and youth both are variable experiences, that the Othering of old age is a social construction, and that a greater understanding and awareness of how age relations work is both necessary and desirable, so people of all ages may be granted similar access to the social location of *the human*. With so many researchers working to reinvent the wheel, it sometimes feels like age studies scholarship spends as much time spinning in place as it does moving forward. Moreover, researchers in the biological and social sciences create theories similar to those in the humanities,[1] generating a notable amount of cross pollination among the work of critical gerontologists, medical humanities, and age studies scholars. Additional interdisciplinary collaboration could advance critical understandings more rapidly.

As in many humanities-based scholarly groups, members of the Gerontological Society of America, the Association for Gerontology in Higher Education, and similar organizations struggle valiantly to create and maintain support for age studies and critical gerontology. Within those organizations, humanities and arts subgroups face a challengingly persistent gap in understanding. Researchers in many fields conflate the differences between humanities-based *interventions* and age studies as a critical *methodology*. Interventions engage elders with art and the humanities, as in the theatre-based performance in Anne Basting's "Penelope Project," Dan Cohen's "Music and Memory" project, Gary Glazner's Poetry Project, and the Scripps Gerontology Center's OMA 2D arts programs. Age studies critical methodologies generate new ideas, expanding the cultural lexicon to include concepts such as those mentioned in this book: age relations, biogerontological textual analysis, conscious aging, gerastology, anocriticism, méconnaissance, otherelders, and reifungsromanae.[2] Age studies scholars and critical and social gerontologists need to combine efforts to create a critical mass that has a broad theoretical foundation and a widespread demonstration of applicability.[3]

Most scholars agree that the experience of aging contains an enormous number of variables, that ageism affects men and women (but it affects them differently), that middle-ageism leads to old-ageism, and that age is an embodied category of social difference. Age is a factor in the life of *every human being*. Each individual needs to be better apprised of how age difference affects their actions and interactions. Age studies collaborations have the potential to connect with race studies and ethnic studies, with mutually beneficial outcomes leading to greater social justice. The possibilities for cross-disciplinary synchronicity apply across the humanities, social sciences, hard sciences, business, public policy, and so on: age is an identity category and age relations play an integral part in our lives from start to finish.

This book explores elements of Caucasian American, Caucasian European, African American, and Native American communities. The ideas of otherprogeny and othereldering, as well as specific concepts in the literature of majority and minority authors, further expand the potential for age studies to have a positive impact on elements of academic and activist work. Analyses of tenets in Latino/a American and Asian American literature and culture could equally enrich age studies models, as may components of literature and culture from Arab, Deaf, Hmong, Jewish, and a myriad of other North American subcultures. How do Banksy, Os Gêmeos, and the many other street artists whose counterculture reputation was made, in part, based on their youthful imprudence, and who now are in their forties, respond to their junior colleagues, and vice versa? For snowboarders, Cirque de Soleil artists, and athletes who do similar work, occupational elderhood begins at younger ages than it does in most other professions, and these sports are new enough to have few elders. Will the fields expand to develop a place for its seasoned former stars? If so, how? During a question-and-answer session at a 2014 Modern Language Association conference panel Age and/as Disability, Harilyn Rousso spoke from the audience to explain that recent medical advances meant no one with her health condition had survived to adulthood until now, so she is at the forefront of a group of people who, medically and socially, are chronicling new territories of elderhood. If Aubrey de Grey's models are sound, the first generations of human beings who can expect to live well beyond their first century of life will contend with similarly unknown psychological and social terrain. These scenarios already exist in works of literary fiction, but despite the valiant efforts of a few scholars, age studies analyses have not kept up with the explosion of new locations from which to consider age relations. What fascinating potential arenas for age studies scholarship!

In literature, as Deats and Lenker explain, "writers have anticipated many of the tenets of contemporary humanistic gerontology" (15); imaginative communication functions as a key component that people use to understand "the phenomenon that they experience [and depict] as reality," so literature and the arts "construct as well as encode the conventional perceptions of individuals" (1). That is, the things that artists see and believe about aging and old age, they include in their literary and other artistic and media productions, and when these works reach a broad audience, they become part of the audience members' experiences about what old age is, or means. However, literature does more than just preserve and reflect. With narrative, others can see how past events can shape the mind and body as they live through time, and how these elements join to create a psychologically three-dimensional, emotionally rich human being.

Despite this, or perhaps because of it, critical gerontologists and age studies scholars have yet to convince most gerontologists, let alone most academics, that our methodologies are valuable to them. Perhaps, as Toni Calasanti suggests, to fully embrace those methodologies first requires admitting and challenging one's own ageism. Even for those practiced in analytical applications of intellectual concepts, there is very little space between learning something through the "pedagogy of discomfort" that Blackie and Lamb report as so useful and the "pedagogy of mortification" that Woodward describes (*Figuring* xi). Academics and other professionals who care deeply about elders and who may have dedicated their lives to "helping old people" still can find it difficult, even painful, to accept that some of their methods may contribute to the situations they have been working so hard to ameliorate.

Teaching and research will benefit when we learn to balance on the thin line between those pedagogies, beyond our comfort zone, uncomfortable but gratified to contribute to a field that focuses on the "emancipation of older people from all forms of domination" (Moody, "Overview" xv). The humanities are ideally situated to advance this work, because the

> stock-in-trade of the humanities—self-knowledge, historical understanding, imaginative communication, and critical appraisal of assumptions and values—can promote a more intellectually rigorous gerontology in several ways: *heuristically*, by offering new hypotheses for empirical inquiry; *critically*, by revealing values and power relations often concealed in existing methods and findings of empirical research; and *practically*, by offering reflection on the intentions and values realized by human actors in particular cultural settings. (Cole vii–viii, emphasis in the original)

Within and beyond literature and other artistic texts, *age identity* is part of each individual's social location; critically sound analyses will improve understandings of how that identity and the resulting age relations influence individual lives. Literary age studies illuminates both the micro and the macro levels of the effects of age. Critical explorations of age as a category of analysis develop understanding and analysis of the tension between interiority and individuality, and the larger social pressures that sculpt the world individuals navigate as they live through time.

Scholarly engagement with age studies can enrich a broad range of fields as scholars bring these concepts into their teaching, research, and personal lives. Such an exposure also can alter those scholars' understandings of their experiences, exposing many of the pitfalls of positive and negative ageist assumptions. An exploration of the historical and cultural contexts in which aging and age-based roles are created leads to a greater understanding of the social positioning, the change in beliefs over time, and the connections to and separation from historically limiting roles. Mapping other critical theories onto age studies can augment the development of this field, simultaneously connecting these studies to larger understandings of personal identities and their intersections and reviving the concept of age as a nonlinear continuum. Expanding age studies opens up the possibilities for new enactments, portrayals, metaphorical uses, depictions, and studies of the ideas surrounding aging and old age. Those who share the work, share the rewards.

Rewriting Death, Rewriting Life

In 1991, Kathleen Woodward wrote, "to completely rewrite the ideology of the aging body in the West, we would have to rewrite the meaning of death" (*Aging* 19). An acknowledgment of age identity's variability and of the dehumanizing powers of the current cultural response to age may counter the fears and other demarcations separating the youth cult(ure) from the *Other* that individuals become when they are read as aged. Increasing the amount of attention given to age studies might or might not "rewrite the meaning of death," but it can expand understanding about the age-created version of "the problem that has no name." Aging forecloses some of the potential in a person's life, and that loss may be mourned. Ambivalence about aging and old age is nearly universal, but aging also "can feel like a cure," says Margaret Gullette (*Safe* xxv). With so many negative social messages about aging, it would be understandable to consider the cure worse than the disease—but how is that possible when there is no disease, only dis-ease? "To assume defeat from what every one of us as individuals wants suggests we're not asking the right questions" (Dr. Laura P. Fried, interviewed by Pennar). In the creative humanities, such as the visual arts, film, and literature, the texts themselves can lead scholarship beyond current outcomes and into questions of *what if*. . . . The *what if* questions could expand infinitely in almost any direction. As age studies ripens to include more scholars and more cross-disciplinary collaboration, *vital involvement*, for adults, and *reducing ageism*, for the temporarily young, are two areas in which such research can be particularly productive and broadly applicable.

Vital involvement is a theory of improved lifelong healthy psychosocial development via "the self's meaningful engagement with the world outside it. Vital involvement requires a self, an outside environment, and a powerful and reciprocal enough interaction that the influence can be truly mutual" (Kivnick and Wells 46; see also Erickson, Erickson, and Kivnick).[4] This model developed from an analysis of interviews and coding data. Dozens of subsequent quantitative studies further support Erickson, Erickson, and Kivnick's analysis (cf. Bath and Deeg; Bath and Gardner; Bennett; Farquhar; Frick, Irving, and Rehm; Holt-Lunstad, Smith, and Layton; Hyyppä and Mäki; Luo et al.; *PLoS*). Among the research results are the observation that £1.00 spent on social intervention saves £1.20 in healthcare costs (*PLoS*), and that during a given period of time, lack of adequate social relationships is a predictor of physical and mental health and mortality rate (Bath and Deeg; Holst-Lunstad, Smith, and Layton; Hyyppä and Mäki; Luo). As more gerontologists include elements of vital involvement in their research focus, the volume of supporting data swells.

Because of the cumulative negative health effects of ageism, reducing ageism in college-age youths via a cross-disciplinary collaboration among researchers in the medical sciences, the social sciences, and the humanities can have a long-term positive impact on public health. Research by Becca Levy and her colleagues suggests that ageist beliefs influence health and self-care enough to reduce life expectancy by an average of 7.5 years, which is about 10 percent of the average human lifespan (Levy "Eradication"; Levy "Mind"; Levy "Stereotype"; Levy and Langer; Levy and Leifheit-Limson; Levy et al., "Age"; Levy et al., "Longevity"; Levy et al., "Memory"). One of the few interventions that can reduce ageist ideations in college-age students is to have them watch and then engage in a discussion about a video that debunks ageist myths (Ragan and Bowen). Humanities faculty have experience showing and leading discussions about videos, but do not have experience leading age studies discussions.[5] The video in Ragan and Bowen's study was nonfiction, but there may be stories that are even more effective than a documentary. Introducing gerontological literacy in undergraduate general education classes can have a significant, long-term influence on public health and career selection, and may reduce the shortage of gerontologically focused healthcare workers. Cross-disciplinary collaboration can improve the efficacy of this work and measure the long-term impact of variations on this study. Those who tell the story control the history of the future.

The potential health benefits of these two approaches—vital involvement and programs to reduce ageist ideation—are so promising, so exciting, that I puzzle at their omission from the news headlines each day. Collectively, the research in those two areas posits that, when there is something to live for, it is easier to stay alive. That message is the fulcrum with which age studies can lever change. Age is not a destination, it is the journey, and "all good trips are, like love, about being carried out of yourself and deposited in the midst of terror and wonder" (Iyer)—a potentially apt description of aging-into-old-age. Of more immediate relevance is the nervous excitement about what happens as you respond to age studies. This could be the start of a beautiful relationship. Like me, you might fall head over heels into love. Age studies awaits. You get to make the next move.

Notes

Chapter 1

1. This is a much-repeated quotation. The article by Anderson and Dunlap is the initial source.

2. Many scholars have written about this; I first became aware of it via Margaret Gullette's *Declining to Decline*.

3. A term coined by Gullette (*Declining*; see also her "Age Studies" article).

4. I agree with Toni Calasanti and others who suggest that *age studies* and *cultural gerontology* are two terms for the same set of ideas, a duality created by the ideological divide between science and the humanities in academia. Other scholars, such as Ruth Ray, use the term *critical gerontology*, "a critique of the social influences, philosophical foundations and empirical methodologies on which gerontology as a field has been historically constructed" (675).

5. "The mutually constitutative nature of subjectivity and sociality," is Woodward's eloquent way of putting it (*Statistical* 21). Nowhere is this idea more crucially applied than in its effects on the human lifespan. According to research by Becca Levy and her colleagues at the Yale School of Public Health, beliefs about stereotypes of aging and old age influence mortality, morbidity, and quality of life, affecting such functions as memory, balance, gait, and cardiovascular health (Levy), mental health and rate of healing (Adler "Ageism"), and health behaviors in areas such as food selection, weight, seatbelt use, and tobacco use (Beck "Attitudes"). "Thinking positively about aging extends life more than exercise and not smoking" (Levy; Yale; see also Marshall "Thinking"). The combined impact of those effects can add an average of 7.5 years to the lifespan, a 10 percent increase in life expectancy.

6. See Calasanti and Slevin (5–6) for more on age relations.

7. For a visual representation of the changing demographics of the United States, see the American Society on Aging's video, "How the Boomers Will Transform Aging and How Aging Will Transform the Boomers."

8. Earlier models include texts by Calasanti, Chivers, Cohen-Shalev, Cruikshank, Deats and Lenker, Gravagne, Gullette, Hepworth, Oró-Piqueras, Waxman, Wohlmann, Woodward, and Wyatt-Brown and Rossen, as well as chapters in the series of handbooks and subsequent publications that Cole has edited with colleagues. In particular, even though it is not exhaustive, Wyatt-Brown's catalog of categories of literary gerontology continues to be useful: "(1) analyses of literary attitudes toward aging; (2) humanistic approaches to literature and aging; (3) psychoanalytic explorations of literary works and their authors; (4) applications of gerontological theories about autobiography, life review, and midlife transitions; and (5) psychoanalytically informed studies of the creative process" ("Literary" 332).

9. Kriebernegg references Anne Wyatt-Brown's and Roberta Maierhofer's concepts as the foundation for her approach.

10. Bakhtin discusses "why also the so-called positive stereotypes, for example, that old people are mainly wise, mild and caring, are fundamentally negative; both positive and negative stereotypes are basically monologic in their suppression of other potentials" (Berg 23).

11. See Mangum for additional analyses of age and age difference in Dickens's works.

12. In 2012, a previously unknown daguerreotype surfaced, a depiction of two women, one of whom has been identified; scholars are cautiously optimistic that the other will be confirmed as Emily Dickinson herself, at around age thirty.

13. A revised version of that article is now the second chapter of Woodward's *Statistical Panic*.

14. Gullette offers extended discussions of menopause in her "Menopause" article and in *Agewise* (85–102).

15. Within the field of gerontology, there is a debate about whether the field is a data-driven social science, or if such positivist approaches are too narrow (cf., Cole). Some scholars use terms such as *cultural gerontology, critical gerontology,* or *social gerontology* to describe the broader approach; the definitions of each of those terms are themselves contested. Researchers who subscribe to a broader approach are much in the minority. Some scholars argue that by definition, gerontology requires a broad, interdisciplinary approach; thus, they suggest that scholars in the data-driven camp are social scientists who focus on age, rather than gerontologists.

16. The term *age class* was coined by Gullette ("Age" 215).

17. See Deats and Lenker (9–10) for additional discussion about terms.

18. Performativity is about sending cultural messages out to the world through one's actions. "A performative is a semiotic gesture that is a being as well as a doing. Or, more accurately, it is a doing that constitutes a being, an activity that creates what it describes" (Hedges).

19. Cf. Waxman (*From* 9).

20. My age studies scholarship included these concepts even before Anne Basting's excellent *The Stages of Age* was published. Her text offers a thorough, informed exploration of these ideas.

21. See also Loe 10–11 for additional discussion of this terminology.

22. Margaret Gullette takes a different position on this concept in chapter 5 of *Agewise*.

23. See also Gullette, *Agewise* 132, and Laura Hurd Clarke's *Facing Age*.

24. Cf. Estes, and Ovrebo and Minkler for additional age/class analyses.

25. See also Swinnen "Late-Life."

26. Barbara Frey Waxman makes a similar argument about feminist language (*Multicultural* xv).

27. See Hurd Clarke for a study of the effects of the anti-aging industry's messages.

28. See Waxman (*From*) for more on *reifungsroman*; see Marshall ("Thinking") for more on the physical benefits of reducing ageism.

29. Cf. Blackie and Lamb; Cruikshank "Beyond"; Beauvoir; Friedenfels; Greer and Whalen; Gullette; Harris and Dollinger; Masters and Holley; McGuire, Klein, and Couper; Phillipson and Walker (12); and Woodward, *Statistical* 50.

30. The definition is based on Cruikshank's discussion of conscious aging in *Learning to Be Old* (5), with additional influence by Moody (*Aging* 47–49), Schachter-Shalomi and Miller, and http://www.consciousaging.com. This definition allows for, but does not focus on, the spiritual aspects sometimes associated with conscious aging.

31. Mentioned in the Atwood section: Cohen-Shalev, Gutmann, Kastenbaum, Labouvie-Vief, Said, Winkler, and Wyatt-Brown. Cohen-Shalev's theory about late style in film is positioned in opposition to Erickson, Erickson, and Kivnick's idea of late life as a time of ego integrity leading to resolution; Cohen-Shalev suggests instead a trend toward late-life embrace of chaos. Kivnick's recent comments (with Wells) about ego integrity suggest that often scholars respond to that term without engaging the full depth and complexity of the ideas. Hutcheon and Hutcheon's article provides an extended analysis and critique of the concept of late style.

32. Cf. Gullette; Sybylla 213-4; Urla and Swedlund 418.

33. Such a separation was useful for Erdrich personally as well, given that she was in her twenties and thirties when she wrote some of her most well-known texts. Interestingly, some Jewish authors, such as Mike Gold, make similar connections between heritage and wisdom; for Gold, the Jewish proletariat was the most effective actor to create revolutionary social change (Port, "Violent"). Barbara Frey Waxman's research on Holocaust survivors in Jewish American communities suggests that they had a similar goal ("Changing" 45, 58).

Chapter 2

1. Cf. Wohlmann for ideations about old age impacting younger adults.

2. See also Morgan's Foucauldian discussion of the disciplinary power of choice as it applies to aged women's bodies.

3. Controversially, critic Jane Gallop extends Adrienne Rich's concomitant connection of the public/private divide to create a binary trinity, with male/public/mind on one side and female/private/body on the other. Gallop contends that male critics can and do bridge the divide, which she says is easier for them because they are not in danger of being trapped on the less powerful side, but risky because it requires them to relinquish some of their "masculine identity." Her readings of the Marquis de Sade, Freud, and Barthes position them as "men who challenged the classic split in knowledge and who were nonetheless influential thinkers" (7).

4. Many people allude to this split in the course of writing about aging (cf. Waxman, *Multicultural* xv).

5. *Infirmity* is a physical characteristic; *feisty* and *sourpuss* are physical as well as an attitudinal descriptions; *witch* is a character marked by a particular performative, usually negative; *geezer* comes from the word *disguise*.

6. It reverses this perception even as the fantasy of the mind escaping from the body is seen as—and may be—increasing; if the body no longer performs as one expects while one's mind still is sound, one certainly can imagine one's self participating in activities that one is physically no longer capable of accomplishing.

7. Many age studies scholars and literary texts discuss this visual dis-identification, or *méconnaissance*. For an overview of such texts, see Marshall ("Through" 54 and 72, n. 3); also cf. Herfray, cited in Holmlund (145); Woodward, *Aging* (53–72).

8. Even the distinction between the *natural* and the *discursive* body is always already a social construction.

9. People in the opposite situation, wherein the body retains its ability to function while the mind is no longer socially capable, do not generally get to communicate or offer critical considerations of their experiences, although there are some celebrated books in which people chronicle their development of Alzheimer's disease.

10. But not only for them—cf. Ovrebo and Minkler (304–5) for a discussion of ageist stereotypes about sexual function causing identity crises in lesbians.

11. Experientially, in menopause, "the reproductive center of the woman's body . . . moves [or is constructed as moving] from the genital region to the cerebral domain" (Campioni 97). Also, cf. Frueh 62.

12. See also Swinnen "Late-Life."

13. In this society, "biotechnology is considered the enlightened alternative to growing older" (Marshall and Katz, "From" 91; see also Marshall and Katz "Embodied"; Katz and Marshall).

14. Having the power of the Phallus is "an effect of difference" (Ragland-Sullivan 290), a relational position. For the power of the Phallus to have meaning, there must be Phallus-lackers subordinate to the Phallus-havers. Women (Phallus-lackers) become mirrors, allowing men to see their Phallus-power while simultaneously highlighting women's lack. A social degendering removes men from a relational position of power, and thus from social virility. This social degendering can be read as a castration ($-\phi$) or as something more complex. Perhaps Boss's concept of *ambiguous loss* can help explore what it means to "have" or to "be" a symbolic representation of a member that no longer works ($-\Phi$).

15. See Marshall "Through" for an extended discussion of the self/ego impact of these kinds of changes.

16. Kristeva's earlier discussions of marginality were very much gendered: "Kristeva describes her concept of womanhood as a political attitude created by virtue of women's social marginality [. . .]. Among the most excluded, suppressed women have surely been the old women of many races, classes, and cultures; once their childbearing function is fulfilled, these women have customarily been viewed as marginal, or worse, disposable" (Waxman, *From* 187).

17. An appreciation of Kristevan theories is not a necessary precursor to the idea of a re-visioned self. The connections between Kristeva's ideas and age studies are explored at length in Marshall "Through."

18. The (m)Other is not always biologically related, the sustenance is not always literally milk, and the source is not necessarily a female's nipple. Many aspects of attachment theory happen regardless of the caretakers' genetic or performed gender(s).

19. Cf. Rooke for additional discussion of how this construct works in literature.

20. See also Moody "Overview" (xxxi); Gubrium "Voice" (58); Marshall and Swinnen.

Chapter 3

1. Barbara Macdonald (Swallow 197).

2. See Wyatt-Brown ("Gerontology" 343–5) for a discussion of this experience in men.

3. See Rips 87; and Sheehy 7–8, 129, 153, 163.

4. Here I invoke Elizabeth Grosz's idea (from Merleau-Ponty) that "perception is as it were mid-way between mind and body or subject and object, requiring the terms of both categories to be comprehensible" (38).

5. Perhaps authors choose this term because, as the *OED* details, it carries the etymological roots of ascension (specifically, climbing a ladder) and reunites the male and female processes of aging, thus standing in direct contrast to menopause, which etymologically refers to an ending of moon cycles (i.e., periods).

6. See *Agewise* (85–102) for Gullette's extended discussion of what she terms *hormone nostalgia*.

7. Toni Calasanti reminds us of the importance of considering potential involvement of drug companies in these efforts; for instance, Hurd Clarke's research shows that "women's attitudes toward their wrinkles corresponded with the current bounds of medicine" (132).

8. Americans' use of HRT continues to decline. For example, in a 2009–2010 study, of the women over age forty who had gone through menopause, fewer than 5 percent use estrogen or a combination of estrogen and progesterone, a notable decrease from the 22 percent in a 1999–2000 study (Grens).

9. For examples of this myth, see Claman, Greer (*The Change*).

10. The history of this diagnosis has attained near-legendary status among feminists of the 1960s and 1970s. See Greer (*The Change* 239–41).

11. In one of the few studies to look at how the "empty nest" affects both men and women, "fathers reported more depression, insomnia, and somatic symptoms such as backache, headaches, and stomach ailments than the mothers, suggesting that 'the empty nest syndrome' affects fathers even more than mothers" (Boss 15).

12. For additional discussion of this myth, see Martin 174–7.

13. For documentation of the existence of this myth, see Martin.

14. For example, see Mackie, who writes that in coming to menopause, "one is regaled with social expectations that speak only of loss—loss of

Notes

womanliness, of childbearing, perhaps of sexuality; 'death' of the womb, the ovaries; loss of menstruation and of youth," all of which leads to "heavy preponderances of dread, exile, silencing, and doom" (21); see also Barbre 51; Daly 161; Rothfield 33; Sheehy 69.

15. For more on the financial connections, cf. Hurd Clarke; Estes; Gullette ("Menopause"); and Port ("Ages").

16. Northrup frames menopausal symptoms as themselves being messengers, sent from a woman's emotions to her mind via the body, delivering information that the hormonal messengers are no longer capable of bearing. Menopausal symptoms, she says, are messages of inner conflict and discontent (39–42). Women with menopausal symptoms therefore need the skills of reliable technical interpreters (medical personnel). In this formulation, a woman going through menopause has become interpellated as so distanced from her own body as to be a foreigner—or a foreign substance—that needs help inhabiting the body, lest her ignorance of local communication methods cause harm to herself or the host system. Such a formulation heightens the mind/body split, perhaps even creating a three-way split: mind, body, and emotions.

17. For example, see Sheehy 132, 134, 135; Komesaroff et al. 6.

18. Kunow suggests that "in the wake of the biomedicalization of senescence it became *normal for the aged human body to be pathological*" (32, emphasis in the original). For a discussion of how signs of age and even the risk of signs of age have become medical "conditions" in need of treatment, see Marshall and Katz ("Embodied" and "From") and Conrad (163).

19. See Gullette ("Menopause") for a counterargument to this position.

20. The racial, cultural, and socioeconomic effects on menopause would fill an entire volume. For particularly relevant and reasonably pithy examples, see Barbre 40; Bart; Dege 66–7; Greer, *The Change* 64, 67, and 71; Lock; Mackie 21; Martin 173; Sheehy 94; and Sontag 21. Almost no age studies analyses of menopause address intersectional categories in detail.

21. See, for example, Flint's comparison of Cuban and Jewish women's discussions of sexual relations (72).

22. Reader comments taken from amazon.com's customer reviews.

23. "[H]ot flashes, night sweats, vaginal dryness, mood swings, mental fuzziness, headaches, migraines, vaginal infections, bladder infections, incontinence, recurrent urinary tract infections, vaginal wall thinning, decreased sexual response, bilateral pounding headache, recurrent vaginal yeast infections, breast swelling and tenderness, depression, nausea, vomiting, bloating, leg cramps, yellow-tinged skin, and excessive vaginal bleeding" (144).

24. Disability studies scholars have widely critiqued the illogic of the

belief in the body's innate lack of disability; hence the term *temporarily able-bodied*. For more on the connections between age studies and disability studies, see Lamb ("Age") and Marshall ("Ageility").

25. See Singleton for a discussion of a similar emphasis on individuality and personal responsibility in self-help books for men.

26. See Port ("Ages") for a discussion of the history of the ties between aging and economics, and Estes (*Aging* and "Aging") for an analysis of more contemporary connections.

27. Ulrich Beck's *Risk Society* might be useful to readers interested in learning more about the cultural fascination with risk management. See also the discussions of risk in Gullette, *Agewise* (32), Marshall and Katz ("Embodied"), and Woodward (*Statistical* 137, 211, 216–8).

28. See Chris Schilling's work for more on the body as a project.

29. The literary scholars' work is mentioned in earlier chapters; Lois Banner's *In Full Flower* (1992) traces the history of aged women in Western Europe and the United States. Within each time period that she considers, Banner focuses her discussion on a specific individual, using that person's experience to discuss both the positive and negative aspects of living as an aged woman in that particular society. Stephen Katz's *Disciplining Old Age: The Formation of Gerontological Knowledge* displays impressive breadth and depth in a Foucauldian analysis of old age and gerontology, tracing how their emergence and development disciplined the aged body into a distinct, medicalized subject.

30. Although the English version of her book was published long before the other texts in this short list, generally it is not scholars' entrée into the field of age studies.

31. See also Ovrebo and Minkler (299–300) and Slevin for analyses of the connections between old age, sexual orientation, and class.

32. Copper was speaking of feminists in the 1970s and 1980s, but other writers since then, such as Rich (of Macdonald and Rich) and Gullette, have made similar points about more contemporary feminists.

33. See also *Agewise* (147–166).

34. Woodward suggests that when shame reaches a "boiling point," it becomes anger (*Statistical* 84), which feels "infantilizing" (85) but can be productive (83–8).

Chapter 4

1. Cf. Waxman (*From* 38, 62).

2. Although initially published separately, these two novels have since been brought together into one volume, entitled *The Diaries of Janna*

Somers. Hereafter, this single volume is called *Diaries*, and all references and page numbers are to the single-volume edition.

3. An American journal is relevant for the *Diaries* because, as this chapter will detail, Lessing was living in Britain but writing for an American audience. For additional reading on more contemporary perceptions about negative ideations of age, see Cruikshank, Featherstone, and Wernick; Featherstone and Hepworth; Gullette; Hepworth; Hurd Clarke; Katz; and Woodward.

4. For additional discussion of this phenomenon, cf. Woodward (*Statistical* 192–4).

5. The blurring and dismantling of boundaries is a recurring theme in Lessing's work. See, for example, Lessing's commentaries on establishing divisions between different types of thoughts or different parts of life (*Notebooks* xii, 154, 241, 261, 344, 447, 450; *Shade* 267–8, 335, 338). "Great dichotomies undo us" (Lessing, *Shade* 338).

6. See also Ovrebo and Minkler (298–9) for a brief discussion of social and class alienations in *Diaries*.

7. The term *care work* includes personal care as well as "instrumental assistance" and "takes into consideration both the physical and the emotional demands of 'caring for' and the emotional conflicts inherent in 'caring about'" (Zajicek et al. 179).

8. In Britain, Home Helps are a type of worker who go into the homes of the elderly and disabled to cook, shop, clean, and keep company, much like home health aides do in the United States.

9. As in real life, hired caregivers are almost universally female. In my three years working as a home health aide (the American equivalent of Home Help), in a company employing forty such aides, none were male.

10. Lessing employs this device in the *Golden Notebooks* and in her autobiography (*Shade* 102–4), as well.

11. In sharp contrast, through the lack of interiority of Kate and some of her friends, *If the Old Could* explicitly demonstrates the vacuousness of some of the young.

12. In Berg's article, she argues that applying the ideas of *creative understanding* to age creates a concept that is the antithesis of ageism. Ageism is a monologic discourse that narrows the available understandings and means of discussing aging and old age, whereas a creative understanding expands the possibilities for experience, critique, and dialogue about aging and old age.

13. Although not technically eligible to receive Meals on Wheels, nonetheless Maudie eventually accepts their assistance.

14. See Lessing's texts: *Skin* 259, 268, 281–92, 319, 392; *Shade* 28, 81, 218, 226, 264–6, 296, 313, 335; *Notebooks* 69, 86, 146–7, 149.

15. In the later part of her life, Lessing connected her ideas to Sufism.

16. "An individualism that goes against simplification, bureaucracy, institutionalization, invisibility, silence, suppression and anonymity" (*Diaries* 21).

17. For example, "The point of [feminists'] work is to change the world" (Newton and Rosenfelt xv).

18. The existence of a Herland relies heavily on the assumption of gender as a dichotomous variable with clearly definable limits. If one accepts such a premise, the *Diaries* offer readers a world in which characters, because they are not defined in terms of man/center versus woman/other, become relationally genderless. In the equation of articulated difference, gender suddenly carries less weight. See Woodward ("Performing") for more on the effects of single-gender productions.

19. Lessing briefly explored this in *The Golden Notebook* as well (202).

20. Suleiman suggests that *roman à thèse* plotlines fall into the categories of exemplary, apprenticeship, and/or confrontation (vii).

21. *Shade* 336.

22. "It is always the individual, in the long run, who will set the tone, provide the real development in society" (Lessing, *Prisons* 72).

23. "This is the worst of the legacies from the First World War: the thought that if we are a race that cannot learn, what will become of us?" (Lessing, *Skin* 10).

24. In her introduction to the single-volume version, in which Lessing reveals herself as the author, she said that trying to publish under a pseudonym was an experiment and a statement about the vagaries of the publishing and reviewing industry (*Diaries* vii–xii). The first two publishers to whom her agent pitched the manuscript, the publishers with whom Lessing usually worked at that point, rejected the manuscript, one saying that it was "too depressing to publish"; eventually, the book was signed by the same publisher that had first printed her books (E. McDowell). In writing as someone else, Lessing said, she also could use a different writing style, "and it did turn out that as Janna Somers I wrote in ways that Doris Lessing cannot" (*Diaries* viii). Although some of the manuscript's reader reports were, according to Lessing, "very patronizing and very nasty," once in print, reception was more positive; reviewers said the novels had "wit," "compassion," "a lovely pattern," and "courage" (E. McDowell). Lasdun offers an engaging twenty-first-century postscript to the publication history.

25. "Her characters are her fiction" (Grumbach 6).

26. For more on anger as a tool of aging, see Woodward ("Against").

27. As writer and literary critic Doris Grumbach labels Lessing's audience.

28. Also, Lessing's mother's name was Maude, whom the family called Jane. Maudie in the *Diaries* was born the same year as Lessing's mother (see *Under My Skin*).

29. "Maudie enclosed in the 'thick black shell' of an old coat and Jane in a 'carapace of clothes'" (*Diaries* 92, 234, 112).

30. "Strong, independent, aggressive, stubborn" (Berg 21).

31. A citizenship in which "populations subjected to different regimes of value enjoy different kinds of rights, discipline, caring, and security" (Ong 217).

Chapter 5

1. See also Ovrebo and Minkler (299–305) for a brief discussion of lesbians and old age.

2. Clifton did not standardize the capitalization in her poetry, much like e. e. cummings. When quoting her poems, I follow her capitalization schema.

3. See also Ovrebo and Minkler (301–5) for a brief discussion of African American women and old age.

4. According to a 2008 survey, 84 percent of African American teenagers and 88 percent of all African Americans "have tremendous respect for the opinions and desires of their elders" (Jones).

5. "As with the truths of our time, this is not to say that they were invariably followed, or that everyone accepted them. In other words, my focus is upon the truths of that time, not upon whether people actually" did or did not do something (Sybylla 217 n.10).

6. As discussed in the next chapter, Louise Erdrich echoes this concept in *Last Report on the Miracles at Little No Horse*, specifically in the dedication (n.p.) and on p. 133.

7. See also Holloway and Demetrakopoulos (23); see Waxman ("Changing History") for a discussion of literature that reflects slavery's impact on African American motherhood.

8. See also Christian (213–4) and hooks (46) on the importance of home and intergenerational information sharing in African American communities.

9. Traditional Christian theology takes a similar stance, but the observance of such theology differs significantly from the theory of it.

10. For examples, see chapter 3; Greer, *The Change* 247; Kaplan,

"Trauma" 185; Marshall, "Through"; Martin 167; Pearlman; Randall 187; and Woodward, *Aging*, among others.

11. For example, Black women tend not to see menopause as a time of changing power relations (Agee 81).

12. Cf. Heglar and Refoe 140.

13. See also Holladay's reading of the poem (*Wild* 64-5).

14. As Meridel LeSueur's writing does.

15. See the volume edited by Komesaroff, Rothfield, and Daly, as well as chapter 3, for additional information on Caucasian American experiences of menopause.

Chapter 6

1. Contact (with a capital C) is the time of the initial interaction among Native American and European American cultures.

2. See Copper and Macdonald and Rich for alternate views on thinking about grandmothers as sources of wisdom.

3. Even as the traditions, literature, and opinions of people from different First Nations may be dissimilar, U.S. policies created a similar situation for too many Native American populations. Thus, the situations that such regulations create and the literary responses to the policies may usefully be considered from what Craig Womack calls a "pan-Indian" perspective.

4. Shomaker, a gerontologist, documents this tradition in the Navajo nation. Such patterns are becoming more prevalent and more legally and socially accepted. In the United States, there are almost 2.5 million grandparents responsible for grandchildren. Of these, nearly 1 million have had this responsibility for five or more years (Gillaspy).

5. Pomo was a Native nation located in northern California.

6. See also Swinnen ("One") for a discussion on the functions of *age bending*, a term she coined in "*Benidorm Bastards*."

7. Although it is not specifically focused on First Nation communities, see Kaminsky for a Bakhtinian exploration of the intergenerational rift created by the cultural changes transferring family functions to state institutions.

8. Texts from authors such as Ella Cara Deloria (1889-1971) and Ignatia Broker (1919-1987), who were elders as well as writers, encourage cultural continuity more traditionally than later texts do. Those authors are older than the others listed here, and neither one was a novelist (i.e., a person whose vocation is nonacademic writing) in the sense that some contemporary Native American writers are novelists. If one accepts the

claim that N. Scott Momaday's 1969 *House Made of Dawn* opened the doors to a wider readership of Native-produced fiction, then those whose lives would be devoted to writing generally had to have not yet devoted their lives to something else. In 1969, Owens and Silko were twenty-one, Sarris was seventeen, Erdrich was fourteen, and Alexie was three.

9. Cf. Castillo for an analysis of this disagreement. Also note the history of using stories to foil cultural appropriation. For example, Greg Sarris suggests that people he knows may have fabricated new stories for the anthropologists who came to learn traditional tales. Erdrich does not have a reputation for deliberately withholding stories, and her stories are so obviously fabricated that people do not usually focus on them when seeking historical data. Rather, Silko has accused Erdrich of over-ahistoricizing (Castillo).

10. This text can be considered representative for several reasons. Several Native American scholars who suggested Native-authored, age-studies-relevant texts mentioned *Report*. I read all the books they recommended. *Report*'s plotline covers most of a lifespan. Erdrich publishes a book every year or so, penning children's literature, poetry, short stories, and nonfiction; scholars will find no shortage of additional material against which to test the ideas in this chapter. Her writing receives critical acclaim in Native and non-Native communities; she was nominated for a Pulitzer and has won literary prizes, including the National Book award, the O'Henry Award, the Pushcart Prize, and the Lifetime Achievement Award from the Native Writers' Circle of the Americas. Her books receive popular as well as critical acclaim: her novels are the most-reviewed Native American literary fiction at amazon.com, and they have made the *New York Times* bestsellers list each decade starting in the 1980s. The wide reach of her writing makes this analysis applicable to a broad range of Native American literature in the public sphere.

11. Schweninger's close ecofeminist reading of Fleur and Pauline Puyat across several texts complicates these ideas, exploring their locations as both oppressors and Others (37–50).

12. The story's web page does not mention the tale's nation of origination; however, one of the stories characters is Kukumat, a Yuma God.

13. "'Keep remembering or you will die.' Remembering also meant being conscious" (Deloria, *Waterlily* 73; see also 71). *Waterlily*, which Deloria wrote in the 1940s, is about personal and cultural survival. On a literal level, this passage informs readers about the importance of literally not losing consciousness. It also has metaphorical resonance with twenty-first-century responses to people who have Alzheimer's disease; several

nations respond to Alzheimer's disease by holding funerals for a person whose memory is gone even as the body survives (Boss).

Chapter 7

1. Cf. Meredith Minkler, Carroll Estes, and the authors whose work appears in their *Critical Gerontology*; and Vern Bengston, K. Warner Schaie, and the contributors to their *Handbook of Theories of Aging*. With challenges similar to those of the self-help texts, gerontological theories sometimes reinscribe the very stereotypes they set out to debunk, as happened with the now-outmoded concept of disengagement theory and the psychosocial life tasks model (see Erickson, Erickson, and Kivnick). For an overview of the arc of disengagement theory, see Victor Marshall (450); see Coleman and Jerome for a summary of similar theories.

2. Additional concepts of interest in age studies include ageility studies, the new erotics of desire, and the versive gaze.

3. Age studies organizations such as ENAS, the European Network in Aging Studies, established in 2010, and NANAS, the North American Network in Aging Studies, established in 2013, strive to create ongoing, viable connections through which scholars can ask questions and exchange theories and other information.

4. Some people, myself included, have misunderstood Erickson, Erickson, and Kivnick's theories about vital involvement as being too rigidly prescriptive. Kivnick's 2013 GSA presentation and 2014 article (with Wells) were helpful in bringing me to reconsider this concept. I am indebted to her for a conversation in which she thoughtfully responded to my inexpert questions, as well as for her initial work shaping this developmental model.

5. Pedagogical models such as Learning AdvantAge can help prepare liberal arts and humanities faculty members for those discussions (www.agingstudies.org).

Works Cited

AARP. "Myths About Menopause." *AARP*. AARP, 2003. Web. 27 Apr. 2003.
Adler, Jerry. "Turning 60." *Newsweek* 146.20 (14 Nov. 2005): 50–8. Print.
Adler, Tina. "Ageism: Alive and Kicking." *Observer* 26.7 (Sept. 2013). Web. 20 Sept. 2013.
Agee, Eve. "Menopause and the Transmission of Women's Knowledge: African American and White Women's Perspectives." *Medical Anthropology Quarterly* 14.1 (March 2000): 73–95. Print.
Akers, Karen. "Generational Marketing: More Boom for Your Buck." *Imprint Magazine* Winter 2001. Web. 3 Feb. 2002.
Alcoff, Linda. "The Problem of Speaking for Others." *Who Can Speak: Authority and Critical Identity*. Ed. Judith Roof and Robyn Weigman. Urbana: U of Illinois P, 1995. 97–119. Print.
Alexie, Sherman. *The Absolutely True Diary of a Part-Time Indian*. New York: Little, 2009. Print.
——— . *Indian Killer*. New York: Warner, 1998. Print.
——— . "The Joy of Reading: Superman and Me." *LA Times* 19 Apr. 1998. Web. 23 Aug. 2012.
Allen, Paula Gunn. "Indian Summer." *Long Time Passing: Lives of Older Lesbians*. Ed. Marcy Adelman. Boston: Alyson, 1986. 183–91. Print.
Anderson, Susan Heller, and David W. Dunlap. "New York Day by Day: Author to Readers." *New York Times* 25 Apr. 1985, Late City Final ed.: B3. Web.
Angus, Jocelyn, and Patricia Reeve. "Ageism: A Threat to 'Aging Well' in the 21st Century." *Journal of Applied Gerontology* 25.2 (Apr. 2006): 137–52. Print.
Arber, Sara, and Jay Ginn. *Gender and Later Life*. Newbury Park, CA: Sage, 1991.
Banner, Lois W. "The Twentieth Century: Menopause and Its Meanings."

In Full Flower: Aging Women, Power, and Sexuality. New York: Vintage Books, 1992. 273–310.

Barbre, Joy. "Meno-Boomers and Moral Guardians: An Exploration of the Cultural Construction of Menopause." *Menopause: A Midlife Passage*. Ed. Joan Callahan. Bloomington: Indiana UP, 1993. 23–35. Print.

Barrett, Anne, and Laura Cantwell. "Drawing on Stereotypes: Using Undergraduates' Sketches of Elders as a Teaching Tool." *Educational Gerontology* 33.4 (Apr. 2007): 327–48.Print.

Bart, Pauline. "Portnoy's Mother's Complaints." *The Other Within Us: Feminist Explorations of Women and Aging*. Ed. Marilyn Pearsall. New York: Harper, 1997. 25–36. Print.

Basting, Anne Davis. *The Stages of Age: Performing Age in Contemporary American Culture*. Ann Arbor: U of Michigan P, 1998. Print.

Bath, Peter A., and Alison Gardiner. "Social Engagement and Health and Social Care Use and Medication Use Among Older People." *European Journal of Ageing* 2.1 (Mar. 2005): 56–63. *EBSCOHost*. Web. 29 May 2013.

Bath, Peter A., and Dorly Deeg. "Social Engagement and Health Outcomes Among Older People: Introduction to a Special Section."*European Journal of Ageing* 2.1 (Mar. 2005): 24–30. *EBSCOHost*. Web. 29 May 2013.

Beauvoir, Simone de. *The Coming of Age*. Trans. Trans. Patrick O'Brian. New York: Warner, 1973. Print.

Beck, Melinda. "Attitudes Toward Aging Can Affect How Well We Age." *Wall Street Journal* Online.wsj.com, 17 Oct. 2009. Web. 20 Sept. 2013.

Beck, Ulrich. *Risk Society*. London: Sage, 1992. Print.

Beckett, Joyce, and Delores Dungee-Anderson. "Older Minorities: Asian, Black, Hispanic, and Native Americans." *Gerontological Social Work: Knowledge, Service Settings, and Special Populations*. Chicago: Nelson-Hall, 1992. 277–322. Print.

Bengston, Vern L., and K. Warner Schaie, eds. *Handbook of Theories of Aging*. New York: Springer, 1998. Print.

Bennett, Kate. "Social Engagement as a Longitudinal Predictor of Objective and Subjective Health." *European Journal of Ageing* 2.1 (Mar. 2005): 48–55. *EBSCOHost*. Web. 29 May 2013.

Bennett, Michael, and Vanessa Dickerson, eds. "Introduction." *Recovering the Black Female Body: Self-Representations by African American Women*. New Brunswick, NJ: Rutgers UP, 2000. 1–15. Print.

Berg, Mari-Ann. "Toward a Creative Understanding: Bakhtin and the Study of Old Age in Literature." *Journal of Aging Studies* 10.1 (1996): 15–26. Web. 14 May 2002.

Berkson, D. Lindsay. *Hormone Deception*. New York: Contemporary Books/McGraw Hill, 2000. Print.Biggs, Simon. "Age, Gender, Narratives, and

Masquerades." *Journal of Aging Studies* 18.1 (Feb. 2004): 45–58. Web. 22 July 2005.

Blackie, Michael, and Erin Gentry Lamb. "Courting Discomfort in an Undergraduate Health Humanities Classroom." *Health and Humanities Reader*. Ed. Therese Jones, Lester Friedman, and Delese Wear. New Brunswick, NJ: Rutgers UP, 2014. 490–500.Print.

Bleich, David. "Intersubjective Reading." *New Literary History* 27.3 (1986): 401–21. Web. 18 Dec. 2002.

Blunk, Elizabeth, and Sue Williams. "The Effects of Curriculum on Preschool Children's Perceptions of the Elderly. *Educational Gerontology* 23.3 (Apr./May 1997): 233–41. Web. June 2008.

Borysenko, Joan. *A Woman's Book of Life: The Biology, Psychology, and Spirituality of the Feminine Life Cycle*. New York: Riverhead Books, 1996. Print.

Boss, Pauline. *Ambiguous Loss: Learning to Live with Unresolved Grief*. Cambridge, MA: Harvard UP, 2000. Print.

Brennan, Teresa. "Social Physics: Inertia, Energy, and Aging." *Figuring Age: Women, Bodies, Generations*. Ed. Kathleen Woodward. Indiana UP: Indianapolis. 1999. 131–48. Print.

Broker, Ignatia. *Night Flying Woman: An Ojibway Narrative*. St. Paul: Minnesota Historical Society P, 1983. Print.

Butler, Judith. *Bodies that Matter*. New York: Routledge, 1993. Print.

———. *Gender Trouble: Feminism and the Subversion of Identity*. New York: Routledge, 1990. Print.

Butler, R. *Why Survive? Being Old in America*. New York: Harper, 1975. Print.

Calasanti, Toni. "Bodacious Berry, Potency Wood and the Aging Monster: Gender and Age Relations in Anti-Aging Ads." *Social Forces* 86.1 (Sept. 2007): 335–55. EBSCO. Web. 9 July 2013.

———. "Gender and Old Age: Lessons from Spousal Care Work." *Age Matters: Realigning Feminist Thinking*. Ed. Toni Calasanti and Kathleen Slevin. New York: Routledge, 2006. 269–94. Print.

Calasanti, T., and K. Slevin. *Gender, Social Inequalities, and Aging*. Walnut Creek, CA: Alta Mira Press, 2001. Print.

———, eds. *Age Matters: Realigning Feminist Thinking*. New York: Routledge, 2006. Print.

Callaghan, Dympna. "Vicar and Virago: Feminism and the Problem of Identity." *Who Can Speak: Authority and Critical Identity*. Ed. Judith Roof and Robyn Weigman. Urbana: U of Illinois P, 1995. 195–207. Print.

Campioni, Mia. "Revolting Women: Women in Revolt." *Reinterpreting Menopause: Cultural and Philosophical Issues*. Ed. Paul Komesaroff,

Philipa Rothfield, and Jeanne Daly. New York: Routledge, 1997. 77–99. Print.

Carothers, Suzanne. "Catching Sense: Learning from Our Mothers to be Black and Female." *Uncertain Terms: Negotiating Gender in American Culture*. Ed. Faye Ginsburg and Anna Lowenhaupt Tsing. Boston: Beacon P, 1990. 232–47. Print.

Carstensen, Laura. 2009. *A Long Bright Future: An Action Plan for a Lifetime of Happiness, Health, and Financial Security*. New York: Random House/Crown.

Castillo, Susan Pérez. "Postmodernism, Native American Literature and the Real: The Silko-Erdrich Controversy." *Massachusetts Review* 32.2 (1991): 285. *Academic Search Complete*. Web. 22 June 2014.

Centeno, Juanita. "Chumash." *Wisdom's Daughters: Conversations with Women Elders of Native America*. Ed. Steve Wall. New York: Harper, 1993. 22–45. Print.

Chivers, Sally. *From Old Woman to Older Women: Contemporary Culture and Women's Narratives*. Columbus: Ohio State UP, 2003. Print.

Christian, Barbara. *Black Feminist Criticism: Perspectives on Black Women Writers*. New York: Pergamon P, 1985. Print.

Claman, Elizabeth, ed. *Each in Her Own Way: Women Writing on the Menopause and Other Aspects of Aging*. Eugene, OR: Queen of Swords P, 1994. Print.

Clark, Rachel, Suzanne Snedeker, and Carol Devine. "Estrogen and Breast Cancer Risk: What Is the Relationship?" *Cornell University Program on Breast Cancer and Environmental Risk Factors in New York State*. Cornell, 16 Aug. 2001. Web. 27 Apr. 2003.

Clifton, Lucille. *Blessing the Boats*. Rochester, NY: BOA Editions, 2000. Print.

———. *The Book of Light*. Port Townsend, WA: Copper Canyon P, 1993. Print.

———. *Good News About the Earth: New Poems*. New York: Random House, 1972. Print.

———. *Good Woman: Poems and a Memoir, 1969–1980*. Rochester, NY: BOA Editions, 1989. Print.

———. *Next: New Poems*. Rochester, NY: BOA Editions, 1987. Print.

———. *The Terrible Stories*. Rochester, NY: BOA Editions, 1996. Print.

———. "The Things Themselves." *What We Know So Far*. Ed. Beth Benatovich. New York: St. Martin's P, 1995. 49–56. Print.

———. *Quilting*. Rochester, NY: BOA Editions, 1991. Print.

Coetzee, J. M. *Disgrace*. New York: Penguin, 2000. Print.

Cohen-Shalev, Amir. *Both Worlds at Once: Art in Old Age*. Lanham, MD: UP of America, 2002. Print.

Cohen-Shalev, Amir. *Visions of Aging: Images of the Elderly in Film*. Brighton, UK: Sussex Academic P, 2012 [2009]. Print.

Cole, Thomas R. "Preface." *Voices and Visions of Aging: Toward a Critical Gerontology*. Ed. Thomas R. Cole, W. Andrew Achenbaum, Patricia L. Jakobi, and Robert Kastenbaum. New York: Springer, 1992. vii–xi. Print.

Cole, Thomas R., David D. Van Tassel, and Robert Kastenbaum, eds. *Handbook of the Humanities and Aging*. New York: Springer, 1992. Print.

Cole, Thomas R., Robert Kastenbaum, and Ruth E. Ray, eds. *Handbook of the Humanities and Aging*. 2nd ed. New York: Springer, 2000. Print.

Cole, Thomas R., Ruth Ray, and Robert Kastenbaum, eds. *A Guide to Humanistic Studies in Aging: What Does It Mean to Grow Old?* Baltimore, MD: Johns Hopkins UP, 2010. Print.

Cole, Thomas R., W. Andrew Achenbaum, Patricia L. Jakobi, and Robert Kastenbaum, eds. *Voices and Visions of Aging: Toward a Critical Gerontology*. New York: Springer, 1993. Print.

Coleman, Peter, and Dorothy Jerome. "Applying Theories of Aging to Gerontological Practice Through Teaching and Research." *Handbook of Theories of Aging*. Ed. Vern Bengston and K. Warner Schaie. New York: Springer, 1999. 379–95. Print.

Collins, Patricia Hill. *Black Feminist Thought: Knowledge, Consciousness, and the Politics of Empowerment*. Boston: Unwin Hyman, 1990. Print.

Conrad, Peter. *Medicalization of Society: On the Transformation of Human Conditions into Treatable Disorders*. Baltimore, MD: Johns Hopkins UP, 2007. Print.

Cook-Lynn, Elizabeth. *Why I Can't Read Wallace Stegner and Other Essays: A Tribal Voice*. Madison: U of Wisconsin P, 1996. Print.

Copper, Baba. *Over the Hill: Reflections on Ageism Between Women*. Freedom, CA: The Crossing P, 1988. Print.

Cowley, Malcom. *The View From 80*. New York: Viking Press, 1976.

Cruikshank, Margaret. "Beyond Ageism: Teaching Feminist Gerontology." *Radical Teacher* 76 (Fall 2006): 39–40. Web. June 2008.

———. *Fierce with Reality: An Anthology of Literature on Aging*. Topsham, ME: Just Write Books, 2006. Print.

———. *Learning to Be Old: Gender, Culture, and Aging*. Lanham, MD: Rowman and Littlefield, 2003. Print.

Cypress, Jeannette, Agnes Cypress, and Susie Billie. "Seminole." *Wisdom's Daughters: Conversations with Women Elders of Native America*. Ed. Steve Wall. New York: Harper, 1993. 68–93. Print.

Daly, Jeanne. "Facing Change: Women Speaking About Midlife." *Reinterpreting Menopause: Cultural and Philosophical Issues*. Ed. Paul Komesaroff, Philipa Rothfield, and Jeanne Daly. New York: Routledge, 1997. 159–75. Print.

Deats, Sara Munson, and Lagretta Tallent Lenker, eds. *Aging and Identity: A Humanities Perspective.* Westport, CT: Praeger, 1999. Print.

Dege, Kristi, and Jacqueline Gretzinger. "Attitudes of Families Towards Menopause." *Changing Perspectives on Menopause.* Ed. Ann Voda, Myra Dinnerstein, and Sheryl O'Donnell. Austin: U of Texas P, 1982. 60–9. Print.

Deloria, Ella Cara. *Waterlily.* Lincoln: U of Nebraska P, 1988. Print.

——— . *Speaking of Indians.* New York: Friendship P, 1944. Print.

Delphy, Christine. "For a Materialist Feminism." *Materialist Feminism: A Reader in Class, Difference, and Women's Lives.* Ed. Rosemary Hennessy and Chrys Ingraham. New York: Routledge, 1997. 59–64. Print.

Dickson, Barbara. "Reading Maternity Materially: The Case of Demi Moore." *Rhetorical Bodies.* Ed. Jack Selzer and Sharon Crowley. Madison: U of Wisconsin P, 1999. 297–314. Print.

Dillaway, Heather. "When Does Menopause Occur and How Long Does It Last: Wrestling with Age- and Time-Based Conceptualizations of Reproductive Aging." *NWSA Journal* 18.1 (Spring 2006): 31–60. Print.

Donovan, Kathleen. *Feminist Readings of Native American Literature: Coming to Voice.* Tucson: U of Arizona P, 1998. Print.

Dowling, Colette. *Red Hot Mamas: Coming into Our Own at Fifty.* New York: Bantam Books, 1996. Print.

Downey, Vickie. "Tewa Tesuque Pueblo." *Wisdom's Daughters: Conversations with Women Elders of Native America.* Ed. Steve Wall. New York: Harper, 1993. 2–21. Print.

Elster, Jon. "Clearing the Decks." *Ethics* 91.4 (July 1981): 634–44. Web. 29 Nov. 2005.

Erben, David. "The Sacred Ghost: The Role of the Elder(ly) in Native American Literature." *Aging and Identity: A Humanities Perspective.* Ed. Sara Munson Deats and Lagretta Tallent Lenker. Westport, CT: Praeger, 1999. 129–38. Print.

Erdrich, Louise. *Four Souls.* New York: Harper, 2004. Print.

——— . *The Last Report on the Miracles at Little No Horse.* New York: Harper, 2001. Print.

——— . *Love Medicine.* New York: Harper, 1984/1993. Print.

——— . *Tracks.* New York: Henry Holt, 1988. Print.

Erickson, E. H., J. M. Erickson, and Helen Kivnick. *Vital Involvement in Old Age.* New York: Norton, 1986. Print.

Estes, Carol. "Aging Enterprise Revisited." *The Gerontologist* 33.3 (June 1993): 292–8. Print.

——— . *Aging Enterprise: A Critical Examination of Social Policies and Services for the Aged.* Hoboken, NJ: Jossey-Bass/Wiley, 1979. Print.

Farquhar, Morag. "Elderly People's Definitions of Quality of Life." *Social*

Science and Medicine 41.10 (1995): 1439–46. *EBSCOHost.* Web. 5 June 2013.

Featherstone, Mark, and Andrew Wernick, eds. *Images of Ageing: Cultural Representations of Later Life.* New York: Routledge, 1995. Print.

Featherstone, Mark, and Mike Hepworth. "Images of Ageing." *Ageing in Society: An Introduction to Social Gerontology.* Ed. J. Bond, P. Coleman, and S. Peace. London: Sage, 1993. Print.

"Five Significant Books of 1972." 1972. *New York Times* 3 Dec. 1972: BR1. *EBSCO.* Web. 18 Oct. 2005.

Flint, Marcha. "Male and Female Menopause: A Cultural Put-On." *Changing Perspectives on Menopause.* Ed. Ann Voda, Myra Dinnerstein, and Sheryl O'Donnell. Austin: U of Texas P, 1982. 363–78. Print.

Foucault, Michel. "Body/power." *Power/Knowledge: Selected Interviews and Other Writings, 1972–1977.* Ed. Colin Gordon. Brighton, Sussex, UK: Harvester P, 1980. 55–62. Print.

Freeman, Ellen, et al. "Symptom reports from a cohort of African American and White Women in the Late Reproductive Years." *Menopause: The Journal of the North American Menopause Society* 8.1 (2001): 33–42. Web. 14 May 2003.

Freud, Sigmund. "The 'Uncanny.'" 1919. *The Standard Edition of the Complete Psychological Works of Sigmund Freud.* Vol. 17. Trans. James Strachey. London: Hogarth/Institute of Psycho-Analysis, 1953–74. Print.

Frick, Ulrich, Hyacinth Irving, and Jürgen Rehm. "Social Relationships as a Major Determinant in the Valuation of Health States." *Quality of Life Research* 21 (2012): 209–13. *EBSCOHost.* 29 May 2013.

Friedan, Betty. *The Fountain of Age.* New York: Simon and Schuster, 1993. Print.

Friedenfels, Roxanne. "Long-Lived and Invisible: Old Women and Gender Integration in the Curriculum." *Transformations* 3.2 (Sept. 1992): 73–8. Web. June 2008.

Frueh, Joanna. *Monster/Beauty: Building the Body of Love.* Berkeley: U of California P, 2001. Print.

Gale Group. "Key Terms." 2001. *Gale Encyclopedia of Alternative Medicine.* Gale, 2001. Web. 27 Apr. 2003.

Gallop, Jane. *Thinking Through the Body.* New York: Columbia, 1988. Print.

Garland-Thomson, Rosemarie. "Learning Something Else: Embracing the Dying Body in Doris Lessing's *Diary of a Good Neighbour.*" *Iris* Winter/Spring (1999): 44–7. Print.

Garza, Mannie, Janice Keaffaber, and Cynthia Rich. "We Hold These Truths to Be Self-Evident." *The Old Women's Project.* Old Women's Project, n.d. Web. 21 Apr. 2012.

Gaston, Marilyn Hughes, and Gayle Porter. "Maneuvering Through

Menopause: A Rite of Passage." *Age Ain't Nothing but a Number: Black Women Explore Midlife*. Ed. Carleen Brice. Boston: Beacon P, 2003. 61–70. Print.

Gerdner, L. A., and D. P. Schoenfelder. "Evidence-based guideline. Individualized Music for Elders with Dementia." *Journal of Gerontological Nursing* 36.6 (2010): 7–15. Print.

Gillaspy, Tom. "Minnesota's Changing Demographics." Gerontology 5105. Department of Gerontology, U of Minnesota. 25 Sept. 2002. Lecture.

Gillispie, Virginia. "Reviews for *Learning to Be Old: Gender, Culture, and Aging*." *Rowman and Littlefield*. Rowman.com, n.d. Web. 24 Aug. 2012.

Gimenez, Martha. "The Oppression of Women: A Structuralist Marxist View." *Materialist Feminism: A Reader in Class, Difference, and Women's Lives*. Ed. Rosemary Hennessy and Chrys Ingraham. New York: Routledge, 1997: 71–82. Print.

Glennon, Frances. "Meaty Meadisms About America." *Life Magazine* 47, 14 Sept. 1949: 147–8. Google Books. Web. 3 May 2014.

Göle, Nilüfer. "The Forbidden Modern." *Feminism and the Body*. Ed. Londa Schiebinger. Oxford, UK: Oxford UP, 2000. 465–91. Print.

Graham, Judith. "'Elderly' No More." *The New Old Age* [column]. *New York Times* 19 Apr. 2012. Web. 21 Apr. 2012.

Gravagne, Pamela. *The Becoming of Age: Cinematic Visions of Mind, Body and Identity in Later Life*. Jefferson, NC: McFarland, 2013. Print.

Green, Brent. "Internal Colonialism vs. the Elderly: Renewal and Critique for Gerontological Theory." *Berkeley Journal of Sociology* 23 (1978–1979): 129–50. Web. 25 Mar. 2004.

Greer, Germaine. *The Change: Women, Aging, and the Menopause*. Robbinsdale, MN: Fawcett Books, 1993. Print.

Greer, Germaine. "Women and the Struggle for Human Rights." University of Manitoba, Canadian Museum for Human Rights, Winnipeg, Manitoba. 14 May 2014. Fragile Freedoms: The Global Struggle for Human Rights lecture series. Broadcast on CBC's *Ideas with Paul Kennedy*. CBC.ca/ideas. 28 May 2014. Podcast. 19 June 2014.

Greer, Jane, and Mollie Whalen. "Raising Daughters: A Womb-to-Tomb Heuristic for Examining Women's Lives." *Transformations* 8.2 (Sept. 1997): 104–16. Web. June 2008.

Grens, Kerry. "Hormone Therapy Use Among Women Continues to Drop." *Reuters.com*. 30 Aug. 2012. Web. 30 May 2013.

Grimwade, J., Ian Fraser, and E. Farrell. *The Body of Knowledge: Everything You Need to Know About the Female Cycle*. Melbourne, Australia: William Heinemann, 1995. Print.

Grosz, Elizabeth. "Merleau-Ponty and Irigaray in the Flesh." *Thesis Eleven* 36 (1993): 38–9. Web. 11 Dec. 2002.

Grumbach, Doris. "A Fictional Trio." *The Washington Post* 24 July 1983, final ed. Book World: 6. Web. 14 May 2002.

Gubrium, Jabber F. "Voice and Context in a New Gerontology." *Handbook of the Humanities and Aging*. Ed. Thomas R. Cole, David D. Van Tassel, and Robert Kastenbaum. New York: Springer, 1992. 46–75. Print.

Gullette, Margaret. "Age Studies as Cultural Studies." *Handbook of the Humanities and Aging*, 2nd ed. Ed. Thomas Cole, Robert Kastenbaum, and Ruth Ray. New York: Springer, 2000. 214–34. Print.

———. *Aged by Culture*. Chicago: U of Chicago P, 2004. Print.

———. *Agewise: Fighting the New Ageism in America*. Chicago: U of Chicago P, 2011. Print.

———. *Declining to Decline: Cultural Combat and the Politics of the Midlife*. Charlottesville: UP of Virginia, 1997. Print.

———. "Menopause as Magic Marker: Discursive Consolidation in the United States, and Strategies for Cultural Combat." *Reinterpreting Menopause: Cultural and Philosophical Issues*. Ed. Paul Komesaroff, Philipa Rothfield, and Jeanne Daly. New York: Routledge, 1997. 176–99. Print.

———. *Safe at Last in the Middle Years: The Invention of the Midlife Progress Novel*. Berkeley: U of California P, 1988. Print.

Gulli, Laith Farid. "Menopause." *HealthAtoZ Medical Network*. HealthAtoZ, n.d. Web. 27 Apr. 2003.

Gutheil, Irene, Roslyn Chernesky, and Marian Sherratt. "Influencing Student Attitudes Toward Older Adults: Results of a Service-Learning Collaboration." *Educational Gerontology* 32.9 (Oct. 2006): 771–84. Web. June 2008.

Gutmann, David. *The Human Elder in Nature, Culture, and Society*. Boulder, CO: Westview P, 1997. Print.

Haight, Barbara K., and Jeffrey Dean Webster. *The Art and Science of Reminiscing: Theory, Research, Methods, and Applications*. Washington, DC: Taylor and Francis, 1995. Print.

Hallett, Janice Sundown. "Seneca." *Wisdom's Daughters: Conversations with Women Elders of Native America*. Ed. Steve Wall. New York: Harper, 1993. 140–79. Print.

"Happiness—It's in Your Hands: An AARP Study." *AARP: The Magazine*. June/July 2013: 66. Print.

Harding, Sandra. "Subjectivity, Experience, and Knowledge: An Epistemology from/for Rainbow Politics." *Who Can Speak: Authority and Critical Identity*. Ed. Judith Roof and Robyn Weigman. Urbana: U of Illinois P, 1995. 120–36. Print.

Harris, Lori, and Stephanie Dollinger. "Participation in a Course on Aging: Knowledge, Attitudes, and Anxiety About Aging in Oneself and Others." *Educational Gerontology* 27.8 (Dec. 2001): 657–67. Web. June 2008.

Hazan, Haim. *Old Age: Constructions and Deconstructions.* New York: Cambridge UP, 1994. Print.

Hedges, Warren. "Terms and Definitions." *Swirl: Your Guide to Post-Millennial Paradigms.* IDTC Terms, n.d. Web. 3 Dec. 2003.

Heglar, Charles J., and Annye L. Refoe. "Aging and the African-American Community: The Case of Ernest J. Gaines." *Aging and Identity: A Humanities Perspective.* Ed. Sara Munson Deats and Lagretta Tallent Lenker. Westport, CT: Praeger, 1999. 139–48. Print.

Hendrick Health System. "Menopause." 2002. *The Corporation.* HendrickHealth.org, 2002. Web. 27 Apr. 2003.

Henneberg, Sylvia. Email to the author. 17 Feb. 2003. Email.

Hepworth, Mike. *Stories of Ageing.* Buckingham, UK: Open UP, 2000. Print.

Herfray, C. *La Veillesse: Une Interprétation Psychoanalytique.* Paris: Desclée de Brouwer, EPI, 1988. Print.

Hill, Janet, and Valerie Barnes Lipscomb. "Performing Female Age in Shakespeare's Plays." *Staging Age: The Performance of Age in Theatre, Dance, and Film.* Ed. Valerie Barnes Lipscomb and Leni Marshall. New York: Palgrave Macmillan, 2010. 85–108. Print.

Hill, Michael Oritz. "Following the Thread." *Gathering In.* GatheringIn.com, n.d. Web. 7 Dec. 2002.

Hill-Lubin, M. A. "The African-American Grandmother in Autobiographical Works by Frederick Douglass, Langston Hughes, and Maya Angelou." *International Journal of Aging and Human Development* 33.3 (1991):173–85. EBSCO. Web. 22 July 2013.

"Hispanic Elderly." *Center on Aging Studies Without Walls.* University of Missouri—Kansas City. 29 June 2010. Web. 3 May 2014.

Hogan, Linda. *Solar Storms.* New York: Scribner, 1995.

Holladay, Hilary. "'I Am Not Grown Away from You': Lucille Clifton's Elegies for Her Mother." *CLA Journal* 42.4 (June 1999): 430–4. Web. 9 Apr. 2003.

———. "Songs of Herself: Lucille Clifton's Poems About Womanhood." *The Furious Flowering of African American Poetry.* Ed. Joanne Gabbin. Charlottesville: UP of Virginia, 1999. 281–97. Print.

———. *Wild Blessings: The Poetry of Lucille Clifton.* Baton Rouge: Louisiana State UP, 2004. Print.

Holloway, Karla, and Stephanie Demetrakopoulos. "Remembering Our Foremothers: Older Black Women, Politics of Age, Politics of Survival as Embodied in the Novels of Toni Morrison." *Women and Politics* 6.2 (Summer 1986): 13–34. Web. 9 Apr. 2003.

Holmlund, Chris. *Impossible Bodies: Femininity and Masculinity at the Movies*. London: Routledge, 2002. Print.

Holstein, Martha. "On Being an Aged Woman." *Age Matters: Realigning Feminist Thinking*. Ed. Toni Calasanti and Kathleen Slevin. New York: Routledge, 2006. 313–34. Print.

Holt-Lunstad, Julianne, Timothy B. Smith, and J. Bradley Layton. "Social Relationships and Mortality Risk: A Meta-Analytic Review." *PLoS Medicine* 7.7 (July 2010). *EBSCOHost*. 29 May 2013.

hooks, bell. *Yearning: Race, Gender, and Cultural Politics*. Boston: South End P, 1990. Print.

Hoy, Helen. *How Should I Read This? Native Women Writers in Canada*. Toronto: U of Toronto P, 2001. Print.

Hull, Akasha (Gloria). "Channeling the Ancestral Muse: Lucille Clifton and Delores Kendrick." *Feminist Measures: Soundings in Poetry and Theory*. Ed. Lynn Keller and Cristanne Miller. Ann Arbor: U of Michigan P, 1994. 96–116. Print.

Hurd Clarke, Laura. *Facing Age: Women Growing Older in Anti-Aging Culture*. Lanham, MD: Rowman and Littlefield, 2011. Print.

Hutcheon, Linda, and Michael Hutcheon. "Late Style(s): The Ageism of the Singular." *Occasion: Interdisciplinary Studies in the Humanities* 4 (31 May 2012). Web. 12 Oct. 2012.

Hyyppä, Markku T., and Juhani Mäki. "Social Participation and Health in a Community Rich in Stock of Social Capital." *Health Education Research: Theory & Practice* 18.6 (2003): 770–9. *EBSCOHost*. Web. 29 May 2013.

Iyer, Pico. "Why We Travel." *Salon*. Salon.com. 18 Mar. 2000. Web. 27 May 2010.

Jablonski, Carol J. "The Return Home: Affirmations and Transformations of Identity in Horton Foote's *The Trip to Bountiful*." *Aging and Identity: A Humanities Perspective*. Ed. Sara Munson Deats and Lagretta Tallent Lenker. Westport, CT: Praeger, 1999. 191–200. Print.

Jaggar, Alison. "Love and Knowledge: Emotion in Feminist Epistemology." *Gender/Body/Knowledge: Feminist Reconstructions of Being and Knowing*. Ed. Alison Jaggar and Susan Bordo. New Brunswick, NJ: Rutgers UP, 1992. 145–71. Print.

James, Selma. "Introduction to *The Power of Women and the Subversion of the Community*." *Materialist Feminism: A Reader in Class, Difference, and Women's Lives*. Ed. Rosemary Hennessy and Chrys Ingraham. New York: Routledge, 1997. 33–9. Print.

Jamieson, Sara. "'Now That I Am Dead': P. K. Page and the Self-Elegy." *Canadian Literature* 166 (Autumn 2000): 63–82. Web. 8 Oct. 2003.

John, Robert, Patrice Blanchard, and Catherine Hagan Hennessy. "Hidden Lives: Aging and Contemporary American Indian Women." *Handbook on Women and Aging.* Ed. Jean Coyle. Westport, CT: Greenwood P, 1997. 290–315. Print.

Johnson, Alicia. Personal communication. 29 Apr. 2003.

Jones, Charisse. "Sweeping Study Finds Blacks in U.S. Diverse, Optimistic." *USA Today,* 27 June 2008. Web. 26 May 2013.

Joyner, Mildred, and Eli DeHope. "Transforming the Curriculum Through the Intergenerational Lens." *Journal of Gerontological Social Work* 48.1/2 (2006): 127–37. Web. June 2008.

Kaminsky, Marc. "Story of the Shoebox: The Meaning and Practice of Transmitting Stories." *Handbook of the Humanities and Aging.* Ed. Thomas R. Cole, David D. Van Tassel, and Robert Kastenbaum. New York: Springer, 1992. 307–27. Print.

Kane, Robert. "What's So Good About Aging?" NIA Gerontology Colloquium. University of Minnesota. 7 May 2003. Lecture.

Kaplan, E. Ann. "Trauma and Aging: Marlene Dietrich, Melanie Klein, and Marguerite Duras." *Figuring Age: Women, Bodies, Generations.* Ed. Kathleen Woodward. Indiana UP: Indianapolis. 1999. 171–94. Print.

———. "Resisting Pathologies of Age and Race: Menopause and Cosmetic Surgery in Films by Rainer and Tom." *Reinterpreting Menopause: Cultural and Philosophical Issues.* Ed. Paul Komesaroff, Philipa Rothfield, and Jeanne Daly. New York: Routledge, 1997. 100–26. Print.

Kastenbaum, Robert. "The Creative Process: A Life-Span Approach." *Handbook of the Humanities and Aging.* Ed. Thomas Cole, David Van Tassel, and Robert Kastenbaum. New York: Springer, 1992. 285–306. Print.

Katz, Stephen. *Cultural Aging: Life Course, Lifestyle, and Senior Worlds.* Ontario, Canada: Broadview P, 2005. Print.

———. *Disciplining Old Age: The Formation of Gerontological Knowledge.* Charlottesville, VA: UP of Virginia, 1996. Print.

———. Personal communication. The Pennsylvania State U, State College, PA. October, 1998.

Katz, Stephen, and Barbara Marshall. "New Sex for Old: Lifestyle, Consumerism, and the Ethics of Aging Well." *Journal of Aging Studies* 17.1 (2003): 3–16. *EBSCO.* Web. 3 July 2013.

Kaufert, P. "Menopause as Process or Event: The Creation of Definitions in Biomedicine." *Biomedicine Examined.* Ed. M. Lock and D. R. Gordon. New York: Kluwer, 1988. 331–49. Print.

Kivnick, Helen Q., and Courtney K. Wells. "Untapped Richness in Erik H. Erikson's Rootstock." *The Gerontologist* 54.1 (2014): 40–50. Print.

Komesaroff, Paul. "Medicine and the Moral Space of the Menopausal Woman." *Reinterpreting Menopause: Cultural and Philosophical Issues.* Ed. Paul Komesaroff, Philipa Rothfield, and Jeanne Daly. New York: Routledge, 1997. 54–76. Print.

Komesaroff, Paul, Philipa Rothfield, and Jeanne Daly. "Mapping Menopause: Objectivity or Multiplicity?" *Reinterpreting Menopause: Cultural and Philosophical Issues.* Ed. Paul Komesaroff, Philipa Rothfield, and Jeanne Daly. New York: Routledge, 1997. 3–16. Print.

---, eds. *Reinterpreting Menopause: Cultural and Philosophical Issues.* New York: Routledge, 1997. Print.

Kriebernegg, Ulla. "'It'll Remain a Shock for a While': Resisting Socialization into Long-Term Care in Joan Barfoot's *Exit Lines.*" *Methoden der Alter(n)sforschung: Disziplinäre Positionen und transdisziplinäre Perspektiven.* Ed. Andrea von Hülsen-Esch, Miriam Seidler, Christian Tagsold. Bielefeld: transcript, 2013. 198–208. Print.

Kriebernegg, Ulla. "Ending Aging in the Shtyngart of Eden: Biogerontological Discourse in *A Super Sad True Love Story.*" *Journal of Aging Studies* 27.1 (Jan. 2013): 61–70. Print.

Kristeva, Julia. *Powers of Horror.* New York: Columbia UP, 1982. Print.

Kunow, Rüdiger. "Chronologically Gifted? Old Age in American Culture." *Amerikastudien: American Studies, A Quarterly* 56.1 (Winter 2011): 23–44. Print.

Labouvie-Vief, Gisela. "Positive Development in Later Life." *Handbook of the Humanities and Aging.* 2nd ed. Ed. Thomas R. Cole and Ruth E. Ray. New York: Springer, 2000. 365–80. Print.

Lacan, Jacques. *Ecrits: A Selection.* Trans. Alan Sheridan. New York: Norton, 1977. Print.

Lamb, Erin Gentry. "'20 Is the New 65': Pedagogical Approaches to Reconciling the Future Self and the Aging Other Through Life as a Story." NWSA Convention, Cincinnati Convention Center, Cincinnati, OH. 20 June 2008. Conference presentation.

———. "'Polyester Pants and Orthopedic Shoes': Introducing Age Studies to Traditional Undergraduates." *Age, Culture, Humanities* 1 (2014): 223-38. Print.

Lamb, Erin Gentry, chair. "Age and/as Disability Panel: Michael Bérubé, Lennard J. Davis, Jane Gallop, Rüdiger P. Kunow, and Kathleen Woodward." MLA Convention, Chicago, 11 Jan. 2014. Age Studies Discussion Group roundtable.

Laqueur, Thomas. "Female Orgasm, Generation, and the Politics of Reproductive Biology." *Representations* 14 (Spring 1986): 1–82. Web. 10 May 2003.

Lasdun, James. "Doris Lessing and the Perils of the Pseudonymous Novel." *New Yorker blog*. New Yorker, 23 July 2013. Web. 24 July 2013.

Laverdure, Betty. "Ojibway." *Wisdom's Daughters: Conversations with Women Elders of Native America*. Ed. Steve Wall. New York: Harper, 1993. 94–131. Print.

Lawrence, Margaret. *The Stone Angel*. Toronto, ON: McClelland and Stewart, 1964. Print.

LeGuin, Ursula. "At the Party." *Women and Aging: An Anthology by Women*. Ed. Jo Alexander, Debi Berrow, Lisa Domitrovich, Margarita Donnelly, and Cheryl McLean. Corvallis, OR: Calyx Books, 1986. 85. Print.

———. "The Light." *Women and Aging: An Anthology by Women*. Ed. Jo Alexander, Debi Berrow, Lisa Domitrovich, Margarita Donnelly, and Cheryl McLean. Corvallis, OR: Calyx Books, 1986. 84. Print.

Lehman, Harvey. "Creative Production Rates of Present Versus Past Generations of Scientists." *Journal of Gerontology* 17 (1962): 409–17. Web. 29 Apr. 2002.

Lentricchia, Frank. "Last Will and Testament of an Ex-Literary Critic." *Lingua Franca* (Sept./Oct. 1996): 59–67. EBSCOhost. Web. 17 May 2014.

Lessing, Doris. *The Diaries of Jane Somers* [contains *The Diary of a Good Neighbour* and *If the Old Could* . . .]. New York: Vintage/Random, 1984a. Print.

———. *The Golden Notebook*. New York: Harper, 1962. Print.

———. "An interview with Doris Lessing." With Susan Stamberg. *Doris Lessing Newsletter* 8.2 (1984b): 3–4, 15. Print.

———. *Love, Again*. New York: Harper, 1995. Print.

———. *The Prisons We Choose to Live Inside*. New York: Harper, 1987. Print.

———. *Under My Skin: Volume One of My Autobiography. To 1949*. New York: Harper, 1994. Print.

———. *Walking in the Shade: Volume Two of My Autobiography. 1949–1962*. New York: Harper, 1997. Print.

LeSueur, Meridel. "Remarks from the 1983 Poetry Reading." *Women and Aging: An Anthology by Women*. Ed. Jo Alexander, Debi Berrow, Lisa Domitrovich, Margarita Donnelly, and Cheryl McLean. Corvallis, OR: Calyx Books, 1986. 9–19. Print.

———. *Ripenings*. Old Westbury, NY: The Feminist P, 1982. Print.

Levy, Becca. "Eradication of Ageism Requires Addressing the Enemy Within." *Gerontologist* 41.5 (Oct. 2001): 578–9. EBSCO. Web. Aug. 2009.

———. "Mind Matters: Cognitive and Physical Effects of Aging Self-Stereotypes." *Journal of Gerontology B: Psychological Sciences*, 58 (2003): 203–11. EBSCO. Web. Aug. 2009.

———. "Stereotype Embodiment: A Psychological Approach to Aging." *Current Directions in Psychological Science*, 18 (2009): 332-36. *EBSCO*. Web. 25 Nov. 2012.

Levy, Becca, Alan B. Zonderman, Martin D. Slade, and Luigi Ferrucci. "Age Stereotypes Held Earlier in Life Predict Cardiovascular Events in Later Life." *Psychological Science* 20.3 (Mar. 2009): 296-8. *EBSCO*. Web. Aug. 2009.

———. "Memory Shaped by Age Stereotypes Over Time." *Journal of Gerontology B: Psychological Sciences* 67.4 (2012): 432-6. *EBSCO*. Web. 25 Nov. 2012.

Levy, Becca, and Ellen Langer. "Aging Free from Negative Stereotypes: Successful Memory in China and Among the American Deaf." *Journal of Personality & Social Psychology* 66.6 (June 1994): 989-97. *EBSCO*. Web. Aug. 2009.

Levy, Becca, and Erica Leifheit-Limson. "The Stereotype-Matching Effect: Greater Influence on Functioning When Age Stereotypes Correspond to Outcomes." *Psychology and Aging* 24.1 (Mar 2009): 230-3. *EBSCO*. Web. Aug. 2009.

Levy, Becca, Martin Slade, Suzanne Kunkel, and Stanislav Kasl. "Longevity Increased by Positive Self-Perceptions of Aging." *Journal of Personality & Social Psychology* 83.2 (Aug. 2002): 261-70. *EBSCO*. Web. Aug. 2009.

Lewis, Peter. "Marxism-Feminism Now." *Durham University Journal* 53.1 (January 1992): 139-41. Web.14 May 2002.

Lipscomb, Valerie, and Leni Marshall, eds. *Age on Stage: Performances of Age and Aging in Theatre, Dance, Film, and Advertising*. New York: Palgrave Macmillan, 2010. Print.

Lock, Margaret. *Encounters with Aging: Mythologies of Menopause in Japan and North America*. Berkeley: U of California P, 1993. Print.

Loe, Meika. *Aging Our Way: Lessons for Living from 85 and Beyond*. New York: Oxford UP, 2011. Print.

Looser, Devoney. Women Writers and Old Age in Great Britain, 1750-1850. Baltimore, MD: Johns Hopkins UP, 2008.

Luo, Ye, et al. "Loneliness, Health, and Mortality in Old Age: A National Longitudinal Study. *Social Science and Medicine*. 74 (2012): 901-14. *EBSCOHost*. Web. 17 May 2014.

Lutkehaus, Nancy. *Margaret Mead: The Making of an American Icon*. Princeton, NJ: Princeton UP, 2008. Print.

Macdonald, Barbara and Cynthia Rich. *Look Me in the Eye: Old Women, Aging, and Ageism*. Minneapolis: Spinsters Ink, 1983. Print.

Mackie, Fiona. "The Left Hand of the Goddess: The Silencing of Menopause as a Bodily Experience of Transition." *Reinterpreting*

Menopause: Cultural and Philosophical Issues. Ed. Paul Komesaroff, Philipa Rothfield, and Jeanne Daly. New York: Routledge, 1997. 17–31. Print.

Maierhofer, Roberta. "American Studies Growing Old." *Crossing Borders: Interdisciplinary Intercultural Interactions*. Ed. B. Kettemann and G. Marko. Tübingen, Germany: Narr, 1999. Print.

Mance, Ajuan Maria. "Re-locating the Black Female Subject: The Landscape of the Body in the Poetry of Lucille Clifton." *Recovering the Black Female Body: Self-Representations by African American Women*. Ed. Michael Bennett and Vanessa Dickerson. New Brunswick, NJ: Rutgers UP, 2000. 123–40. Print.

Mangum, Teresa. "Dog Years, Human Fears." *Representing Animals*. Ed. Nigel Rothfels. Indiana UP, 2002: 35–47. Print.

———. "Literary History as a Tool for Gerontology." *Handbook of the Humanities and Aging*. Ed. Thomas Cole, Ruth Ray, and Robert Kastenbaum. 2nd ed. New York: Springer, 2000. 62–76. Print.

———. "Longing for Life Extension: Science Fiction and Late Life." *Journal of Aging and Identity* 7.2 (June 2002): 69–82. Web. June 2008.

———. Telephone interview. 21 July 2008.

Mansfield, Phyllis Kernoff, and Ann Voda. "From Edith Bunker to the 6:00 News: How and What Midlife Women Learn About Menopause." *Faces of Women and Aging*. Ed. Nancy Davis, Ellen Cole, and Esther Rothblum. New York: Harrington Park P, 1993. 89–104. Print.

Manson, JoAnn E. "Overview of Menopause." *Menopause.org*. 2012. Web. 18 July 2013.

Marshall, Barbara, and Stephen Katz. "The Embodied Life Course: Post-Ageism or the Renaturalization of Gender?" *Societies* 2 (Oct. 2012): 222–34. Web. 14 Dec. 2012.

———. "From Androgyny to Androgens: Resexing the Aging Body." *Age Matters: Realigning Feminist Thinking*. Ed. Toni Calasanti and Kathleen Slevin. New York: Routledge, 2006. 75–98. Print.

Marshall, Leni. "Ageility Studies: The Interplay of Critical Approaches in Age Studies and Disability Studies." *Alive and Kicking at All Ages: Health, Life Expectancy, and Life Course Identity*. Ed. Ulla Kriebernegg, Roberta Maierhofer, and Barbara Ratzenböck. Bielefeld, Germany: Verlag. 21–40. Print.

———. "Thinking Differently About Aging: Changing Attitudes Through the Humanities." *The Gerontologist*. In press. Print.

———. "Through (With) the Looking Glass: Lacan and Woodward in Méconnaissance, the Mirror Stage of Old Age." *Feminist Formations* 24.2 (Aug. 2012): 52–76. Print.

Marshall, Leni, and Aagje Swinnen. "'Let's Do It Like Grown-Ups': A Filmic Ménage of Age, Gender, and Sexuality." *Aging, Media, and Culture*. Ed. C. Lee Harrington, Denise Bielby, and Anthony R. Bardo. Lantham, MD: Lexington Books/Rowman and Littlefield. 157–68. Print.

Marshall, Victor. "Analyzing Social Theories of Aging." *Handbook of Theories of Aging*. Ed. Vern Bengston and K. Warner Schaie. New York: Springer, 1999. 434–58. Print.

Martin, Emily. *The Woman in the Body: A Cultural Analysis of Reproduction*. Boston: Beacon P, 2001. Print.

Masters, Julie, and Lyn Holley. "A Glimpse of Life at 67: The Modified Future-Self Worksheet." *Educational Gerontology* 32.4 (Apr. 2006): 261–9. Web. July 2008.

Masters, Ken. "Old Woman Spider." *Cherokee Images: Tribal Art and Culture*. CherokeeImages.com, 1996–2010. Web. 7 Dec. 2002.

McCluskey, Audrey. "Clifton's Children's Books." *Black American Women Poets and Dramatists*. Ed. Harold Bloom. New York: Chelsea House, 1996. 48–51.

McDonald, Katrina Bell, and Elizabeth M. Armstrong. "De-Romanticizing Black Intergenerational Support: The Questionable Expectations of Welfare Reform." *Journal of Marriage and Family* 63.1 (Feb. 2001): 213–23. Print.

McDowell, Deborah. "Recovery Missions: Imaging the Body Ideals." *Recovering the Black Female Body: Self-Representations by African American Women*. Ed. Michael Bennett and Vanessa Dickerson. New Brunswick, NJ: Rutgers UP, 2000. 296–317. Print.

McDowell, Edwin. "Doris Lessing Says She Used Pen Name to Show New Writers' Difficulties." *New York Times* 23 Sept. 1984, Metropolitan ed., sec. 1: 45. *LexisNexis Academic*. Web. 26 July 2012.

McGee, Micki. *Self-Help, Inc*. New York, Oxford UP, 2005. Print.

McGuire, Sandra, Diane Klein, and Donna Couper. "Aging Education: A National Imperative." *Educational Gerontology* 31.6 (June 2005): 443–60. Web. July 2008.

Meadows, Robert, and Kate Davidson. "Maintaining Manliness in Later Life: Hegemonic Masculinities and Emphasized Femininities." *Age Matters: Realigning Feminist Thinking*. Ed. Toni Calasanti and Kathleen Slevin. New York: Routledge, 2006. 295–312. Print.

Meisner, Brad A. "A Meta-Analysis of Positive and Negative Age Stereotype Priming Effects on Behavior Among Older Adults." *Journals of Gerontology Series B: Psychological Sciences & Social Sciences* 67B.1 (Jan. 2012): 13–7. *Academic Search Complete*. Web. 20 Sept. 2013.

Merck StayWell Co. "Understanding Menopause—Feeling Good in a

New Stage of Life: Estrogen and Your Health." 2001. *Merck & Co.* MerkSource.com, 2001. Web. 27 Apr. 2003.

Miller, Jane. "Doris Lessing and the Millennium." *Raritan: A Quarterly Review* 18.1 (Summer 1998): 133–45. Web. 14 May 2002.

Minkler, Meredith, and Carroll Estes, eds. *Critical Gerontology: Perspectives from Political and Moral Economy.* Amityville, NY: Baywood, 1999. Print.

Moody, Harry R. *Aging: Concepts and Controversies.* Thousand Oaks, CA: Pine Forge P, 2009. Print.

Moody, Harry R. "Overview: What Is Critical Gerontology and Why Is It Important?" *Voices and Visions of Aging: Toward a Critical Gerontology.* Ed. Thomas R. Cole, W. Andrew Achenbaum, Patricia L. Jakobi, and Robert Kastenbaum. New York: Springer, 1993. xv–xli. Print.

Morgan, Kathryn Pauly. "Women and the Knife: Cosmetic Surgery and the Colonization of Women's Bodies." *Hypatia* 6.3 (Autumn 1991): 25–53. EBSCO. Web. 9 July 2013.

Morrison, Toni. *Jazz.* New York: Knopf, 1992. Print.

Naples, Nancy A. "Activist Mothering: Cross-Generational Continuity in the Community Work of Women from Low-Income Urban Neighborhoods." *Gender and Society* 6.3 (Sept. 1992): 441–63. Web. 9 Oct. 2002.

Narayan, Uma. "Working Together across Difference: Some Considerations on Emotions and Political Practice." *Hypatia* 3.2 (1988): 31–48. Web. 5 Sept. 2007.

Newman, Jane. "Place and Race: Midlife Experience in Harlem." *Welcome to Middle Age! (And Other Cultural Fictions).* Ed. Richard Shweder. Chicago: U of Chicago P, 1998. 259–93. Print.

Newton, Judith, and Deborah Rosenfelt. *Feminist Criticism and Social Change.* New York: Methuen, 1985. Print.

Nickerson, Betty. *Old and Smart: Women and the Adventure of Aging.* Madeira Park, BC: Harbour, 1991. Print.

Nixon, Elisha, et al. "'Staying Strong': How Low-Income Rural African American Women Manage Their Menopausal Changes." *Women and Health* 34.2 (2001): 81–95. Web. 9 May 2003.

Northrup, Christiane. *The Wisdom of Menopause.* New York: Bantam Doubleday Dell, 2003. Print.

Oates, Joyce Carol. *A Widow's Story: A Memoir.* New York: Ecco, 2011. Print.

Ong, Aiwa. *Flexible Citizenship: The Cultural Logics of Transnationality.* Durham, NC: Duke UP, 1999. Print.

Ortiz, Simon. "Introduction: Wah Nuhtyuh-yuu Dyu Neetah Tyahstih (Now It Is My Turn to Stand)." *Speaking for the Generations.* Ed. Simon Ortiz. Tucson: U of Arizona P, 1998. xi–xix. Print.

Oró-Piqueras, Maricel. *Ageing Corporealities in Contemporary English Fiction: Redefining Stereotypes.* Saaarbrücken, Germany: Lambert, 2011. Print.

Osteoporosis Education Project. "Osteoporosis Glossary." *Osteoporosis Education Project.* BetterBones, 2002. Web. 27 Apr. 2003.

Ovrebo, Beverly, and Meredith Minkler. "The Lives of Older Women: Perspectives from Political Economy and the Humanities." *Voices and Visions of Aging: Toward a Critical Gerontology.* Ed. Thomas R. Cole, W. Andrew Achenbaum, Patricia L. Jakobi, and Robert Kastenbaum. New York: Springer, 1993. 289–308. Print.

Owens, Louis. *Mixedblood Messages: Literature, Film, Family, Place.* Norman, OK: U of Oklahoma P, 1998. Print.

Palmore, Erdman. "Three Decades of Research on Ageism." *Generations* 29.3 (Fall 2005): 87–90. Web. July 2008.

Pattock, Mary. "Voters Who Come in from the Web." *Reach* (Summer 2012): 2. Print.

Patterson-Rudolph, Carol. *On the Trail of Spider Woman: Petroglyphs, Pictographs, and Myths of the Southwest.* Santa Fe, NM: Ancient City P, 1997. Print.

Pearlman, Sarah. "Late Mid-Life Astonishment: Disruptions to Identity and Self-Esteem." *Faces of Women and Aging.* Ed. Nancy Davis, Ellen Cole, and Esther Rothblum. New York: Harrington Park P, 1993. 1–12. Print.

Pennar, Karen. "Unafraid of Aging." *New York Times,* 25 June 2012. Science section. Web. 8 Aug. 2013.

Peterson, Carla. "Forward." *Recovering the Black Female Body: Self-Representations by African American Women.* Ed. Michael Bennett and Vanessa Dickerson. New Brunswick, NJ: Rutgers UP, 2000. ix–xvi. Print.

Pezzulich, Evelyn. "Coming of Age: The Emergence of the Aging Female Protagonist in Literature." *Doris Lessing Studies* 24.1&2 (Summer/Fall 2004): 7–10. Print.

Phillipson, Chris, and Alan Walker. *Ageing and Social Policy: A Critical Assessment.* Farnam, UK: Gower Publishing, 1987. Print.

Piercy, Marge. "Something to Look Forward To." *Women and Aging: An Anthology by Women.* Ed. Jo Alexander, Debi Berrow, Lisa Domitrovich, Margarita Donnelly, and Cheryl McLean. Corvallis, OR: Calyx Books, 1986. 86. Print.

Pipher, Mary. *Reviving Ophelia: Saving the Selves of Adolescent Girls.* New York: Ballantine, 1995. Print.

PLoS Medicine Editors. "Social Relationships Are Key to Health and Health Policy." *PLoS Medicine* 7.8 (Aug. 2010). *EBSCOHost.* Web. 29 May 2013.

Pogrebin, Letty Cottin. *Getting Over Getting Older: An Intimate Journey.* Boston: Little, 1996. Print.

Port, Cynthia. "'Ages Are the Stuff': The Traffic in Ages in Interwar Britain." *NWSA Journal* 18.1 (Spring 2006): 138–61. Print.

———. "'Violent and Sentimental by Turns': The Gendered Discourses of Mike Gold." *Shofar: An Interdisciplinary Journal of Jewish Studies.* 32.2 (Jan. 2014): 88–115. Print.

Ragan, Amie, and Anne Bowen. "Improving Attitudes Regarding the Elderly Population: The Effects of Information and Reinforcement for Change. *The Gerontologist* 41.4 (2001): 511–5. EBSCOHost. Web. 23 Sept. 2013.

Ragan, Pauline. "Crimes Against the Elderly: Findings from Interviews with Blacks, Mexican Americans, and Whites." *Justice and Older Americans.* Ed. Marlene Young Rifai. Lexington, MA: Lexington Books, 1977. 25–35. Print.

Ragland-Sullivan, Ellie. *Jacques Lacan and the Philosophy of Psychoanalysis.* Chicago: U of Illinois P, 1986. Print.

Ramel, Gordon. "Some Tarantula Myths." *EarthLife Web.* EarthLife.net, n.d. Web. 6 Dec. 2002.

Randall, Margaret. "From: The Journals." *Women and Aging: An Anthology by Women.* Ed. Jo Alexander, Debi Berrow, Lisa Domitrovich, Margarita Donnelly, and Cheryl McLean. Corvallis, OR: Calyx Books, 1986. 127–30. Print.

Ray, Ruth. "A Postmodern Perspective on Feminist Gerontology." *The Gerontologist* 36.5 (1996): 674–80.

Rich, Adrienne. *The Dream of a Common Language: Poems 1974–1977.* New York: Norton, 1978. Print.

Richeson, Jennifer A., and J. Nicole Shelton. "A Social Psychological Perspective on the Stigmatization of Older Adults." *When I'm 64.* Ed. Laura L. Carstensen and Christine R. Hartel. Washington, DC: National Academies Press, 2006. 174–208. Print.

Rips, Jill. "Who Needs a Menopause Policy?" *Menopause: A Midlife Passage.* Ed. Joan Callahan. Bloomington: Indiana UP, 1993. 79–91. Print.

Roberts, Marcus. *Analytical Marxism: A Critique.* London: Verso, 1996. Print.

Robinson, Stephanie, Robert Briggs, and Desmond O'Neill. "Cognitive Aging, Geriatrics Textbooks, and Unintentional Ageism." *Journal of the American Geriatrics Society* 60.1 (2012): 2183–2185. Print.

Roof, Judith, and Robyn Weigman, eds. "Part 2: Speaking Parts." *Who Can Speak: Authority and Critical Identity.* Urbana: U of Illinois P, 1995. 93–5. Print.

Rooke, Constance. "Old Age in Contemporary Fiction: A New Paradigm of Hope." *Handbook of the Humanities and Aging*. Ed. Thomas Cole, David Van Tassel, and Robert Kastenbaum. New York: Springer, 1992. 241–57. Print.

Rothfield, Philipa. "Menopausal Embodiment." *Reinterpreting Menopause: Cultural and Philosophical Issues*. Ed. Paul Komesaroff, Philipa Rothfield, and Jeanne Daly. New York: Routledge, 1997. 32–53. Print.

Rowe, John, and Robert Kahn. *Successful Aging*. New York: Pantheon Books, 1998. Print.

Rowles, Graham. "AGHE President's Message." *Association for Gerontology in Higher Education: aghexchange*. 35.2 (2012): 1–16. Print.

Rubenstein, Roberta. "Feminism, Eros, and the Coming of Age." *Frontiers: A Journal of Women's Studies* 22.2 (2001): 1–19. Web. 8 Oct. 2003.

Rushing, Andrea. "Clifton's Early Verse." *Black American Women Poets and Dramatists*. Ed. Harold Bloom. New York: Chelsea House, 1996. 50–1. Print.

Russell, Karen. *St. Lucy's Home for Girls Raised by Wolves*. New York: Vintage, 2007. Print.

Rybarczyk, Bruce. "Using Reminiscence Interviews for Stress Management in the Medical Setting." *The Art and Science of Reminiscing: Theory, Research, Methods, and Applications*. Ed. Barbara K. Haight and Jeffrey Dean Webster. Washington, DC: Taylor and Francis, 1995. 205–218. Print.

Said, Edward. *On Late Style: Music and Literature Against the Grain*. New York: Vintage, 2007. Print.

Sandoval, Chela. *Methodology of the Oppressed*. Minneapolis: U of Minnesota P, 2000. Print.

Sarris, Greg. *Keeping Slug Woman Alive: A Holistic Approach to American Indian Texts*. Berkeley: U of California P, 1993. Print.

Sarton, May. *As We Are Now*. New York: Norton, 1992. Print.

——— . *The Magnificent Spinster*. New York: Norton, 1985. Print.

Savishinsky, Joel. *Breaking the Watch: The Meanings of Retirement in America*. Ithaca, NY: Cornell UP, 2002. Print.

——— . "First Impressions and Last Words: Condensing Elderly Lives into Three-Line Haiku." *Anthropology and Aging Quarterly* 27.4 (2006): 5–8. Web. July 2008.

——— . "Lighting the Match: Using Haiku to Teach About Aging." *Gerontology and Geriatrics Education* 27.4 (2007): 55–68. Web. July 2008.

——— . Telephone interview. 21 July 2008.

Schachter-Shalomi, Zalman, and Ronald S. Miller. *From Age-ing to Sage-ing: A Profound New Vision of Growing Older*. New York: Grand Central, 1997. Print.

Schiebinger, Londa. "Introduction." *Feminism and the Body*. Oxford, UK: Oxford UP, 2000. 1–24. Print.

Schilling, Chris. *The Body and Social Theory*. London: Sage, 1993. Print.

Schlib, John. "Autobiography After Prozac." *Rhetorical Bodies*. Ed. Jack Selzer and Sharon Crowley. Madison: U of Wisconsin Press, 1999. Print. 202–217.

Schweninger, Lee. "A Skin of Lakeweed: An Ecofeminist Approach to Erdrich and Silko." *Multicultural Literatures Through Feminist/Poststructuralist Lenses*. Ed. Barbara Frey Waxman. Knoxville: U of Tennessee P, 1993. 37–56. Print.

Search for Good Health. "Menopause and Andropause." *Search for Good Health*. SearchForGoodHealth.com, 7 Apr. 2003. Web. 27 Apr. 2003.

Seyersted, Per. "Two Interviews with Leslie Marmon Silko." *American Studies in Scandinavia* 13 (1981): 17–33. Web. 18 Dec. 2002.

Sheehy, Gail. *Menopause: The Silent Passage*. New York: Pocket Books, 1993. Note: The book stems from a magazine article (Gail Sheehy. "The Silent Passage: Menopause." *Vanity Fair* (October 1991): 222–7, 252–63) and readers' responses to that article. Print.

Shomaker, Dianna. "Transfer of Children and the Importance of Grandmothers Among the Navajo Indians." *Journal of Cross-Cultural Gerontology* 4 (1989): 1–18. Web. 18 Dec. 2002.

Silko, Leslie Marmon. *Almanac of the Dead*. New York: Penguin, 1992. Print.

———. *Ceremony*. New York: Penguin, 1977. Print.

Simonds, Wendy. *Women and Self-Help Culture: Reading Between the Lines*. Piscataway, NJ: Rutgers UP, 1992. Print.

Singleton, Andrew. "'Men's Bodies, Men's Selves': Men's Health Self-Help Books and the Promotion of Health Care." *International Journal of Men's Health* 2.1 (Jan. 2003): 57–72. EBSCO. Web. 7 July 2013.

Slevin, Kathleen. "The Embodied Experiences of Old Lesbians." *Age Matters: Realigning Feminist Thinking*. Ed. Toni Calasanti and Kathleen Slevin. New York: Routledge, 2006. 247–68. Print.

Smith, Caroline. *Cosmopolitan Culture and Consumerism in Chick Lit*. New York: Routledge, 2007. Print.

Sollors, Werner. "A Critique of Pure Pluralism." *Reconstructing American Literary History*. Ed. Sacvan Bercovitch. Cambridge, MA: Harvard UP, 1986. 250–79. Print.

Sontag, Susan. "The Double Standard of Aging." *The Other Within Us: Feminist Explorations of Women and Aging*. Ed. Marilyn Pearsall. New York: Harper, 1997. 19–24. Print.

Sooktis, Lena. "Northern Cheyenne." *Wisdom's Daughters: Conversations with Women Elders of Native America*. Ed. Steve Wall. New York: Harper, 1993. 46–67. Print.

Srivastrava, Sarita. "'You're Calling Me a Racist?': The Moral and Emotional

Regulation of Antiracism and Feminism." *Signs* 31.1 (2005): 29–62. *EBSCO*. Web. 9 July 2013.
St. John, Martha. "Healing." *Gifts of Age: Portraits and Essays of 32 Remarkable Women*. Ed. Charlotte Painter. San Francisco: Chronicle Books, 1985. 61–65. Print.
Steinem, Gloria. *Revolution from Within: A Book of Self-Esteem*. Boston: Little, 1993. Print.
Stock, Robert. "Senior Class: Removing the Stigma from the O-Word." *New York Times* Home and Garden, 7 Mar. 1996. Web. 21 Apr. 2012.
Suleiman, Susan Rubin. *Authoritarian Fictions: The Ideological Novel as a Literary Genre*. Princeton, NJ: Princeton UP, 1983. Print.
Swallow, Jean. "Both Feet in Life: Interviews with Barbara Macdonald and Cynthia Rich." *Women and Aging: An Anthology by Women*. Ed. Jo Alexander, Debi Berrow, Lisa Domitrovich, Margarita Donnelly, and Cheryl McLean. Corvallis, OR: Calyx Books, 1986.
Swinnen, Aagje. "*Benidorm Bastards*, or the Do's and Don'ts of Aging." *Aging, Performance, and Stardom: Doing Age on the Stage of Consumerist Culture*. Ed. Aagje Swinnen and John Stotesbury. Berlin: Lit Verlag, 2012. 7–14. Print.
———. "Late-Life Masculinity in *Wandering Streams*, by Pascal Rabaté." *Ageing and Society*. In revision. Print.
———. "'One Nice Thing About Getting Old Is that Nothing Frightens You.' From Page to Screen: Rethinking Women's Old Age in Howl's Moving Castle." *Narratives of Life: Mediating Age*. Ed. Heike Hartung and Roberta Maierhofer. Berlin: Lit Verlag, 2009. 167–82. Print.
Sybylla, Roe. "Situating Menopause Within the Strategies of Power: A Genealogy." *Reinterpreting Menopause: Cultural and Philosophical Issues*. Ed. Paul Komesaroff, Philipa Rothfield, and Jeanne Daly. New York: Routledge, 1997. 200–24. Print.
Tiger, Virginia. "Ages of Anxiety: *The Diaries of Jane Somers*." *Spiritual Exploration in the Works of Doris Lessing, CSSFF, Contributions to the Study of Science Fiction and Fantasy*. Ed. Phyllis Perrakis. Westport, CT: Greenwood P, 1999. 1–16. Print.
Turner, Bryan. "Aging and Identity: Some Reflections on the Somatization of the Self." *Images of Aging*. Ed. Mike Featherstone and Andrew Wernick. London: Routledge, 1995. Print.
U.S. Census, 2010: Age and Sex Composition in the United States (C2010BR-03). 2010 Census Brief by Lindsay M. Howden and Julie A. Meyer. May 2011. Web. 26 Aug. 2012.
U.S. Census, 2010: Percent Distribution of the Projected Population by Selected Age Groups and Sex for the United States: 2010 to 2050. 14 Aug. 2008. Web. 26 Aug. 2012.

U.S. Census, 2010: Projections of the Population by Selected Age Groups and Sex for the United States: 2010 to 2050. 14 Aug. 2008. Web. 26 Aug. 2012.

Urla, Jacqueline, and Swedlund, Alan. "The Anthropometry of Barbie: Unsettling Ideals of the Feminine Body in Popular Culture." *Feminism and the Body*. Ed. Londa Schiebinger. Oxford, UK: Oxford UP, 2000. Print. 397–428.

Vines, G. *Raging Hormones, Do They Rule Our Lives?* London: Virago P, 1993. Print.

Wall, Cheryl A. "Sifting Legacies in Lucille Clifton's *Generations*." *Contemporary Literature* 40.4 (Winter 1999): 552–74. Web. 9 Apr. 2003.

Waxman, Barbara Frey. "Changing History Through a Gendered Perspective: A Postmodern Feminist Reading of Morrison's *Beloved*." *Multicultural Literatures Through Feminist/Poststructuralist Lenses*. Ed. Barbara Frey Waxman. Knoxville: U of Tennessee P, 1993. 57–83. Print.

———. *From the Hearth to the Open Road: A Feminist Study of Aging in Contemporary Literature*. Westport, CT: Greenwood P, 1990. Print.

———. "Literary Texts and Literary Critics Team Up Against Ageism." *A Guide to Humanistic Studies in Aging: What Does It Mean to Grow Old?* Ed. Thomas Cole, Ruth Ray, and Robert Kastenbaum. Baltimore: Johns Hopkins UP, 2010. 83–104. Print.

---, ed. *Multicultural Literatures Through Feminist/Poststructuralist Lenses*. Knoxville: U of Tennessee P, 1993. Print.

Weibel-Orlando, Joan. "Elders and Elderlies: Well-Being in Indian Old Age." *American Indian Culture and Research Journal* 13:3&4 (1989): 149–70. Web. 18 Dec. 2002.

———. "Grandparenting Styles: Contemporary American Indian Experience." *The Cultural Context of Aging: Worldwide Perspectives*. Ed. Jay Sokolovsky. Westport, CT: Bergin and Garvey, 1997. 139–55. Print.

Winkler, Mary. "Walking to the Stars." *Handbook of the Humanities and Aging*. Ed. Thomas Cole, David Van Tassel, and Robert Kastenbaum. New York: Springer, 1992. 258–84. Print.

Wisker, Gina. "'Disremembered and Unaccounted For': Reading Toni Morrison's *Beloved* and Alice Walker's *The Temple of My Familiar*." *Black Women's Writing*. Ed. Gina Wisker. New York: St. Martin's, 1993. 78–95. Print.

Wohlmann, Anita. *Aged Young Adults: Age Readings of Contemporary American Novels and Films*. Bielefeld, Germany: Verlag, 2014. Print.

Womack, Craig. *Red on Red: Native American Literary Separatism*. Minneapolis: U of Minnesota P, 1999. Print.

Woodward, Kathleen. "Against Wisdom: The Social Politics of Anger and Aging." *Cultural Critique* 51 (Spring 2002): 186–218. Web. 19 Mar. 2003.

———. *Aging and Its Discontents: Freud and Other Fictions.* Indianapolis: Indiana UP, 1991. Print.
---, ed. *Figuring Age: Women, Bodies, Generations.* Indianapolis: Indiana UP, 1999. Print.
———. "Performing Age, Performing Gender." *NWSA Journal* 18.1 (Spring 2006): 162–89. Print.
———. "Reviews: *Declining to Decline. Cultural Combat and the Politics of the Midlife.*" Brandeis. Brandeis Scholars Gullette Reviews, n.d. Web. 18 Oct. 2005.
———. *Statistical Panic: Cultural Politics and the Poetics of Emotion.* Durham, NC: Duke UP, 2009. Print.
———. Telephone interview. 24 July 2008.
———. "Youthfulness as a Masquerade." *Discourse* (Fall/Winter, 1988/89): 119–42. Web. 28 Dec. 2004.
Wyatt-Brown, Anne. "Literary Gerontology Comes of Age." *Handbook of the Humanities and Aging.* Ed. Thomas R. Cole, David D. Van Tassel, and Robert Kastenbaum. New York: Springer, 1992. 331–51. Print.
———. "Resilience and Creativity in Aging: *The Realms of Silver.*" *A Guide to Humanistic Studies in Aging: What Does It Mean to Grow Old?* Ed. Thomas Cole, Ruth Ray, and Robert Kastenbaum. Baltimore, MD: Johns Hopkins UP, 2010. 57–82. Print.
Wyatt-Brown, Anne, and Janice Rossen, eds. *Aging and Gender in Literature: Studies in Creativity.* Charlottesville: U of Virginia P, 1993. Print.
Thompson, E. H., Jr. "Guest Editorial." *Journal of Men's Studies* 13 (2004): 1–4. EBSCOhost. Web. 6 May 2014.
Yale School of Public Health. "Thinking Positively About Aging Extends Life More than Exercise and Not Smoking." Press Release. Yale University Office of Public Affairs and Communications. 29 July 2002. Web. 22 Sept. 2013.
Zajicek, Anna, Toni Calasanti, Cristie Ginther, and Julie Summers. "Intersectionality and Age Relations: Unpaid Care Work and Chicanas." *Age Matters: Realigning Feminist Thinking.* Ed. Toni Calasanti and Kathleen Slevin. New York: Routledge, 2006. 175–97. Print.

Index

AARP, 12, 47, 108
abject(ion), 36–8, 40
Achebe, Chinua, 5
activism, ix, 2–3, 6, 15–6, 18, 40, 59, 62, 70, 82, 92–3, 105, 116, 143, 147; activist action, 3, 25, 46, 58, 70, 89, 92, 123, 145; social change, 9, 12, 15–6, 18, 20–3, 28, 45, 55, 57, 69–71, 80, 83–5, 87, 90, 92–3, 109, 119–20, 131, 152, 156n17, 156n7. *See also* civil rights
adolescent, 16, 28, 82
adult, 11, 28, 61, 151, 156n1; adulthood, 1, 10, 14, 38, 148
African American. *See* race
age: age relations, 2, 139, 145–9, 153n6; middle age, 7, 10–2, 14, 23, 41–2, 57–8, 63, 80, 89–91, 114, 121, 147; old age/aged, 5–6, 10, 13, 18–20, 22, 27–40, 56, 58–61, 63, 69, 70, 76, 91, 95, 97, 103, 105, 110–3, 115, 119, 136–7, 141, 146, 150, 156n2, 159n18, 160n29; youth/young, vii, 1–2, 5, 9–17, 21, 23, 29–30, 38–9, 42, 49, 61–5, 69–70, 73–7, 80–1, 85, 91–2, 98, 102, 107, 110, 115, 119, 121, 123, 134, 136, 139–141, 148,
151, 156n1, 161n11. *See also* child; elder
age studies, ix, 1–26, 39–43, 57, 59, 62, 65–70, 86, 92–6, 116, 139, 143–52, 153nn3–4, 155n20, 159n20, 160n24, 160n30, 165n10, 166nn2–3; analysis, vii, 1–18, 22, 25–7, 41, 56, 59–62, 70, 86, 92, 94–7, 109, 119, 141, 143, 146–50, 153n4, 154n15, 157n9, 159n20, 166n1; theory, ix, 4, 9, 13–4, 19, 25–40, 61–3, 66–7, 151, 155n31, 157n18, 166n1
Aged by Culture (Gullette), 14, 39
ageism. *See under* discrimination
agency, 20, 27, 32–8, 58, 92–3, 111–2, 120. *See also* subject
Agewise (Gullette), 3, 4, 8, 11, 14, 16, 47, 154n14, 155nn22–3, 158n6, 160n27, 160n33
aging studies, 2, 8, 18, 166n3. *See also* age studies
Alexie, Sherman, 123, 129–30, 165n8
Althusser, Louis, 32, 141
ambiguous loss, 20, 41, 43, 64–7, 102, 157n14. *See also* Boss, Pauline

America(s), 3, 5, 11–2, 21, 25–6, 32, 39, 43–4, 46, 58, 63, 71, 82, 93, 96–7, 109, 113, 125, 130, 154n7, 165n10. *See also* North America; United States
anti-aging, 14, 32, 58, 62, 155n27
Arber, Sarah, 10
Asian American, 147. *See also* race
Atwood, Margaret, 5–6, 14, 17, 155n31
autobiography, 21, 63, 81, 154n8

Basting, Anne, 147, 155n20
Beauvoir, Simone de, 13, 59–60, 93, 155n29
Beck, Ulrich, 33, 160. *See also* risk
Biggs, Simon, 7, 9
binarity, 2, 27–34, 110, 153n4, 156n3; mind-body split, 19, 29–35, 105, 111, 159n16
Black. *See* race: African American
bodily ability. *See* disability
Boss, Pauline, 64–5, 102, 157n14, 158n11, 166n13. *See also* ambiguous loss
Britain, 161n3, 161n8
Broker, Ignatia, 122, 126, 164n8
brother. *See* family role: sibling
Butler, Judith, 27–31, 34, 37–8
Butler, Robert, 3, 63

Calasanti, Toni, 10, 34, 110, 145, 148, 153n4, 153n6, 154n8, 158n7
care work, 9, 21, 47, 54, 65–6, 72–7, 81–2, 92, 100, 104, 109, 114, 122, 137, 139–140, 142, 151, 157n18, 161n7, 161n9
Carstensen, Laura, 39
Cartesian. *See* binarity

Caucasian American. *See under* race
child, 27–8, 47, 50, 60–1, 63, 74, 78, 81–2, 86, 99–104, 121–2, 126, 136–8, 140, 165n10. *See also* age; family
childbearing, 66, 102, 157n16, 159n14
childhood, 1, 38
Chivers, Sally, 154n8
choice, 18, 19, 27, 31–4, 38, 40–1, 50, 84, 86, 138, 156n2
Christian, 99, 111, 134, 138, 163n9. *See also* religion
Christian, Barbara, 163n8
civil rights movement (U.S.), 94, 104
Civil War, U.S., 26, 101. *See also* slavery
class, 5, 12, 21, 59–60, 63, 74, 86, 90, 92, 94, 98, 103–4, 107, 113, 146, 155n24, 157n16, 160n31, 161n6. *See also* economics; socioeconomics
classism, vii, 21. *See also* discrimination
Clifton, Lucille, 17, 21–3, 93–117, 119, 163n2
Coetzee, J. M., 5
Cohen-Shalev, Amir, 6, 154n8, 155n31
Cole, Thomas, 149, 154n8, 154n15
Collins, Patricia Hill, 105, 142
communism. *See under* economics
community, 20–1, 23, 58, 64, 93, 98, 100–8, 116–7, 121–37, 140–1. *See also* otherelder
Contact, 119, 130–1, 138, 140, 164n1. *See also* race: Native American

Index

Copper, Baba, 13, 59–61, 93, 105, 160n32, 164n2
Cruikshank, Margaret, 14, 43, 59, 63–4, 154n8, 155nn29–30, 161n3; *Learning to be Old*, ix, 14, 43, 63, 155n30
cultural analysis. *See* literature: literary analysis
culture, 2–4, 7, 10, 20–2, 27–39, 45–6, 51, 53, 58, 78, 93–8, 100, 103–7, 110–6, 121–34, 140, 142, 147, 157n16, 164n1; cultural capital, 12, 14, 21, 32, 34–36, 42, 49–51 (*see also* discrimination; normative; Other; power, visibility); cultural continuity/transmission, 22, 119, 124–7, 141; cultural studies, vii, 4–8, 15, 23, 37, 53, 60, 64, 96, 106, 109, 124, 143, 149. *See also* literature: literary analysis; social construction

Daly, Jeanne, 41, 45, 52–3, 159n14, 164n15
daughter. *See under* family role
death/dying, 9, 11, 14, 26, 38, 41, 47, 60–6, 72–4, 79–80, 94, 97–8, 102, 113, 127, 134–9, 143, 145, 150–1, 153n5, 159n14
Deats, Sara Munson, 59, 148, 153n8, 155n17
decline, 8, 27, 32, 34, 39, 45, 63, 105, 136, 15n8
Declining to Decline (Gullette), 14, 62, 153n2
Deloria, Ella Cara, 124, 127, 131, 143, 164n8, 165n13
Demetrakopoulos, Stephanie, 93, 96–100, 109, 115, 163n7
dependence, 11–2, 17, 20, 23, 46, 63, 71, 73, 81, 85, 114, 142, 163n30
Diary of a Good Neighbour (Lessing), 21, 69–92, 160n2, 161n3, 161n6, 162n16, 162n18, 162n24, 163nn28–9
Dickens, Charles, 5, 154n11
Dickenson, Emily, 5, 154n12
Dillaway, Heather, 7, 20, 45, 48, 65
disability/ability, viii, 8, 10–1, 15, 20–23, 29–38, 45, 48–55, 59–65, 71, 73, 75–8, 80–1, 85–6, 105, 108, 112, 125–6, 133, 136, 148, 151, 155n28, 156nn5–6, 157n9, 159n24, 161n7; mental ability/health, 8, 15, 29, 30, 34, 46–55, 64–5, 72, 74–6, 79, 108, 126, 130, 148, 151, 153n5, 156n5, 159n23, 161n7
discrimination/prejudice, 3, 5, 10, 14, 20–1, 25, 49, 59, 61–3, 81, 96, 115, 154n10; ageism, viii, 3, 8–9, 11, 14–6, 21, 23, 29, 33, 39, 48, 58–64, 69, 71–3, 80, 90–3, 102, 107, 109, 111–2, 122, 136, 147–8, 151, 153n5, 155n28, 157n10, 161n12, 166n1; classism, vii, 21; homophobia, 3, 56; racism, 3, 9, 16, 21, 25, 61, 81, 93–4, 104, 106, 109, 113, 115–6, 141; sexism, viii, 3, 16, 56, 61. *See also* culture: cultural capital; power; visibility
discursive, 27–8, 30–2, 34, 156n8

economics, 7, 13–4, 18, 53, 57–9, 70, 73, 83, 85, 88, 92, 107, 129, 136, 159n20, 160n26; classism (*see under* discrimination); communism, 71, 82, 84;

economics (*continued*), Marxism, 78, 83–4; materialism, ix, 8, 21, 70–8, 82–6, 98, 105, 112, 119, 129; sexual economy, 36; socialism, 82–5. *See also* class; socioeconomics

elder, vii, 1, 9, 12–3, 17, 20–2, 25, 29–30, 36–9, 43, 56, 61, 71, 74, 78, 80, 83, 92–5, 98, 101, 108, 113, 119–30, 133, 136, 139–43, 146–9, 161n8, 163n4, 164n8. *See also* age; otherelder

emotional health. *See* disability: mental health

Erdrich, Louise, 17, 22–3, 119–20, 123–5, 129–30, 133–42, 156n33, 163n6, 165nn8–10; *Last Report on the Miracles at Little No Horse*, 119–20, 124, 133–4, 137–42, 163n6, 165n10

Estes, Carol, 14, 155n24, 159n15, 160n26, 166n1

ethnicity. *See* race

ethics, 30–2, 38, 83, 87, 100, 105, 119, 140–2

Europe, 6, 26, 98, 160n29

European American. *See* race: Caucasian

European Network in Aging Studies (ENAS), 166n3

family, vii, ix, 18, 21–2, 49–50, 64–5, 71–4, 81–2, 85–6, 97–104, 107–8, 114, 121–6, 129, 131, 137–8, 140–1, 164n7

family role: daughter, 21–2, 43, 62, 67, 72–3, 81–2, 103–4, 108, 117, 137, 142; father, 62, 101, 104, 138, 140, 158n11; grandchild, 34, 164n4; grandparent, 34, 56, 60, 108, 122–7, 133, 141–2, 164n2, 164n4; mother, 16, 22, 25–6, 37, 43–4, 47, 60–3, 67, 74–5, 79–82, 96, 99, 103–8, 114–7, 122, 124, 127, 137, 142, 158n11, 163n28, 163n7; partner/spouse, 47, 49, 66, 72, 77, 79, 85–6, 108, 114; relative, other, 77, 91, 107, 140, 145, 155n26, 158n10; sibling, 67, 74–9, 101, 103, 106–7, 116–7, 121, 128; son, 75, 82, 103–4, 112, 140, 142. *See also* elder; generations; otherdaughter/otherson; otherelder; othermother/otherfather

fashion, 3, 62, 70, 91–2, 126, 135, 163n29

father. *See under* family role

Featherstone, Mark, 7, 161n3

female. *See under* gender

feminism, viii, 6, 9, 13–6, 19–20, 23–9, 35, 45–6, 52, 56–65, 75, 82, 85–6, 104, 116, 125, 145, 155n26, 158n10, 160n32, 162n17, 165n11. *See also* activism

film, 5, 14, 17, 35, 38, 79, 126, 150, 152, 155n31

First Nation. *See* race: Native American. *See also* Contact

Foucault, Michel, 27, 112

Freud, Sigmund, 13, 27–8, 66, 156n3

Friedan, Betty, 13, 16

Gallop, Jane, 156n3

Garland-Thomson, Rosemarie, 81, 91

gay. *See* queer; sexuality

gender, vii, 1–9, 17–28, 31–40, 49, 56, 59–63, 69, 71, 74, 81–2, 85–6, 91–6, 103–6, 110, 113–6, 119, 135–6, 139, 145–6, 157n14,

157n16, 156n18, 162n18; female, 2, 6–7, 15, 20–2, 29, 31, 34–8, 45, 48, 57, 85–6, 90, 101–2, 105–10, 125, 134–6, 156n3, 157n18, 158n5, 161n9; male, 2, 29, 31, 35–6, 45, 48, 54, 85–6, 90, 104, 134–5, 156n3, 158n5, 161n9

generations, ix, 7, 12, 21–2, 26, 78, 91, 97, 101, 103, 113–4, 117, 121–3, 127, 137–43, 148, 163n8, 164n7; genealogy, 59, 103. *See also* age; family role

gerontology, viii, 4–5, 9, 11, 14, 19, 23, 58, 71, 146–9, 153n4, 154n8, 154n15, 160n29, 166n1

Ginn, Jay, 10

grandparent/grandchild. *See under* family role

Gravagne, Pamela, 154n8

Greer, Germaine, 42, 45, 48, 52, 56, 108, 155n29, 158nn9–10, 159n20, 163n10

Grosz, Elizabeth, 36–7, 158n4

Gubrium, Jaber, 158n20

Gullette, Margaret, 3–4, 7–11, 14, 16, 27, 45, 47, 54, 59, 62–3, 150, 153nn2–3, 154n8, 154n14, 155n16, 155nn22–3, 155n29, 155n32, 158n6, 159n15, 159n19, 160n27, 160n32, 161n3; *Aged by Culture*, 14, 39; *Agewise*, 3, 4, 8, 11, 14, 16, 47, 154n14, 155nn22–3, 158n6, 160n27, 160n33; *Declining to Decline*, 14, 27, 62, 153nn2–3

hair color, viii, 1, 12, 18, 29, 33–4, 78, 95, 109–11, 145

Heath, Kay, 5, 7

Henneberg, Sylvia, 96

Hepworth, Mike, 7, 154n8

heritage, 22, 93–4, 116, 126–7, 156

heterosexual. *See* sexuality

Hispanic, 147. *See also* race

Holladay, Hilary, 96, 99, 116, 164n13

Holloway, Karla, 93, 96–100, 109, 115, 163n7

Holstein, Martha, 9

hooks, bell, 163

homophobia, 3, 56. *See also* discrimination

homosexual. *See* queer; sexuality

human, 4, 20, 27–30, 33–4, 38, 66, 70, 74, 78–9, 85–90, 100, 109, 112, 119–28, 131, 141–50 153n5, 159n18

humanities, viii, 7–9, 11, 14, 20, 59, 92, 96, 146–51, 153n4, 154n8, 166n5

Hurd Clarke, Laura, 30, 32, 35, 50, 89, 155n23, 155n27, 158n7, 159n15, 161n3

husband. *See* family role: partner/spouse

Hutcheon, Linda and Michael, 155n31

identity, 1–2, 4–5, 8–10, 13–17, 20, 26–28, 34–7, 40–2, 47, 55–6, 59, 62, 70, 95–7, 106, 109, 112, 115–6, 119, 129, 131–2, 135–6, 141, 145–50, 156n3, 157n10

independence. *See* dependence

inscription, 19, 32, 33, 40

interdisciplinary, 22, 92, 146, 154n15

intersectional, 4, 17, 19–21, 31, 34, 64, 77, 93, 96, 116, 126, 159n20

invisible. *See* visibility

Jaggar, Alison, 16

Kahn, Robert, 58–9
Kaplan, E. Ann, 44, 163n10
Katz, Stephen, 14, 34, 59, 146, 157n13, 159n18, 160n27, 160n29, 161n3
Kivnick, Helen, 151, 155n31, 166n1, 166n4
Komesaroff, Paul, 41, 46, 55, 107, 159n17, 164n15
Kriebernegg, Ulla, 4
Kristeva, Julia, 27, 36–7, 157nn16–7
Kunow, Rüdiger, 19, 145, 159n18

Lacan, Jacques, 27–8, 37
Lamb, Erin Gentry, 11, 14, 29, 39, 149, 155n29, 160n24
Last Report on the Miracles at Little No Horse (Erdrich), 119–20, 124, 133–4, 137–42, 163n6, 165n10
late life. *See* age; elder
Latino/a, 147. *See also* race
Lawrence, Margaret, 6
Learning to be Old (Cruikshank), ix, 14, 43, 63, 155n30
LeGuin, Ursula, 13
Lenker, Lagretta Tallent, 59, 148, 154n8, 155n17
lesbian. *See* queer; sexuality
Lessing, Doris, 6, 17, 21, 23, 69–92, 161n3, 161n5, 161n10, 162–3nn14–29; *Diary of a Good Neighbour*, 21, 69–92, 160n2, 161n3, 161n6, 162n16, 162n18, 161n24, 163nn28–9
LeSueur, Meridel, 13, 164n14
Levy, Becca, 9, 151, 153n5

Lipscomb, Valerie, 7, 14; *Staging Age*, 14
literature, viii, 2–9, 12–23, 26, 43, 48, 52, 59, 67, 69, 87, 92, 94–6, 109–10, 112, 116, 125, 132, 145–150, 154n8, 159n19, 163n7, 164n3, 165n10; literary analysis, 4–5, 13–5, 19, 21–2, 48, 52, 84, 87, 92, 147, 163n27; myth, 14, 28, 39, 44–55, 64, 72, 88, 97–8, 107–9, 114–5, 125, 151, 158n9, 158nn12–3
Lock, Margaret, 18, 20, 46, 65, 93, 159n20
Loe, Meika, 3, 155n21
Looser, Devoney, 7
Lukács, György, 90

Macdonald, Barbara, 6, 13, 36, 59–62, 93, 105, 158n1, 164n2
Maierhofer, Roberta, 63, 154n9
male. *See under* gender
Mangum, Teresa, 16, 154n11
Mann, Thomas, 87–8
Marshall, Barbara, 14, 34, 157n13, 159n18, 160n27
Marshall, Leni, 15, 30, 37–8, 65, 153n5, 155n28, 156n7, 164n10, 157n15, 156n17, 158n20, 160n24, 164n10; *Staging Age*, 14
Martin, Emily, 45, 47–50, 108, 158nn12–3, 159n20, 164n10
Marxism. *See under* economics
materialism. *See under* economics
Mead, Margaret, 47
méconnaissance, 147, 156n7
medical, 7–8, 19, 44–56, 63, 92, 106–7, 148, 151, 159n16, 159n18, 160n29; medical humanities,

11, 146; medical-industrial complex, 14, 50, 107; medicine, 45, 51, 54–5, 106, 116, 158n7; treatment, 8, 12, 45–6, 48, 50–1, 54, 159n18

men. *See* gender: male

mental health. *See under* disability

menopause, 7–8, 10, 14, 16–7, 20, 35–6, 41–67, 93, 102, 107–9, 112–5, 154n14, 157n11, 158n5, 158n8, 158–9nn14–6, 159nn19–20, 164n11, 164n15

middle age. *See under* age

mind-body split. *See under* binarity

minority, 3, 21, 96, 147, 154n15. *See also* race

mirror, viii, 3, 30, 36, 38, 157n14

Modern Language Association (MLA), 5, 148

Moody, Harry, 39, 149, 155n30, 158n20

Morrison, Toni, 6, 96, 99

mother. *See under* family role

movie. *See* film

myth. *See under* literature

Native American. *See under* race. *See also* Contact

nature, 20, 29, 31, 33–4, 38, 102

normative, 2, 12, 14, 16, 19–20, 26–30, 33, 35, 38, 49–50, 78, 81, 93, 136, 159. *See also* culture; Other

North America, 5, 7, 18, 29, 33, 29, 44, 46, 51, 53, 115–6, 129, 147, 166n3. *See also* America; United States

North American Network in Aging Studies (NANAS), 166n3

old. *See under* age

Old Women's Project, 12, 84

Oró-Piqueras, Maricel, 72, 154n8

Ortiz, Simon, 131

Other, The, viii, ix, 9, 13, 23, 25–31, 37–8, 58, 60, 70–1, 78, 91, 93, 103, 105, 141, 146, 150, 157n18, 162n18, 165n11. *See also* culture; discrimination; normative

Otherdaughter/otherson, 21–2, 72–3, 81–2, 104, 117, 142, 147

otherelder, 22, 105, 127, 133, 139–40, 142, 147. *See also* community; elder

othermother/otherfather, 22, 104–8, 117, 122, 127

Owens, Louis, 121, 130, 132, 165n8

pagan, 113, 134, 138. *See also* religion

partner. *See under* family role. *See also* queer

pedagogy, 4, 8, 11, 16, 21, 23, 26, 28–9, 48, 60, 63–4, 92, 125–7, 133, 149, 151–2, 166n5; class, 16, 26, 60, 92, 152; school, 48, 63, 78, 94, 137

performance actions, 2–3, 10–1, 14, 19–20, 25, 27, 29, 33, 35, 46, 56–60, 70, 74–5, 77, 84, 89, 92, 98–9, 105, 119, 123–4, 128–9, 135, 137–8, 145–7, 155n18, 156n6, 157n18

performative, 19–20, 27, 29, 34–5, 38, 41, 58–9, 69, 77, 155n18, 156n5, 157n18

Pezzulich, Evelyn, 15

Phallus, The, 36, 157n14

Phillipson, Chris, 155n29

physical ability. *See* disability

Piercy, Marge, ix, 13
Pipher, Mary, 16
Pogrebin, Letty Cottin, 56–7
Port, Cynthia, 156n33, 159n15, 160n26
power, 2, 9, 12–4, 17, 21–2, 26–7, 32–8, 42, 45–6, 50–3, 56–7, 60–3, 81, 85–9, 92, 98–101, 107, 110, 112–3, 116–7, 122–8, 133, 138–41, 146, 149–50, 156n2, 157n14, 164n11. See also culture; cultural capital; discrimination; visibility
prejudice. See discrimination
psychology, 13, 15, 19–20, 31, 37, 48, 58, 64, 75–6, 85, 102, 108, 129, 148, 151, 154n8, 166n1

queer, 8, 23, 25, 31, 41. See also sexuality

race/ethnicity, 1, 5, 9, 21–3, 59, 71, 74, 76, 81, 86, 92–5, 102–3, 106, 115, 125, 143, 146–7, 157n16; African American/Black, 19, 21–2, 41, 61, 81, 93–117, 147, 163nn3–4, 163nn7–8, 164n11; Asian American, 147; Caucasian American/European American/White, 5, 19, 21, 25, 43–4, 95–110, 113, 115, 123–4, 130–40, 147, 164n1, 164n15; Hispanic/Latino/Latina, 147; Native American/First Nation, 19, 22, 65, 93–4, 119–43, 147, 164n1, 164n3, 164n5, 164nn7–8, 165n10
racism. See under discrimination
RaglandSullivan, Ellie, 157n14
Ray, Ruth, 153n4
reifungsroman, 15, 69, 95, 111, 147, 155n28. See also Waxman, Barbara Frey

relationships, vii–viii, 1–2, 19, 21–2, 29, 67, 71, 77, 79–88, 100–7, 110, 119, 123, 125, 127, 131–4, 106, 137, 139, 141, 145–52. See also age relations; family; family role
relatives. See family role
religion, 60, 87, 98–9, 111, 113, 134, 138, 147, 156n33, 159n21, 160n21, 163n9
reproduction, 35, 45–7, 50, 82, 85, 99, 101–2, 104, 110, 122, 157n11
research, viii, 3–8, 13–8, 21, 45, 58, 62, 83, 93, 96, 108, 122, 127, 146, 149, 152, 153n5, 154n15, 158n7
resistance. See activism
Rich, Adrienne, 52, 156n3
Rich, Cynthia, 6, 12–3, 59–62, 84, 93, 105, 160n32, 164n2
ripening, ix, 15, 22, 112, 150. See also reifungsroman
risk, 12, 32, 58, 100, 156n3, 159n18, 160n27
roman à thèse, 21, 71, 86–90, 162n20
Roof, Judith, 26
Rooke, Constance, 66, 158n19
Rothfield, Philipa, 41, 46, 51–2, 107, 159n14, 164n15
Rowe, John, 58–9
Rowles, Graham, 9

Sandoval, Chela, 132
Sarris, Greg, 123, 129–30, 140, 165nn8–9
Sarton, May, 6, 13, 62
Savishinsky, Joel, 18, 93
Schiebinger, Londa, 53
scholarship. See pedagogy; research
self-image, 42, 105–6, 112. See also identity

Index

senior. *See* elder. *See also* age
sexism. *See under* discrimination
sexuality, 22, 25, 27–8, 31, 35–8, 47, 50, 56, 59–61, 95, 101–2, 104–5, 110–2, 135, 139, 157n10, 159n14, 159n21, 159n23, 160n31; sex, 77, 101–2, 111, 134–6, 157n10. *See also* queer
Shakespeare, William, 26
Sheehy, Gail, 42, 44, 47, 49, 108, 114, 158n3, 159n14, 159n17, 159n20
sibling. *See under* family role
Silko, Leslie Marmon, 123, 127–8, 130, 133, 141, 143, 165nn8–9
sister. *See* family role: sibling
slavery, 94, 97, 191, 101–6, 163n7. *See also* Civil War; discrimination; race
Slevin, Kathleen, 10, 110, 153n6, 160n31
Staging Age (Lipscomb and Marshall), 14
Steinem, Gloria, 56
social capital. *See* culture: cultural capital
social change. *See under* activism
social construction, 2, 4, 7–9, 17–20, 23, 27–8, 32, 36, 38, 40, 48, 51–7, 61–4, 67, 71, 76–85, 88, 93, 99–106, 109, 115–6, 119, 134, 145–8, 153n4, 156n8, 157n11
socialism. *See under* economics.
socioeconomics, 18, 53, 59, 107, 159n20. *See also* class; economics
son. *See under* family role
Sontag, Susan, 159n20
spouse. *See under* family role: partner
stage. *See* performance

Steinem, Gloria, 56
subject/object, 17, 19, 27–8, 32–8, 40–1, 89, 103–4, 110, 112–3, 153n5, 158n4, 160n29
Suleiman, Susan Rubin, 86–90, 162n20
Swinnen, Aagje, 13, 38, 155n25, 157n12, 158n20, 164n6

teaching. *See* pedagogy
theatre, *See* performance
Tiger, Virginia, 91
time, 10, 12, 14, 19, 22, 28–9, 32–3, 41–2, 45, 65, 73–4, 78, 80, 89, 91, 95, 97, 99, 103–5, 111, 116, 121, 125, 128, 134, 141–3, 146, 148–50; chronology, 1, 4, 7, 10–2, 22, 41, 45, 69–71, 74, 80, 110, 123, 127, 134, 136, 139–40; lifetime, 17, 105, 165n10

United States, 3, 46, 97, 154n7, 160n29, 161n8, 164n4. *See also* America; North America

versive gaze, 166n2
visibility/invisibility of old age, 1–2, 4, 13–5, 26–7, 36–8, 53, 58, 61, 66, 69, 72, 84–6, 95, 106, 109, 145, 162n16. *See also* culture: cultural capital; discrimination; Other; power

Wall, Cheryl, 97, 103–4
Waxman, Barbara Frey, 9, 15, 17, 39, 59, 69, 91, 154n8, 155n19, 155n26, 155n28, 156n33, 156n4, 157n16, 160n1. *See also* reifungsroman
Weigman, Robyn, 26
Wernick, Andrew, 161n3

Western cultures, 10, 21, 27, 29, 31, 33–4, 45, 53, 115, 126
White. *See* race: Caucasian
wife. *See* family role: partner/spouse
wisdom, 5–6, 22, 53, 55, 95, 98–9, 122, 125, 156n33, 164n2
witch, 29, 38, 77–8, 156n5
Wittig, Monique, 27–8
Wohlmann, Anita, 154n8, 156n1
Womack, Craig, 164n3
women. *See* gender: female

Woodward, Kathleen, 4, 6, 9, 13–4, 16–7, 23, 32, 36, 42, 57, 59, 65–6, 93–4, 141, 149–50, 153n5, 154n8, 154n13, 155n29, 156n7, 160n27, 160n34, 161nn3–4, 162n18, 163n26, 164n10
wrinkles, viii, 18, 32, 33–4, 41, 115, 136, 158n7
Wyatt-Brown, Anne, 6, 59, 154n8, 155n31, 158n2

young/youth. *See under* age